T0328545

SKEPTIC'S GUIDE TO JESUS

Skeptic's Guide to Jesus

Christopher Cumo

Algora Publishing
New York

Library of Congress Cataloging-in-Publication Data —

Names: Cumo, Christopher author.
Title: A skeptic's guide to Jesus / Christopher Cumo.
Description: New York : Algora Publishing, 2016. | Includes bibliographical
    references.
Identifiers: LCCN 2016037691 (print) | LCCN 2016037892 (ebook) | ISBN
    9781628942347 (soft cover : alk. paper) | ISBN 9781628942354 (hard cover :
    alk. paper) | ISBN 9781628942361 (pdf)
Subjects: LCSH: Jesus Christ--Rationalistic interpretations. | Jesus
    Christ--Historicity. | Faith and reason--Christianity.
Classification: LCC BT304.95 .C86 2016 (print) | LCC BT304.95 (ebook) | DDC
    232.9--dc23
LC record available at https://lccn.loc.gov/2016037691

Printed in the United States

Table of Contents

PREFACE

This book is part confession. This literary genre goes back to Augustine, bishop of Hippo in North Africa and Catholic saint, but my agenda differs from that of Augustine so many centuries ago. Augustine lived at a time when the Christian Church was beginning to flex its muscles and make bold claims. Today we live in the "twilight of the gods," to borrow the title of one of Friedrich Nietzsche's last works. Religion as a general construct peaked long ago, probably before the Enlightenment, and is now in retreat. This period of decline and demise makes essential at long last a realistic treatment of Jesus of Nazareth.

My meeting with the ghost of this legendary figure occurred decades ago. As an Italian by birth and upbringing, I was early baptized into the Catholic Church. My parents were very pious and I attended Mass weekly and on all holy days and prayed at meals and at night. My parents expected rigid devotion to the Church and, of course, to Jesus. So often was the phrase used that for many years I thought this person's full name was Jesus Christ. I was mistaken. Jesus is the Latin name for Joshua, which was evidently a common name in first century CE Judea. Christ is not a name at all, but simply a statement of faith. Christ is short for Christos, meaning the anointed one or messiah. It is a claim that Jesus was the long sought holy man who would free the Jews from oppression.

I am not alone in finding Jesus' name puzzling. The canonical gospels do not record an instance of a person addressing the man as Jesus. Rather terms like "rabbi" or "teacher" are used. Only the gospel authors apply the designation Jesus, which really means just Joshua, as we have seen. There were probably many Jewish men with this name, at least one of whom happened to have been crucified during the reign of Pontius Pilate.

Perhaps at the core of our difficulty is our tendency to allow faith to overtake reason in matters that relate to Jesus. It seems strange that we demand science or history or any of a number of disciplines to be rational, but we absolve religion of this requirement. This is an unfortunate state of affairs because it prevents us from seeing Jesus as something other than a god who was the product of a virgin birth and who rose from the dead. Until we can think critically about these matters, we will always allow darkness to triumph over light. This book tries to illuminate Jesus' life by demanding a rational inquiry about it. Such rationality is badly needed today.

I'm not sure how long I might have held onto these beliefs, but then, at age 43, my mother died. I was 15 at the time and didn't know how to reconcile the notion of a good, just, loving God with such a tragedy. My immediate concern was that she have a peaceful afterlife. At this juncture I did something radically different than all my previous behaviors would have suggested. I was then in a Catholic high school. Nowhere in the curriculum had I read any portion of the bible, though I knew from theology class that Jesus was supposed to have preached about life after death. So without any urging from anyone, I decided to confront Jesus through the only medium I then knew in existence, the gospels. In using the term gospels, I referred to the canonical texts in the New Testament: the accounts given the names Matthew, Mark, Luke, and John. I did not know then that there are many more accounts of Jesus' life that the Catholic Church chose not to incorporate into the New Testament. The reasons for exclusion will become clear in later chapters.

I borrowed a copy of the bible from the local library and read these four accounts in little more than a single sitting. True, I found several passages in which Jesus spoke of eternal life, particular in the gospel of John. The message seemed comforting, but only in part. I found myself unable to square the biblical accounts with the reality I knew. The large number of miracles struck me, even as a teen, as implausible. The idea of a virgin birth contradicted what I was learning about reproductive biology in school. In short, as I was immersing myself in the sciences, I was not able to make sense of much that I read in the gospels. I began to wonder whether these accounts were fanciful rather than historical.

This tension only worsened as I made my way through college and graduate school. This was not solely due to my interest in the sciences, for in college philosophy began to interest me. I read with great care the atheistic existentialists and before them, Nietzsche of course. Nietzsche had trained his guns on the life-denying forces of Christianity but said comparative little about Jesus. I found myself wanting to turn the tables by scrutinizing the life of Jesus and ignoring the larger religious context so far as that was possible.

In fact this is impossible to do, but I upheld it as an ideal at the time. All the while I was in search of a method of inquiry that would lay bare Jesus' life.

I eventually found what I believe to be the most probative way of examining Jesus. I was now in graduate school and extended my orbit to include not merely philosophy and the sciences, but also history. In my training as a historian of science, I not only sharpened my understanding of the Scientific Method but also gained a firm grasp of historical methods. That is, I began to use scientific and historical methods to test assertions.

I now wish to test the assertions about Jesus. I want to know whether the Jesus of the written records could withstand the scrutiny of the sciences and history. This inquiry forms the core of this book.

The difficulty of a book like this is the attempt to reach as large a number of readers as possible. Doubtless my ideas will not infuriate atheists or agnostics, but Christians are likely to be another matter. Anytime a person relies on dogma at the expense of evidence, the result is likely to be a narrow-minded rejection of any path that deviates from what faith defines as the true path. I intend as much as possible to ignore rejection of this kind because I do not intend to write within the compass of faith. A very long time ago humans had little more than faith to guide them. I do not intend to write for this mindset but to entertain other methods of understanding what we call reality. The sciences, philosophy, and history will be our guides. I hope that their rigor will appeal to those who remain intellectually curious and open-minded.

INTRODUCTION

This book has grown out of the conviction that the methods of history in particular and of the sciences secondarily have not been applied forcefully enough to an investigation of Jesus. The name has resonated throughout Western civilization, which for some centuries was held together by the glue of Christianity, the religion founded upon the teachings and actions of Jesus to the extent that it may be possible to infer them from the written record.

We will scrutinize this written record. One may claim to derive much from the study of his life. One might, for example, point to the ethics that the gospels promoted. They are presumably an example of the way Christians ought to live, though Italian diplomat and author Niccolò Machiavelli was correct to observe that if one behaves like Jesus when no one else is doing so, one will only be trampled for trying. The selfishness and self interest that Russian-Jewish American novelist and philosopher Ayn Rand promoted seems to guide human behavior much more often than does altruism. Others will maintain that Jesus was the most important figure in history. This kind of claim has the taint of hyperbole. Why should one reckon Jesus more important than Buddha or Confucius? For that matter, why is Jesus more important than Edward Jenner, whose vaccination program led ultimately to the eradication of smallpox, once a horrible killer? Other examples might abound but they are unnecessary to make the claim that it is possible to overrate Jesus.

It is true, however, that Jesus (or at least the ideas one gleans about him through the canonical gospels) has been the inspiration for much of the great art and music of the Western world. Who can hear Bach's "St. Matthew Passion" without some recognition of the sublime and perhaps even the divine? There are examples even in the United States of atheists flocking to a church to hear a Bach cantata or another piece of sacred music. It is difficult to deny that such an experience is spiritual. A devotion to Bach's music does not, of course, prove anything about Jesus. It is merely a testament to Bach's genius. Much Christian art in Rome, Florence and other major cities are expressions of an intense devotion to Jesus. They too bring us near a mystical experience. Through the Renaissance nearly every major artist in the West expressed some aspirations toward the religious. Sometimes—the art of Flemish painter Hieronymus Bosch is an example—this art is not easy to interpret, just as the religious impulse itself is not easy to pin down. In these ways, then, the memory of Jesus has only grown more intense even as his life as a historical figure can no longer be made out with any certainty.

Nonetheless, I will play by the rules of Christians in accepting for the purpose of scrutiny that Jesus was history's most important figure. If such a claim is at least remotely possible, then nothing can be more important than a book that attempts to determine what can and cannot be known about him. As a civilization we are in desperate need of such a book. It may once have sufficed to claim knowledge about Jesus through faith, but we must now see that such a claim is illogical and impossible. To know something is to claim evidence for holding a postulate as true. I may walk around town all day proclaiming, for example, that a triangle is a four sided, four-angled figure. You who truly have knowledge will not take me seriously. You will refer to the definition of a triangle to affirm that it is a three sided, three angled figure, the sum of whose angles equals 180 degrees. By appealing to a foundational definition, you know what a triangle is. This knowledge is a form of truth because even on Mars a triangle will be the figure you defined earlier.

Let's try to apply this reasoning to an attribute of Jesus. One may choose among many, though let me begin with the assertion that Jesus was god, the central statement of Christianity. The actual formula of the Nicene Creed holds that Jesus was both man and god. I will concede to Jesus the property of having been a man. But can the same claim be made of his divinity? Consider a basic property of god as not being subject to death. That is, if god exists he must not be subject to limitations, among them death.[1] The cessation of life is the most emphatic limit one may conceive. Now the four gospels of the New Testament, the canonical gospels, all agree that Jesus died when the Romans crucified him. But this is to impose a limit on Jesus when no limit is permissible for a divine being. Jesus cannot then have both died and been god. Because it seems fairly well established that Jesus did die, he cannot have been god. Logic, then, can cut through religious propaganda.

---

[1] Richard Swinburne, *Was Jesus God?* (Oxford: Oxford University Press, 1994) 6.

The person of faith will sweep aside my every word and claim belief nonetheless. But even if one grants this person the freedom to believe, such belief is not knowledge. It depends on no evidence and no appeal to definition or logic. In fact a statement of faith is all that one can grasp in the absence of evidence or rationality. Faith may have been necessary in the remote past when humans knew precious little about their world. But in modernity it is more hindrance than help. We live in a world of verification. I know, for example, that I can bicycle at only about 15 miles per hour because I have closely estimated my distance after an hour's exertion. On the other hand, by watching the speedometer in my 2006 Chevy Colorado, I know I can travel 100 miles per hour. In no case need I invoke faith because the tangible combination of distance and time yields reliable measurements. (In no case, however, should the knowledge that my truck can travel 100 miles per hour provoke me to approximate such speeds on American highways.)

With this said, I intend to subject the life of Jesus to a modern critique that relies heavily on the methods of history and the sciences. My thesis is that we can know—and I write of knowledge not belief—almost nothing about Jesus from the sources available to us. Note, however, that I do not go so far as to claim that Jesus never existed. There appears to have been more written about Jesus in antiquity than about Greek philosopher Plato. I do not doubt that Plato existed, so I should not place an unfair burden on those who believe that Jesus existed as well. But the analogy is imperfect. One important aspect of Plato is that he left a corpus or writings and was clearly among history's most dazzling stylists. On the other hand, Jesus, like Plato's mentor Socrates, left no writings of his own. For a historian this absence is a blow because it is hard to believe that any writing could match the observations of Jesus himself, had he left anything approximating Plato's legacy.

My critique is ordered in seven chapters. Chapter 1 assesses the sources of Jesus' life story as we know it: the canonical gospels, the Gnostic gospels, the infancy gospel of Thomas and some lesser-known documents. The essential point is that there are no true historical records of Jesus. The gospels, whether canonical, Gnostic, or infancy, do not qualify. To take one example, the gospel of Mark is generally agreed to be the earliest account of Jesus' life. Yes, some of Paul's letters may be older, but they provide almost no information about Jesus. In fact, Paul did not know Jesus and so cannot have been a witness to his activities. Mark dates between about 70 and 90 CE, depending on what one reads. Even if one allows the early date of 70 CE, some four decades had already elapsed since Jesus' death, making doubtful any claim that the author (and we have no idea who wrote Mark) could have been an eyewitness to Jesus' activities. There are many more reasons for doubting that this or any other text could be a primary source.

The second chapter will examine what little was written in the centuries immediately after Jesus' death about his birth. Of all that was written about Jesus in the first two centuries after his death, only two passages, one in Matthew and the other in Luke, place Bethlehem as the birthplace. Moreover the historical evidence from Roman antiquity makes the birth narrative in Matthew and Luke highly improbably, if not impossible. In this context the story of a virgin birth merits scrutiny.

The third chapter examines the elusive years of Jesus' childhood. Even a casual reading makes obvious that the first two centuries after Jesus' death say almost nothing about his childhood, with good reason. This is an example of humanity's abhorrence of a vacuum. Because Jesus' childhood was a blank slate, someone had to try to write something intelligible on it. The result was the later infancy gospel of Thomas, which merits attention even though the text is much too recent to tell us anything about the actual childhood, which, like most of Jesus' life appears lost to history. Other infancy narratives will receive treatment as well.

The fourth chapter grapples with Jesus' ministry, an apparently short and tumultuous series of events. The miracle accounts deserve scrutiny. Indeed, what the gospels omit in facts they make up for in miracles. There are too many to make necessary or desirable an analysis of each one. The miracle accounts in John, the last of the canonical gospels, particularly the raising of Lazarus, deserve some commentary if we are to understand their relationship to the claims about Jesus. It will be important to link the resurrection accounts one finds in Old and New Testaments to similar accounts in religious texts popular in the Mediterranean Basin during and after Jesus' life.

Chapter 5 attempts to review the literature about Jesus' death and resurrection. The account of his death does not trouble me inordinately because death is the end of every life, no matter how well or poorly lived. Moreover it is an organic fact strong enough to earn the distinction of being a law. Every mosquito dies. Every dragonfly dies. Every salamander dies. Every human dies and so forth. Death cannot be evaded no matter what one thinks and hopes. My perspective about the resurrection accounts will occupy most of this chapter. Details are not essential in this introduction, though one might note in passing that the gospel of Thomas mentions nothing about the resurrection. If the resurrection is the central event in human history, why did this author omit it? Why did he not reinforce the message of the canonical gospels? Other Gnostic accounts treat the resurrection as more symbol than substance. Even Paul of Tarsus appears not to have had an encounter with a physical Jesus, although the canonicals require just this sort of physical resurrection. If the religious texts do not agree, how are we to view the claims of Jesus' resurrection today?

Chapter 6 gives theologians and pro religion scientists their due. It outlines the belief of prominent theologians and one physicist. But it is not a dry recitation of information. My aim is to combat the assertions of these people given the argument this book presents. Yes, theologians sometimes go on the offensive, but there is no reason why this book cannot respond in kind. The result is a renewal of my earlier arguments to stymie the natural instincts of theologians. Remember that they are not neutral but are invested in the Jesus worldview, one that places faith above knowledge. I argue that this premise is mistaken.

The final chapter, treating Jesus in purely human terms, announces the death of god. Nietzsche deserves credit for having forged this slogan as a weapon against Christianity, and it remains a forceful notion today. The questions Nietzsche posed in the nineteenth century remain largely unanswered today. If the notion of Jesus as god is dead, who should grieve this passing? More important, how should we fashion a stronger, more durable civilization apart from the man who ought not to remain the central figure in history? Does Western civilization remain a cohesive notion without Jesus and all he has been made to represent over the centuries? The time has come to acknowledge the finality of Jesus' death and, in turn, our own.

CHAPTER 1. TOWARD AN UNDERSTANDING OF THE SOURCES

In their quest for reliability, the methods of history place stiff requirements on our sources of information. These will become evident throughout this chapter. The problem with the sources about Jesus is that they do not conform to historical standards. The sources therefore are almost worthless. As a result it is extremely difficult to draw valid conclusions about Jesus' life. The best one may be able to do is acknowledge that the sources about Jesus are a kind of theology rather than history. We can know, therefore, what early Christians thought about the theological issues that surrounded Jesus. But we can know almost nothing about him as a person. This information shapes our entire understanding of Jesus throughout this chapter and throughout this book. In any case the search for Jesus must begin with the sources.

The Sources

The sources are not as easy to define as one might suppose. Theologians have written much about Jesus. Are these sources? They are, but of a particular type. They are what historians label secondary sources in opposition to primary sources. Here is how the system should work. Suppose a person wishes to write a history of the Vietnam War. Imagine that he or she did not serve in combat during the war. He or she then cannot have been an eyewitness to the war. This limitation does not pose an insuperable barrier as long as the writer reads what Vietnam Veterans wrote about the war and perhaps interviews people from this divisive period in U.S. history. This person's history will constitute a secondary source of its own because it draws from primary sources, meaning those sources written or described by eyewitnesses to the war. In this context it will be even better if the writer knows Vietnamese so that he or she may include Vietnamese perspectives about the war. The question we want to answer is whether one can apply the same method to Jesus. Is it possible to find eyewitness accounts about Jesus that will allow the historian to write a history of his life? This question will occupy us in this chapter and throughout this book. In historical terms we cannot allow Jesus' partisans to push us from the path leading to the rigorous methods of history. Cheap theology cannot substitute for history, even though some evangelicals may tell you otherwise. Stripped to essentials, the historical method is a method of reasoning, to which we now turn.

Principles of Reasoning

Over the last two millennia theologians have dominated the debate over the life of Jesus. I do not aim to show malice on their part, but they have naturally focused on issues important to theology. For example they do not seek to prove that Jesus was god. They proceed to take this information at face value, wondering instead how the divine and human elements of Jesus commingled. They recount miracles as putative proof of Jesus' colossal importance in human history. Such doings should cause the mind to ponder whether such an event as a miracle is possible. In all cases theologians assume all first principles to be true. That is the miracles articulated in the canonical gospels, merely by being stated are presumed true. A better approach would be to question all foundational principles until one accrues sufficient evidence to defend them. Mere assertion is not enough. Along these lines one must ask whether the gospels are more than aggregates of assertions.

I want to be fair in my polemic by reminding the reader that ancient literature is full of unexamined first principles. Even as dazzling a writer and intellectual as Greek philosopher Plato was susceptible to such errors. He wrote about the gods as though they existed when his first task should have been a proof of polytheism.[1] An even more intriguing series of statements comes from the *Phaedo*, a magnificent dialogue from Plato's middle period. Here, in four ways, Plato attempted to prove the immortality of the soul.[2] He apparently took for granted that such an entity existed in the first place. We cannot indulge in such luxuries. The soul must be proven to exist before its immortality can be proven. Language must do real work before it is entitled to belief. Words have meaning only if they correspond to an aspect of reality.

---

[1] Plato, *Apology*, in *The Great Dialogues of Plato* (New York: New American Library, 1955) 427.
[2] Plato, *Phaedo*, in *The Great Dialogues of Plato* (New York: New American Library, 1955) 472-490.

I am not in favor of devaluing the notion of proof. Large parts of mathematics, geometry is an example, depend on rigorous proofs. By appealing to the definition of a triangle I can assure the reader that it has three, not two or four, sides and its angles total 180 degrees. This is simply the outcome of the desire to hold a definition as inviolable. When one speaks of souls and gods, however, matters are far more difficult. Greek philosopher Aristotle seems to have been right that we derive an enormous amount of information through the senses. Because the soul and gods are thought to be immaterial, the senses cannot apprehend them. Proving their existence is therefore a strenuous affair. The tenor of our times seems to hold that no past attempt to prove the existence of the soul and gods has succeeded. According it seems fair, regardless of what the theologians say, to doubt the existence of the soul and gods. To be clear I do not propose that one may disprove these notions with certainty, only that an attitude of skepticism is proper. Then again, skepticism may lead to atheism, and this too is a principle worth defending. The days of theodicies should not be part of the modern world.

Method and the Historian

From the outset I will not try to propose that Jesus never existed, but that the evidence for his life is threadbare. This statement should surprise no one. Even in modernity plenty of people live under the radar so to speak. A curt obituary greets their death. Even if one tried, one could scarcely learn much more about them, despite living in an era of massive record keeping. Jesus then was scarcely different from most people who glide through life today without making a ripple. This supposition that Jesus' life is largely unknown and unknowable leads to a search for evidence. As noted earlier, I propose to examine Jesus through the lens of history. Given that he was likely a historical figure, it seems appropriate to attempt to describe him with the tools of the historian. One might inquiry how such a historical approach is possible.

Let me answer with a pair of modern examples. Consider first that a historian wishes to write a biography of President Barack Obama. Such a task should be possible sometime after the end of his presidency, when voluminous documents become available for study. But not all documents have equal value. Imagine that one would have access to the emails that the president received and those that without a doubt he wrote of his own accord. These would be extremely valuable in revealing how President Obama approached various issues that confronted him. Also important would be any genuine correspondence between members of the House and Senate, Democrat and Republican, and the president. Caution is necessary. A focus on exclusively Democratic sources would likely depict the president in too favorable a light whereas an emphasis on Republican sources would likely be too negative. That is, a historian is expected to try to be balanced and impartial. Notice that theologians are not impartial about Jesus, a reflection that should give us pause.

Another source of information about President Obama might be his speeches, but again caution is warranted. The president has speechwriters, making it very difficult to determine whether a particular sentence or paragraph in a speech fully represents the president's agenda. Obviously a portion, perhaps a very large one, of the ideas in a speech are meant to be understood as depicting the ideas of the speech-maker. Of course, one must consider the possibility that a trained speechwriter operating at the highest level of government must be extremely skilled at articulating the ideas given to a president to present. To what degree, then, might a document created by one of President Obama's subordinates reflect his own insights with such fidelity that it is permissible to credit these thoughts to the president?

Fortunately the age in which Jesus lived provided a good answer. Aristotle comes first to mind. The Roman orator and politician Cicero described the glories of Aristotle's dialogues.[1] None, however, survives. What have survived are the treatises, which possibly began their lives as Aristotle's lecture notes. Remember that Aristotle founded the Lyceum and so must have had various pedagogical duties.[2] Consider the treatise devoted to ethics. Ethics is a branch of philosophy that aims to instruct one on how best to live life. This treatise bears the title of the *Nicomachean Ethics* because Aristotle's son, Nicomacheus, is thought to have written or at least edited this treatise in its final form.[3] Yet Aristotle is considered the author because Nicomacheus was faithful in rendering Aristotle's ideas accurately.

Antiquity provides a second example. A stoic philosopher Epictetus is credited as author of the *Discourses of Epictetus*. Yet it is well known that the writer was a follower of the stoic named Arrian.[4] Arrian was a successful philosopher in his own right. In the case of Epictetus, as with Aristotle, Arrian was so accurate a transcriber of Epictetus' ideas that these ideas can be properly credited to Epictetus. By the standards of antiquity, we should favor President Obama as the author of his speeches even though other men and women wrote them.

---

[1] Henry B. Veatch, *Aristotle: A Contemporary Appreciation* (Bloomington and London: Indiana University Press, 1974) 10.

[2] Robert S. Brumbaugh, The Philosophers of Greece (Albany: State University of New York Press, 1981) 173.

[3] Richard Kraut, "Aristotle's Ethics," The Stanford Encyclopedia of Philosophy (Spring 2016). Plato.Stanford.edu/archives/spr2016/ethics/Aristotle-ethics.

[4] Epictetus: The Discourses as Reported by Arrian, the Manual, and Fragments," archives.org/pstream/epictetusdiscour01/epicuoft/epictetusdiscour01_djvu.text.

The problem is how to relate these concerns with the Jesus accounts. I will argue that Jesus never had any speechwriters or ghostwriters of the caliber of Nicomacheus and Arrian. We can be sure that these people and materials were never at hand during Jesus' time. If Jesus had speechwriters or some mechanism of preserving his thoughts, one would expect a more or less uniform understanding of him. This is far from what one finds, even shrinking our sample to the four canonical gospels.

The issue is the way Jesus addresses his audience. In the synoptic gospels—Matthew, Mark, and Luke—Jesus tends to speak in parables, short pithy stories designed to teach a lesson. Yet the Jesus of the fourth gospel, John, departs almost wholly from this approach, choosing instead long speeches about his putative divinity.[1] Where did John get this different material, some 70 years after Jesus' death? If there were no records of speeches, or ghostwritten material, how could the authors of John have any idea what Jesus actually said? The answer is that they could not have known and so must have fabricated these speeches. This is not the mark of legitimate history.

Consider another example. As with President Obama, it should be possible, at least hypothetically, for a historian to write a biography of Paris Hilton. Again, one must search for the written sources. Paris Hilton claims to have written books, but the fact that many celebrities employ ghostwriters makes dubious her claim. These ghostwriters certainly did not have the relationship to Paris Hilton that Nicomacheus had with Aristotle or Arrian with Epictetus. In the ancient cases, the ghostwriters had a carefully cultivated intellectualism that lent them to be the conduits of others' ideas, and they respected their subjects and intended to portray them faithfully. Paris Hilton's ghostwriters were likely little more than hired computers. They must have had little stake in what Paris Hilton actually said or did. Their purpose was to entertain. Beyond this consideration, the media have occasionally managed to secure brief interviews with her, but usually while she is en route to a posh location and not serious about saying anything substantive. One has as well, I suppose, the sex tapes, but it is difficult to see their historical merit. This is not to say that they have no value as entertainment or eroticism. In fact, if these traits are at the core of Hilton, then perhaps they merit attention after all. But one can find eroticism everywhere. To say that it was a component of her life is simply banal. In short, absent a series of lengthy and serious interviews, we appear to have little information about Ms. Hilton. She comes off more as an icon of plutocratic decadence than as a person who has revealed much about her life suitable for a biography. The case of Paris Hilton underscores the difficulties

---

[1] John 15: 1-27 (New American Bible) for example.

that even a modern subject, in the information age, may pose to the historian. How much more problematic become these concerns when one retreats to the antiquity of Jesus?

I wish to summarize the goals and problems of the historian in an effort to magnify the lessons that must guide us throughout the rest of this book. First, the historian must know what a person thought and did to make his or her biography possible. We noted that the emails that President Obama wrote must be insightful in this regard. It is much more difficult to know anything about a person who has left no written record.

We will examine Jesus in this regard. Here it is enough to note the ubiquity of this problem. Greek philosopher Socrates, for example, wrote nothing and we might know almost nothing about him, but for the substantive writings of his pupil Plato.[1] Even then, interpretation is not easy. As the example of Socrates and Plato suggests, without written information from the source itself, some eyewitness testimony is essential. Obviously Plato was such an eyewitness. In the case of President Obama, any Republican or Democratic leader of stature has firsthand knowledge and opinions about the president.

An account from the subject of a biography, where possible, and eyewitness accounts of him or her, are known as primary sources. One may name other types of primary sources, but the elaboration of Jesus' life does not require an exhaustive treatment of historical methods. The basics will suit us well. As historians in training, we must apply the criterion of primary sources to the life of Jesus.

Please consider the large premises that are guiding our inquiry. We are seeing the value of primary source-eyewitness accounts in understanding the past. These principles apply to the sciences as well. Today, scientists interested in the issue of climate change want to know how the climate was in the past. A promising new study is underway in the United States whereby scientists wish to find out what the climate was like in the Pacific Northwest in the late nineteenth century. How is such knowledge to be gained? The answer is to comb through thousands of pages of journals and ships' logs to understand what sailors witnessed in this region. Through eyewitness testimony of this type, scientists are learning that the climate in the Pacific Northwest was colder in the late nineteenth century than it is today. How is this phenomenon possible? One theory is that we have only ourselves to blame for spewing enormous amounts of greenhouse gases into the atmosphere. To be blunt, the burning of fossil fuels is ruining our habitat. There are other theories, also from reputable sources, that note the existence of long-term natural cycles of warming and cooling. Not all the evidence is in.

---

[1] Francis M. Cornford, *Before and After Socrates* (Cambridge: Cambridge University Press, 1932) 54-55.

In drawing our conclusions, we must make a proper reading of eyewitness accounts and analysis of physical evidence. We want such accounts in our examination of Jesus.

Historical Methods and the Nature of the Sources about Jesus

That is, we must determine whether Jesus or eyewitnesses (or both) wrote anything about him. Our task, simple as it may seem, has immediate hazards. Any theologian will point us to the New Testament. Opening it, we find that the very first book is the gospel according to Matthew. The fourth is the gospel according to John. For the purposes of full treatment, the New Testament contains just four gospels, the other two being Mark and Luke.

For the moment I wish to single out Matthew and John because theologians make special claims about them. By tradition, theologians have attributed the gospel of Matthew to the apostle Matthew, the tax collector who obeyed Jesus' summons to follow him.[1] In the same vein, the gospel of John is attributed to one of the most senior apostles, John, the beloved disciple.[2] It seems fair to assume that Jesus really did surround himself with a group of acolytes. Perhaps two were named the local equivalent of "Matthew" and "John." If the above were true, because Matthew and John would have had firsthand knowledge of Jesus, their gospels should be eyewitness accounts of Jesus' life.

But matters are not so simple. I think a compelling two-part argument can weaken the case for eyewitness testimony by anyone. Let me start with a biological argument because in many ways biology is destiny. This argument is tied to the dating of the gospels. For this portion, I wish to reintroduce Mark and Luke, in addition to Matthew and John, so that we might attempt a rough chronology of the four canonical gospels. The question of dating is extremely difficult. We do not possess in tangible form anything that was written about Jesus in the first century CE, the century in which Jesus lived. In fact the earliest full manuscripts date to the mid fourth century, probably more than 300 years after Jesus' death.[3] The attempt to date the canonical gospels earlier is therefore a supposition, not a fact. Even if we grant these suppositions, being mindful that they are anything but ironclad, theologians tend to place Mark as the first gospel, asserting its composition about perhaps 60 to 65 CE, though competent people prefer a date closer to 70 CE.[4]

---

[1] Bart D. Ehrman, *The New Testament: A Historical Introduction to the Early Christian Writings*, 5th edition (New York and Oxford: Oxford University Press, 2012) 114-115.

[2] Ibid., 195.

[3] Ehrman, *The New Testament*, 20.

[4] "The Gospel According to Mark," New American Bible, 1139.

Note that, from the outset, this chronology, placing Mark first, violates the order in the New Testament which places Matthew first.

One might state that the New Testament contains some letters from Paul of Tarsus. Such letters would be well within the frame of the first century. The problem is that they tell us little about Jesus. Yes, Paul claims that Jesus rose from the dead, but he gives us no details about Jesus' life. What is absent from Paul is Jesus the historical person. For this reason I wish here to exclude Paul from treatment. Were we to take Paul seriously, we would encounter the additional difficulty that Paul was not an eyewitness to Jesus' life. Yes, Paul claimed to have had a vision of Jesus, but we know nothing about what actually happened because Paul revealed so little about the event.[1] What might have been called a vision was likely a hallucination. To put matters bluntly, Paul did not see the risen Jesus. He may have thought he did. By the time of Paul's experience, Jesus had been long dead.

The dating of Matthew is particularly important because to theologians it represents eyewitness material about Jesus. There must be great temptation to put Matthew as early as possible to make it seem like a primary document. Some scholars have tried to do just that, asserting that a partial gospel of Matthew dates from the 50s CE. Once Mark was circulated in the 60s, Matthew the apostle borrowed from it to fill any gaps in his gospel, creating a full-length account of Jesus. The problem is that the "early Matthew" thesis has no evidence for so early a date. Most scholars put Matthew (and Luke as well) between 80 and 85 CE.[2] I will argue that this dating is extremely important. Last came John, which may date as early as 90 or as late 100 CE.[3] This dating too is important because theologians hold John to be an eyewitness account.

Now, basic biological data must come to the fore. In his classic *Essay on the Principle of Population*, British cleric Thomas Malthus argued that humans tend to outrun their food supply. Results are catastrophic as famine, disease and warfare kill enough people to bring the population back in line with the food supply.[4] These checks on population operated not just in the eighteenth century but also for large periods of history. Antiquity was no different. The result was a short lifespan. Infant mortality was high.

For our purposes, one of the best-documented cases came from Malthus' eighteenth century. German composer Johann Sebastian Bach always had enough money to feed his family; yet diseases killed 10 of his 20 children

---

[1] Acts 9: 1-48 (New American Bible)
[2] "The Gospel According to Matthew," New American Bible, 1080, 1083.
[3] "The Gospel According to John," New American Bible, 1207.
[4] Thomas Malthus, *An Essay on the Principle of Population* (Oxford: Oxford University Press, 2000), 3.

before they reached adulthood.[1] Bach's children were not alone to suffer this fate. Churchyards in England are full of rows of little tombs inscribed with the name John, as a father tried desperately to pass on his name. In antiquity many Senate families, the richest of the rich, failed to produce a surviving son despite having all the resources in the world. The family thus lost its seat in the Senate. By this mechanism new names populated the Senate with each generation.

Studies of ancient Egypt and Rome put life expectancy at about 40 to 45 years for men and 30 to 35 years for women.[2] Of those who reached age 15, a significant accomplishment given high mortality, half died before the age of 45. To reach the age of 40 in antiquity and the Middle Ages marked one as an old person. This sketch does not preclude the possibility of exceptional longevity. Greek philosopher Plato is thought to have lived to age 80.[3] One must remember however that Plato was an aristocrat who never suffered hunger.

Matthew and John cannot have had such wealth. As commoners affiliated with a preacher who appears to have had no money, the apostles would have suffered all the slings and arrows of outrageous fortune. Would Matthew and John have lived long enough to write the two gospels? Matthew would have had to survive to age 80 to 85 and John would have had to approach a century. We have already seen that infant mortality was very high. Given the evidence from Bach's family, let's estimate the number at ½. Furthermore, we know that about half of all people who survived to age 15, well past infancy, died before age 45. That is, taking infant mortality (½) times mortality to age 45 (½), one arrives at the figure that only ¼ survived to age 45. That is, ¾ of all people died by age 45. Notice my generosity. The number should be before age 45, but I'm allowing longevity to 45.

Consider now that Matthew and John would have needed to survive roughly twice this long to have been able, even in biological and demographic terms, to have lived long enough to write their putative gospels. The probability of death before these ages must have been much higher than ¾. Matthew's lifespan would have to have been no shorter than that of Plato. John would have needed to exceed Plato's lifespan by at least a decade. To put matters simply, the claim that the apostles Matthew and John wrote eyewitness accounts of Jesus is extremely improbable. The short life spans in

---

[1] "How Many of Johann Sebastian Bach's Children Grew Older than 18 Years? www.bachonbach/100-johann-sebastian-bach-faq-a/faq-27-how-many-of-bach-s-kids-became-older-than-18.

[2] "Human Lifespans Have Not Been Constant for the Last 2000 Years." Johnhawks.net/weblog/reviews/life_history/age-specific-mortality-lifespan-bad-science-2009.html

[3] "Preface," in The Great Dialogues of Plato (New York: New American Library, 1955) 8.

antiquity almost surely consigned them to death decades before they could have written the gospels that carry their names.

How did the gospels acquire the names of Mark, Matthew, Luke and John, then? The answer may lie in the desire to produce authoritative documents about Jesus. The authors of the gospels were not eyewitnesses to Jesus' life.[1] Nonetheless they wished their documents to be convincing. A shortcut along this route, taking the gospel of John as an example, is to create the impression that the apostle John actually wrote the document even though he was surely dead by the time the writing was done. With a now illustrious pedigree, the gospel of John could claim to be authoritative, in a way that would be impossible were it known that some literate but undistinguished person wrote it.

Appeals to authority are not integral to just antiquity. Consider modern popular culture. Is there any product that Denver Broncos quarterback Payton Manning does not endorse? Advertisers could recruit you or me to endorse, say, Domino's Pizza, but why would anyone listen to us? By using Payton Manning, the equivalent of the apostle John, rather than us, in a nation saturated with popular culture, Domino's Pizza acquires an authority it would otherwise lack. The gospels rely on this same pattern of name recognition hybridized with celebrity. In other words, these were not historians per se, but propagandists.

But we have more than biology and demography to consider. A second line of evidence, leading from the literature itself, is no less emphatic in ruling out the probability that any of the gospel accounts could have been eyewitness accounts. Our attention remains on the four canonical gospels. We will consider the Gnostic gospels and other materials in a later section. The historian is right to demand written accounts of Jesus. History differs from archeology in requiring written records to bolster any conclusion about the past. Writing developed about 5000 years ago in Sumer, a region in what is today Iraq, with its independent development in Egypt about the same time. It is clear, then, that Jesus must have lived about 3000 years after the invention of writing, and so we should expect written accounts of such an outstanding figure. Again, a quick glance at the New Testament reveals four such accounts.

Let us scrutinize them. The first point is that the New Testament that you may or may not hold in your hand is the product of almost 2000 years of scholarship, translation and commentary. As historians, we would benefit from studying the original documents themselves at the time they were produced. In doing so, we encounter a series of surprises. The first, and perhaps it should be no surprise, is that we have no autographs (in the

---

[1] Ehrman, *The New Testament*, 19.

sense of documents written by the original author) of these four gospels or indeed any gospel. An autograph is a precious commodity because it is the actual text that the author wrote. To consider an example from American history, we do not have the autograph of the Declaration of Independence that Thomas Jefferson drafted at the beginning of July 1776. What we have is the document that the Continental Congress debated and approved on July 4, 1776. Autographs, then, are scarce. Without an autograph it is not possible to be certain of an author's intent. We don't know, therefore, what the original gospel writers intended to say. In a basic sense, the gospels are open to various interpretations that have fueled 2000 years of scholarship and commentary because we do not have the originals.

Perhaps another example might help. Musicologists have many of the autographs of Bach's compositions. After his second marriage, these autographs become exceedingly beautiful, as they are in the hand of his second wife, Anna Magdalena Bach. But if the music is in her hand, how can it be an autograph of Bach? It appears that Bach had the practice of dictating his music to Anna, making her hand an extension of his. Consider the contrary case: that Bach wrote no music, just as Jesus and Socrates wrote nothing about their lives. Imagine that oral traditions circulated about what Bach's music must have sounded like and that only 40 years or so after his death did anyone write down the putative contents of this music. How reliable would such texts be? Yet this is exactly the situation that confronts us in reading and interpreting Mark's gospel, and the later gospels are even more problematic.

Instead, as the foregoing analogy to Mark's gospel suggests, we have manuscripts of the gospels.[1] A manuscript is produced by a copyist. The first manuscripts must have been copied from the original autographs or speeches, but they too do not exist. In a sense, it is shocking to base whole religions on fundamental documents that do not exist, but time exacts a cost. The autographs and the manuscripts must have been printed on sheets of opened papyrus stems or similar material. Papyrus was an all-purpose plant in antiquity and its use by authors and copyists was ubiquitous. To be sure it was less durable than parchment or today's paper, and this circumstance accounts for the fact that much that was written does not survive in any form. To return to the first century CE, the period when Jesus lived, the Roman writer Pliny the Elder was enormously prolific according to those who knew him, but only a single work, albeit a long, multi volume one, survives to the present, his *Natural History*.

Given that so much has been lost, it is necessary to ask what we have regarding the gospels. Autographs and first manuscripts are out of play, and

---

[1] Ibid., 20-22.

the earliest documents that survive to the present are very small fragments of a gospel. Consider the gospel of John, which we have dated to 90 or 95 CE, perhaps even 100 CE. Since we do not have an original version, an autograph, only later transcriptions, we have nothing from the 90s CE. This means that we have no copy of John even from the end of the century when Jesus lived. The first inkling of John comes from a fragment of papyrus the size of a credit card and dating to perhaps 125 CE, nearly a century after Jesus' death.[1] That means about three generations later. Because the fragment contains such a tiny portion of John, it is not possible to know much about the original account.

In dating such writings, chronologists rely partly on the testimony of ancient authorities like second-century scholars Papias and Irenaeus. Perhaps even more important are textual references in the canonical gospels themselves. Consider the synoptic gospels of Mark, Matthew and Luke. Note that Mark contains no reference to the Roman destruction of the Jewish temple in Jerusalem in 70 CE. This omission likely means that the author of Mark had no knowledge of this event and so Mark must date before 70 CE. Matthew and Luke, however, claim that Jesus predicted this destruction and so these accounts were written after 70 CE.

In fact no complete manuscript of any of the canonical gospels is known from any earlier than 350 CE, more than 300 years after Jesus' death. These late manuscripts tell us two vital pieces of information. First, they are anonymous. That is, they do not claim to have an author. So the putative authors Mark, Matthew, Luke and John do not come to us from the earliest available sources. To take the case of the apostle John, for example, why would he, given his prominence and authority, not have affixed his name to the gospel he supposedly wrote? Remember that the gospels are a kind of argumentative essay. They desire to persuade the reader that Jesus performed many miracles, including rising from the dead, and so he is god. These are ambitious claims that demand an authoritative author. Who could have been more authoritative than a man who Jesus chose as a disciple and who was likely privy to Jesus' most intimate thoughts? Yet the gospel's manuscripts are silent. That is, they give us no reason to suppose that they are really eyewitness accounts, at least in the cases of Matthew and John, of Jesus' life.

If we have no reason to suppose that Mark, Matthew, Luke and John wrote the gospels that now bear their names, two issues arise. We must try to determine who really wrote these documents and how they ended up with their current names. Regarding our first issue, our prospects are nil. Without documentary evidence from the sources that exist, we cannot

---

[1] Ibid., 195-196.

know who wrote these gospels. Some might not decry such circumstances because much ancient literature is anonymous, but this misses the point that many significant texts bear the authors' names. We know Greek mathematician Euclid's writings, the plays of Greek dramatist Sophocles, the medical texts of Greek physician Galen, the astronomy and geography of Greek scholar Claudius Ptolemy of Alexandria, Egypt, the histories of Greek authors Herodotus and Thucydides and of Roman historian Tacitus, and of course the work of Pliny the Elder and the dialogues of Plato. One might expand this list substantially, but the point is that it is troubling to place one's faith in Jesus when no one knows who wrote the texts about him. Without knowing anything about the author, we can have no confidence in his authority, relationship to Jesus, activities, prior or later writings, or any of a host of other attributes that might allow one to gauge this author's comments about Jesus. The situation is no different today. Were a scholar to discover an anonymous play the media might not herald the find, but if it was a lost play by American dramatist and Nobel laureate Eugene O'Neill the news would captivate many people inside and outside academe.

Naming the Gospels

If the gospels are anonymous, how did they acquire their names? We have already made a first attempt to answer this question and are now prepared to launch a second salvo. Remember that after Jesus' death, a movement arose to make him the center of a new religion or perhaps a modification of Judaism, Christianity. Remember too that this new Church took up the hierarchies and administrative structure of the Roman Empire of which it was a part. This meant that leaders and scholars who were thought to have merit were in a position to make many decisions about how to understand Jesus. These men gave the gospels the authors that they never had.

One must note at the outset that these men lived centuries after Jesus' death and so could have no eyewitness insights into the man. Among these leaders was the second-century Church authority and scholar Papias, who appears to have been the first to weave the name Mark into the narrative of the earliest gospel.[1] It's not clear where Papias derived this name, but it may have been from oral stories that had circulated about this gospel. Of course Mark is not among the names of the apostles, so no attempt could be made to credit him as an eyewitness to Jesus' life. Papias got around this problem by linking Mark to Peter, an important disciple for a number of reasons. Peter of course must have been an eyewitness, so that even though Mark was not,

---

[1] Craig L. Blomberg, *Can We Still Believe the Bible? An Evangelical Engagement with Contemporary Questions* (Grand Rapids, MI: Brazos Press, 2014) 77.

it would help if he could be claimed to have derived his information straight from Peter.

According to tradition Mark was thought to be an assistant to Peter. But here, language arises as an issue. Peter was portrayed as a simple fisherman. Because he could converse with Jesus, Peter, like Jesus, must have spoken Aramaic, a language of commoners in Palestine. But the gospel of Mark was written in Greek. Whoever he was, it is not easy to assert that Mark was fluent in both Greek and Aramaic. The gospel of Mark must have been written in Greek in order to reach a wider, international audience. The link between Mark and Peter therefore appears tenuous. Those who followed Papias nonetheless held onto the Mark myth. At the end of the second century Irenaeus, bishop of Lyon, France, reiterated Papias' assertion of Mark as author of the earliest gospel. Clement, bishop of Alexandria, Egypt, dated the gospel by affirming that Mark wrote it during Peter's lifetime. If Emperor Nero executed Peter between roughly AD 64 and 68, then the gospel of Mark must date to about the mid 60s. Given the paucity of evidence, there is no reason to suppose that the author of this gospel wrote much later or much earlier, particularly since, as we have seen, the linkage between Mark and Peter is weak.

Still later, from biblical commentator and translator Jerome, a saint in the Catholic Church, emerged the tradition that Mark died in Alexandria about 62 CE, pushing Mark even earlier than Clement had allowed. This legend had interesting consequences. In antiquity there was a grave in Alexandria whose occupant was thought to be the evangelist Mark. Meanwhile in Italy, the decline of the Roman Empire left numerous cities in control of their own destinies, at least for a time. Venice in the northeast emerged as a commercial and seafaring power. The plutocrats of Venice realized that to be truly great, they needed a symbol of greatness. By some convoluted logic, the Venetians determined that greatness would come if they stole Mark's body from Egypt and entombed him in Venice. The plan succeeded, and Venice built Saint Mark's Square to proclaim its possession of Mark, or at least his bones. Of course there is no reason to suppose that any person with any connection to any gospel had ever been entombed in Egypt and later Italy.

Papias and Irenaeus averred that the apostle Matthew wrote his gospel during the lives of Peter and Paul of Tarsus. This reckoning gave a date again of about 60 to 65 CE since both Peter and Paul were executed about the mid 60s. The church attributed the third gospel to Luke. By tradition Luke was a physician and a companion of Paul. His status as physician, true or not, probably means very little. Medical training was not rigorous and would have been little valued in the writing of the life of Jesus. The connection to Paul also means less than one might suppose. Despite his claim of a vision,

Paul came to Christianity after Jesus' death. Paul had never known Jesus and was therefore not an eyewitness to his life. Even if all that is said about Luke is accurate, he could not have had access to firsthand knowledge of Jesus. In the beginning of the gospel of Luke, the author admits he used other sources, which we would have to expect of a man who had no direct knowledge of the events. Luke claims to have had access to eyewitness accounts of Jesus, but he never reveals these sources. Again we have no way of verifying Luke's statements and, without evidence, caution should guide us. To Luke is also attributed the Acts of the Apostles, an account of the early church after Jesus' death. The failure to cite one's sources creates a chasm between scholarly expectations in antiquity and modernity. By modern standards nothing Luke or his gang of believers wrote could ever be remotely close to scholarship.

The final canonical gospel, John, is fascinating in many ways because of the information that is found nowhere else in the study of Jesus.

The author, we have seen, was thought to have been the apostle John. Biological and demographic data show that it is highly improbable that he was alive when the gospel attributed to him was written. Even Papias admitted that so much time had elapsed since the death of Jesus that John was likely disqualified as author of the gospel attributed to him.

We do not know who wrote the gospels. We do not know how close, if at all, these authors were to Jesus. We cannot evaluate their credentials as putative authorities about Jesus. We can say, however, that the New Testament contains no firsthand accounts of the life of Jesus. That is, a chasm exists between what we might like to know about Jesus and the material that has survived to modernity. Because of the nature of these sources, we know almost nothing about Jesus, and we cannot know more. What exist instead are texts of a legendary figure.

Jesus and Socrates

Let me tackle the problem of eyewitness accounts from a different vantage point. One might parallel the connection between Jesus and the authors of the canonical gospels with the link between Socrates and Plato. A brief overview of Socrates and Jesus reveals points in common. Socrates was an itinerant teacher in Athens, Greece, and appears to have had very little money. He focused much of his teachings on how people should strive to live. Jesus appears to share these characteristics, having been an itinerant teacher in Judea. He too does not appear to have had much money and his ministry focused on the right way to live, at least to an extent. Like Jesus, Socrates gathered around him a group of acolytes. The difference is that one of Socrates' followers, Plato, was an eyewitness who wrote what appear to have been firsthand accounts of Socrates' life. This differentiates Socrates from Jesus, who had no eyewitness biographers. Plato was the son of aristocrats and had every advantage in his upbringing. Like any privileged youth, Plato had a sound education and found an affinity for the methods and intellectual rigor of Socrates. Jesus had no such aristocrat in his immediate entourage.

Yet even so, the task of finding the historical Socrates in his pupil's dialogues is not easy. Let us consider just two of Plato's dialogues, the *Apology* and *Phaedo*. The *Apology* is largely a series of monologues and so does not fit easily with many of Plato's other writings. It may have been the first work of Plato and so is an early dialogue-monologue. The *Phaedo* is a middle dialogue that Plato wrote many years after the *Apology*. Just as the writings about Jesus are varied, so the *Apology* and *Phaedo* give us different accounts of Socrates.

Of the two, the *Apology* seems to be closer to the historical Socrates. It presents Socrates as the wisest man in Athens because he alone knew the full extent of his ignorance.[1] Other people supposed that they had knowledge but did not, whereas Socrates never entertained this illusion. He was an incessant questioner who sought to help others give birth to knowledge. A classic portion of the *Apology* will help us note the differences between it and the *Phaedo*. In the *Apology*, Socrates comes to the topic of death and the afterlife. Sticking to his self-depiction as a man without knowledge, Socrates professes that he knows nothing about death and the afterlife.[2] Death may simply be oblivion in which the deceased has eternal sleep untroubled by dreams. What could be more desirable, Socrates wonders? On the other hand death might be a portal to the afterlife. This option too would please Socrates, since he would be able to question the gods and to expose their ignorance.

The *Phaedo* is different. To see these differences one must return to the beginning of the *Apology*, where Plato lists himself as one of the onlookers at Socrates' trial. Now, on the last day of Socrates' life as depicted in the *Phaedo*, Plato announced that he was too ill to be present.[3] It is as though Plato has abjured his eyewitness status at the end of Socrates' life. Instead, the *Phaedo* emerges with a complicated framing device so that the story of Socrates' death comes to Plato through a chain of people, so wrote Plato. Almost immediately one encounters a different Socrates in the *Phaedo*. He is still a questioner, but one who rises beyond this status by supplying copious knowledge to the men gathered around him. He is no longer ignorant. If one could count Socrates an agnostic in the *Apology*, this stance is nowhere present in the *Phaedo*. Socrates is now certain about the existence of an afterlife and claims four ways to prove the immortality of the soul.

---

[1] Plato, *Apology*, 427.
[2] Ibid., 445-446.
[3] Plato, *Phaedo*, 462.

How does one account for the two Socrates, both sketched by a man who was an eyewitness to his life? There are no easy answers. Even in the *Apology*, Plato did not likely make any record of the long speeches he attributes to Socrates. He must have written about Socrates in a way that convinced Plato that he was doing justice to the memory of his mentor. What changed between the *Apology* and the *Phaedo* must be time and the maturation of Plato's own ideas, which he put in the mouth of Socrates. That suggests that the four proofs for the immortality of the soul must be Plato's ideas and are probably not original to Socrates. In this respect Plato must have created fiction of his own. None of this is meant to denigrate Plato, only to show that putative eyewitness accounts may not be as faithful to the person as one might hope, whether they aggrandize or diminish the subject. How much less reliable are the accounts of Jesus, based as they are on putative sources that contain no eyewitness material!

The Method of Doubt

Turn to the gospels with this thought in mind. Here the problems multiply because one has no eyewitness accounts at hand. Every sentence becomes suspect. One must be especially vigilant when one comes to extraordinarily events. In the gospel of John for example Jesus raised Lazarus from the dead. Extraordinary events demand extraordinary evidence. Billions of people have died over time. Today thousands of humans die every day, yet we can pinpoint no resurrections from the dead. We are right to inquire about the Lazarus syndrome. What evidence supports it? Why does this miracle occur only in John and nowhere else in the written record about Jesus? Is this a case of the latest gospel containing the greatest legendary material? If by now you are questioning the accuracy of the gospels, you are on the correct path. We will focus additional attention on the Lazarus story in chapter 4.

Let us return to another problem with the gospels, and indeed with all ancient texts. I want to approach this problem in terms of what might be called the publication process. Contrast might help us grasp the essential features. Today the process is relatively straightforward. An author, finalizing a book, sends it, usually electronically, to the publisher. An editor or editors set to work to ensure in house style. At the end of editing the author usually has two chances to scrutinize the final copy in hopes of catching every last typographical error. With the final changes in place, the publisher issues copies of the book to sellers, online and brick and mortar. These copies are all identical. Even if one or two typos survive, these will be reproduced in every copy of the book so that a person in North Dakota will have exactly the same text before him or her as someone in Florida.

The publication process in antiquity, if it may be called that, was very different. In antiquity everything depended on hand labor. An author made an autograph letter by letter over some span of time. If the autograph proved worthy of preservation because of its contribution to knowledge, a problem immediately arose. The papyrus scroll was not the most durable writing surface. In the Levant, where Jesus lived, arid conditions dried the scroll so that it could become nearly black, obscuring the writing in the process. Before desiccation ruined the scroll, someone had to copy it as a way of preservation. The process of copying was fraught with danger. Consider the autograph for example. In antiquity no one had invented a space between words and punctuation or capital letters where appropriate. The autograph, then, was a series of line in which all letters were crammed next to one another. It was up to the reader to make sense of what might appear to be a jumble of letters. The person who copied the autograph had to be particularly vigilant, because the act of moving from autograph to manuscript might involve the loss of letters and even lines of text particularly when this task was repeated to the point of fatigue.

A loose analogy might borrow from genetics. The building blocks of deoxyribose nucleic acid (DNA) are nucleotide bases, large sugar molecules. The bases may be altered just as letters and lines were in the process of making a manuscript. In the biological world such alterations are known as mutations. Because mutations are chance events, they seldom benefit the cell. In many cases the cell dies and the body has eliminated the deleterious mutation. In other cases one is not so fortunate. The uncontrolled replication of a cell by mutation in the rate of growth benefits the cell at the expense of the body. The unfortunate person has cancer.

Just as an organism can have its genetic material altered, so humans alter an autograph in the process of copying it. In a sense their errors multiply as though they were a cancer. The accruing of errors further complicates the interpretation of any ancient text. Different errors occurred at different rates and in different places. Manuscripts of, say, the gospel of Mark, were circulated in some parts of the Mediterranean Basin, the core of the Roman Empire. Errors would accrue in one area and a second set of mistakes in another. The result was that when manuscripts of Mark could be compared, each differed from the other and certainly from the autograph, though we have seen that the autograph did not survive. But because the autographs of the gospels are no longer extant, it is not possible amid errors to be sure what the anonymous author or authors meant to convey with precision. In fact mistakes must have occurred very frequently in the early decades of Christianity. The ancient copyists were likely not professionals. They were almost surely Christians who undertook the task out of their sense of pious duty. They were probably not trained to copy documents as scribes for a living and so were inattentive at times and subject to error. Only in the Middle Ages did monks with sufficient training and experience come to shoulder the burden of copying the gospels. The error rate appears to have slowed, but by 1000 years after Jesus' death they were in the business of copying manuscripts that were already cluttered with centuries of mistakes. The task of scholars and biblical commentators has been to find and eliminate errors while trying to preserve as much of what they believed was part of the original first century accounts. Remember, though, that we do not have these documents or know much about the authors. What, then, can we hope to know about Jesus?

These sources represent a paucity of information about Jesus. One might assert that any man who received four life stories must have been significant. Such a person refers to the four canonical gospels, but we have seen that they were not eyewitness accounts and contain a large element of the fanciful. Remember the raising of Lazarus as such an example. Yet they are almost all one can consult regarding early accounts, though, as we have seen, they were not early. In fact, if one puts Jesus' death about 30 CE, the number that Luke holds and the number that fits neatly into Pontius Pilate's reign between 26 and 36 CE, and takes the century after his death, namely 30 to 130 CE, the canonical gospels are just about all one has.[1] True, we will toward the end of this chapter turn to a significant statement about Jesus in the *Annals* of Roman historian Tacitus and other second century sources.

The Canonical Gospels

For the moment let us consider the basics of the canonical gospels. They are called canonical gospels because the early Christian church considered them authoritative and holy and so placed them in their list of holy books, known as a canon, and which we now call the New Testament. Keep in mind that the church made these judgments on religious not historical grounds. The church does not seem to have been concerned with historical accuracy. Rather, if I may put the matter in these terms, the church identified these four gospels as propaganda material to persuade people that Jesus was god. There is no historical information in such an assertion. Keep in mind that this assertion is just that, a speculative claim devoid of evidence. This state of affairs is problematic. How can one gauge the accuracy of a claim that is bereft of evidence? We see this problem with assertions today. They are notorious in sports. One might assert that professional basketball player Lebron James is King James. In fact this talk may have originated with the man himself, but how do we evaluate this claim? Is it an attempt to ramp up

---

[1] Luke 3: 23; Ehrman, *The New Testament*, 238.

publicity? There is no evidence that Mr. James is a hereditary nobleman, so how can he be a king? Yet the appellation has stuck. At least some basketball fans must believe it to some degree. In the end it remains just an assertion.

The analogy with Jesus may not be farfetched. Jesus may have claimed some special status, just as Mr. James has. In both cases the claims are just assertion. The Christian may wish to save face by claiming that the hypothesis that Jesus was god is backed by evidence, namely the miracles. How could Jesus have performed so many miracles and not been god? The problem is that this type of reasoning is circular. Not only is the claim of divinity an assertion the miracles are assertions as well. One group of eyewitnesses wrote an independent account to try to verify that Jesus performed miracle after miracle. To go back to Lazarus, if Jesus raised him from the dead, should not Lazarus have described this experience as a necessary precondition to convincing the reader that the event really happened? Why did Lazarus not write his own gospel? Should he not have been grateful to Jesus and wished to commemorate this event is some grand way? We populate our towns with statues of Civil War veterans who lived comparatively uneventful lives but we have no shrine to Lazarus to memorialize his resurrection. Perhaps Lazarus never rose from the dead. In a larger sense perhaps no one has ever risen from the dead.

We need not compare the canonical gospels verse by verse, but curious statements abound in them. Consider the most basic issue: Jesus' resurrection. It is the putative event upon which Christianity is founded. We will have much more to say in chapter 5. For now consider that the earliest gospel, Mark, does not depict Jesus' appearances to his apostles. One might protest that the last verses do make such statements, but these verses were add-ons, probably in the second or third centuries CE, far too late for an eyewitness account. The earliest manuscripts of Mark end with Mary Magdalene encountering a man at the empty tomb who states that Jesus has been raised from the dead. Mary does not actually see Jesus, even in this friendly account. One might brush aside this evidence by referring to Matthew, Luke, and John, all of which record the presence of a risen Jesus. Remember, however that these are the late gospels, with Matthew and Luke dating no earlier than 80 CE and John no earlier than 90 CE. Over time exaggerations grow into legends and the fanciful becomes spectacular beyond description. Chapter 5 will say more about the illusion of the resurrection, though we have already poked a large hole in the claim.

The canonical gospels are striking in other fundamental differences. For example, aside from the resurrection of Jesus, the raising of Lazarus is the supreme miracle that foreshadows the events after Jesus' death. Guess where this miracle appears? Only in the latest canonical gospel, John, has the process of exaggeration run riot over the text, as we may recall such treatment earlier.[1] Mark, Matthew and Luke do not report this miracle. If it really happened and if the gospel writers wished to convert readers to their faith, why did they omit such a stunning miracle? They did not recall the miracle of Lazarus because it never happened. By the time of John, with all eyewitnesses surely dead, the author could write what he wished without fear of criticism. To John the god Jesus could do anything.

This feature of change over time is not unique to the gospels. Recall the *Apology*, an early dialogue of Plato. In it, his mentor, Socrates, is wise only to the extent that he is fully aware of his ignorance. He is therefore not a source of knowledge, but rather a midwife who helps others give birth to their own knowledge. He is a questioner not a man who has all the answers. Yet by the middle and late dialogues—the *Phaedo* and *Republic* are excellent examples— Socrates has undergone a striking change. He questions people to the point that they admit their ignorance and then gives long speeches to fill his audience with his extensive knowledge. Socrates went from ignorance to one of the most knowledgeable people in all literature. Plato of course was the architect of this change and appears to have acted to use the memory of his mentor to express his own mature thinking. Remember that Plato, by the nature of his relationship to Socrates, was an eyewitness to his life. Yet even in Plato one encounters what must have been distortions to the historical memory of Socrates. This process is much more rampant in sources like the gospels because they are not eyewitness accounts.

My point is that there were no limits to the actions of authors, certainly not in antiquity. This is particularly true, we have seen, because of the lateness of the gospels. It seems strange that the people who followed Jesus and who must have witnessed his many miracles did not write about their rabbi even during his life. Recall for example that Lazarus wrote nothing about Jesus. If all that the gospels claim about Jesus were true, why wouldn't anyone who witnessed his saying and deeds have memorialized them on the spot? It may be that none of Jesus' followers was literate. They appear to have been poor ordinary fishermen and peasants. They likely spoke Aramaic, as did Jesus. Yet the New Testament was written in Greek. How did minimally literate people suddenly learn to write Greek? It also seems possible that during and immediately after Jesus' life no one had an interest in writing his sayings and deeds. This assertion may seem puzzling, but one must remember that the first century CE was a period of apocalyptic thinking. By this I mean that likely Jesus and his followers believed that the world would soon end. They believed that the forces of evil and oppression, evident in the Roman occupation, had pushed the Jews and their god to the limit. Because their

---

[1] John 11: 1-44 (New American Bible)

god was just he could no longer tolerate this evil age and so would soon intervene in history to overthrow evil and usher in the Kingdom of God. One finds this suggestion in full flower in Mark and even in the later Matthew.[1] Both gospels claim that Jesus foretold the terrible signs by which one would recognize the coming end of times. In Mark Jesus appears to have said that some of his followers would not die before god ushered in the Kingdom of God. This may have been an authentic saying of Jesus because his followers appear to have clung to this idea. They may not have written about Jesus because they were so certain that the world was about to end. In this event, the writing of Mark about 65 CE must have marked a milestone. When we calculated life expectancy in antiquity, we concluded that by this date most and probably all of Jesus' followers would have been dead. And yet the world had not ended. This recognition must have led Greek-speaking converts to Christianity to begin to write down the stories of Jesus.

The fact that these converts had not known Jesus makes it imperative to know where they got their information. If one asks the question today of where one found information to write about, say, the history of smallpox, the answer would involve an aggregate of written sources: books, scholarly articles, contemporary journalism, and perhaps the internet. Our schoolchildren are learning that the internet is not just one but the primary source of information about a topic. Hopefully college will disabuse them of this view.

Many of these luxuries were unavailable to the ancients. The immediate problem of the sources of gospels is that they no longer appear to exist. Part of the information may have come from oral traditions, which of themselves would not have survived. Oral traditions would have been notorious for their fluidity. The rumors that surface about athletes and celebrities seldom have value, and the same would have been true about the oral traditions that circulated about Jesus. The earliest gospel, Mark, would have needed sources of some type because the author was not an eyewitness to the events of Jesus' life. The claim that he got his information from Peter seems difficult to believe given that Peter knew how to speak Aramaic and the author of Mark knew how to speak and write Greek. Even the supposition that this author knew Peter has no evidence to support it. Mark therefore must have relied on independent sources. The important point is that we know nothing about such sources because they have not survived. The process is akin to trying to reconstruct the life ways of a species of dinosaur despite having no fossils of it.

What seems to be clear, however, is that Matthew and Luke borrowed from Mark. This statement is repeated as though it is no surprise. I'm

---

[1] Mark 13: 3-8; Matt 24: 3-28.

surprised nonetheless by the claim that this borrowing was natural coupled with the statement that Matthew was an apostle and so an eyewitness to Jesus' life. If Matthew really were an eyewitness, why would he have needed to rely on Mark for information? What occurred in Matthew and Luke was tantamount to plagiarism of Mark. Yet Matthew and Luke share other material that is not found in Mark. From where did it come? The claim is that Matthew and Luke independently took this material from an unidentified written source known as Quelle (Q), which means simply "source."[1] It is important to note that no one over the centuries has ever identified Q. It may once have existed, but at the moment it has as much certainty as our mythical dinosaur.

Other scholars confuse matters further by positing the existence of an M source to which Matthew had access, and an L source to which Luke had access.[2] It is difficult to know how to respond to such speculation except to say that without concrete evidence of these sources, one must suspend belief. Some biblical commentators propose that Matthew, by borrowing from Mark and M, and Luke, by borrowing from Mark and L, were complete. That is, they did not need the existence of Q. So did Q exist or not? These questions can throw one into a fit. The rule is that we should favor assertions for which evidence exists, in which case they are no longer mere assertions. Medical authorities do not posit the existence of a new virus or bacterium without evidence for the pathogen. Why does speculation have such free reign when theological matters are involved? I suspect that the need to believe corrupts our ability to be rational.

When one speaks about the borrowing among Mark, Matthew and Luke, known as the synoptic gospels, the situation is even worse when one confronts John. Here it looks like a repetition of the Socrates problem. Recall that only in the middle and late dialogues does Socrates move from ignorant questioner to man whose long discourses display brilliance. Much the same happens with John's Jesus. Where the Jesus of the synoptics told parables to communicate a pithy message, by John Jesus emerges an as intellectual capable of holding his own with anyone. Gone are the nuggets of parables. In John, Jesus gives long discourses about who he is and why he should be worshipped. From where did all this new information come? The short answer is we do not know. Oral traditions probably would not have been this elaborate or would not have survived so long. Perhaps they are comparatively new traditions to have escaped being encoded in the synoptics and yet to have found a place in John. Again this is all guesswork

---

[1] Ehrman, *The New Testament*, 107.
[2] Ibid.

and little better than speculation. The point is that speculation alone props up the stories of Jesus.

The Gnostic Accounts

The problem enlarges when one begins to realize that the canonical gospels are not all that one has about Jesus. Remember that during the first century after Jesus' death, the canonical gospels are nearly all we have about Jesus. Extend the chronology to the fourth century CE and many more accounts materialize. These accounts, of which there are at least 35 about Jesus, come primarily from a single spectacular find in 1945 in Nag Hammadi, Egypt.[1] These texts, buried and hidden for centuries in the desert, are known as the Nag Hammadi corpus or the Nag Hammadi library. The manuscripts all date to the fourth century, but some of the autographs, which do not exist, must be as old as the second century CE. Egypt may seem an odd place for the discovery of Christian texts. Remember, however, that between the rise of Christianity and the conquest by Islam, Egypt was Christian, even though the interval was comparatively short. These texts will be important throughout this study. Here, a few salient points are in order. The first is that these documents are often characterized as exemplars of Gnostic Christianity. Gnostic derives from the Greek *gnosis*, meaning "knowledge." This terminology is necessary to understand that many Gnostics believed that salvation lay not in the performance of good deeds or the veneration of relics or other behaviors but in the discovery of the full import of the knowledge Jesus taught. This knowledge was not available to everyone but to those who had access to Jesus' hidden teachings, which produced this hidden knowledge.

Although these texts were written in Coptic, the language after the fall of the hieroglyphs and before the conquest of Arabic, the emphasis on knowledge appears to owe a heavy debt to Greek philosophy. Both Plato and Aristotle wrote often about how one acquires knowledge. This is exactly what the Gnostic texts purport to do by helping acolytes acquire the knowledge that Jesus wished them to have. Yet for the most part Plato and Aristotle ignore any hidden aspect to knowledge. Knowledge was plain for everyone to apprehend. With Plato, one simply concentrated the intellect on this knowledge. Of course, in the *Republic* Plato made clear that humans were not always in an ideal position to grasp knowledge, and this idea appears to be part of the Gnostic creed. It is not surprising to find Greek ideas in Coptic texts because Greece had a strong influence on Egypt, just as Egypt influenced Greece. In fact Alexander the Great founded the Greek colony of

---

[1] William C. Placher. *A History of Christian Theology: An Introduction* (Philadelphia: The Westminster Press, 1983) 46.

Alexandria in the Nile delta. It became a leading center of intellectual inquiry, diffusing Greek ideas throughout Egypt.

Many of these texts would surprise the staid Christian. The gospel of Philip likely implies that Jesus and Mary Magdalene had an intimate relationship. I have suggested as much in a previous publication, and if this surmise is true, it goes a long way toward explaining why the author of the gospel of Mark favored Mary as the discoverer of the empty tomb.[1] The insight that Jesus may have had a lover goes much farther than any of the other gospels in humanizing him. It also makes one wonder why the canonical gospels say so little about her. Were the authors uncomfortable with a carnal Jesus? If so, this was the type of historical whitewashing that makes it nearly impossible to know much about Jesus the man.

Perhaps the greatest surprise among the Nag Hammadi texts is the gospel of Thomas. It may be the most important document of its kind. Written possibly as early as the second century CE, the gospel of Thomas is attributed to the apostle Thomas, though in no way could he have been alive. Thomas was thought to be the twin of Jesus. Such language is curious. If Jesus had been born by a virgin mother, as Matthew and Luke insist, then he cannot have had a true twin, at least not an identical one. Keep in mind the existence of two types of twins: identical and fraternal. The identical twin is interesting because he or she is a clone of the other twin, both sharing exactly the same genotype. Any differences between identical twins must be the result of the environment. Fraternal twins, on the other hand, are not genetic equivalents. They are simply siblings that happen to have been born at the same time. These siblings need not be the same sex, whereas identical twins must be of the same sex.

If Jesus had a twin, that twin must have been fraternal to permit the birth narrative in Matthew and Luke to have any hope of standing the scrutiny of chapter 2. In fact, given the birth narrative it would be better to say that Jesus could have had no twin, only a half brother. Once one dispenses with the birth narrative, as we will do in the next chapter, then it is possible that this Thomas might have been Jesus' identical twin. If so the author of the gospel of Thomas must have been eager to adopt this pseudonym to lend credibility to his story. Who better, after all, to understand Jesus' secret knowledge than his own identical twin? Keep in mind that notions of identical and fraternal twins were probably beyond the conception of this ancient writer. If one can account for the naming of this gospel, the details must baffle anyone familiar with the canonical gospels. The gospel of Thomas is a stark account of 114 sayings attributed to Jesus. These saying supposedly reveal Jesus' hidden teachings. Several of these sayings

---

[1] Christopher Cumo, "The Temptation," *Swallow* magazine, 2007, 11-13.

are very similar to what one reads in the synoptics. The issue is continuity. If Thomas was not written until the second century CE, how did it retain material from the comparatively early gospel of Mark? The real shocker, of course, is what Thomas does not include. Miracles are completely absent from the text. There is no story of a virgin birth, no casting out of demons, no healings, no raising of Lazarus from the dead, and no resurrection of Jesus.[1] If all these events happened, why does Thomas not record them? If Jesus was a remarkable person capable of the greatest feats, why does not Thomas say so? The resurrection of the dead transcends anything that anyone can otherwise conceive and yet Thomas fails to note it. This omission makes sense only if Jesus never performed any miracles and especially never rose from the dead. A fully human Jesus is the only match for the fully human portrait Thomas paints. The mere comparison of sources, therefore, yields the gravest doubts about what the canonical gospels claim about Jesus. In addition to our reasoning in the introduction, we now have even stronger grounds for doubting that Jesus could have been god. Other objections will arise as we continue the quest for the historical Jesus.

Other Gnostic gospels dismiss the idea of a bodily resurrection of Jesus so central to the later canonicals like Luke and John. In fact there are few grounds for believing in the resurrected, deified Jesus in these Gnostic texts. The authors suppose that Jesus did not bodily rise from the dead but that the resurrection was somehow spiritual. Jesus appeared in visions—perhaps hallucinations are the proper term—to certain followers. At the outset we need to differentiate vision from hallucination. As I am using the term vision, I am supposing that some external stimulus has caused this sensation. If I have a vision of my truck from afar it must be because I can see my truck as I approach it from a distance. A hallucination, however, is a sensory experience devoid of any external stimulus. If my truck is not really in the distance I must be mistaken or in the grips of psychosis, however brief the episode is. Obviously, if the disciples did not perceive the actual resurrected Jesus, then they experienced a hallucination. This problem is important and will receive fuller treatment in chapter 5.

The results of such analyses have produced a new generation of sober biblical scholars. The renowned Jesus Seminar, an annual meeting of these scholars has produced dramatic if speculative results. Every year these men and women gather to vote for the verses in the gospels that actually record what Jesus said or did. The gospels under consideration are the familiar Mark, Matthew, Luke, and John, and our black sheep Thomas. In one recent showing scholars voted that only 18 percent of Jesus' sayings and 16 percent

[1] "The Gospel According to Thomas," in *The Other Gospels: Accounts of Jesus from outside the New Testament*, eds. Bart D. Ehrman and Zlatko Plese (Oxford: Oxford University Press, 2014) 161-173.

of his deeds are true to these accounts. The vast majority must therefore be fiction. This information is useful, but does it go far enough? We examined the quality of the sources at our disposal to discover time and again that the gospels fail to provide a historical account of Jesus. Why should we believe that even 18 percent of Jesus' sayings and 16 percent of his recorded deeds in these gospels are true? The percentages, as I will try to show throughout this book, must be far lower.

Pagan Sources

Bear in mind that the story of Jesus depends on more than religious sources. There are few, but important pagan sources. I use the term "pagan" with caution. As used today it means little more than primitive, false religious beliefs. I prefer a much narrower use bereft of stigma. A pagan in antiquity was nothing more than a person who was neither Jewish nor Christian. Such a person would be automatically biased against the view that Jesus was god. This stance counterbalances the Christian insistence on divinity. Notice too that Judaism (and later Islam) rejects the divinity of Jesus.

The first fact to apprehend is that no pagan author made a single reference to Jesus during the first century CE, the century in which he lived. These authors wrote about many topics. The omission of Jesus must have meant that he was not important. Yet if he was the miracle worker the gospels claim he must have been consequential. Here is a contradiction. The only way forward is to suppose that Jesus had not been important, an estimation that held true among all pagan authors. The fact that consensus must have turned against Jesus strongly suggests that he was no miracle working wizard.

Only in the second century did a small number of pagans, mostly Roman authors, begin to include remarks about Jesus, but these contain precious little information, again reinforcing the notion that Jesus was not worth space on a papyrus scroll. The first Roman reference to Jesus comes from a letter by Pliny the Younger to Emperor Trajan in 112 CE.[1] Pliny the Younger was the grandnephew of the famous author Pliny the Elder, whom we encountered earlier. Trajan was easily among Rome's most competent military commanders and emperors. He wanted capable people at administrative posts and so appointed Pliny the Younger to one. In this letter, Pliny emphasizes that Jesus had been a man whose followers worshipped him as a god. Pliny must have thought Jesus too inconsequential for more than the most cursory treatment because he says no more. Neither did Trajan reply with any desire to know more about Jesus nor with any

---

[1] Erhman, *The New Testament*, 239.

information of his own. Between the two of them Pliny and Trajan appear to have known almost nothing about Jesus.

An even more mysterious potential reference comes from the Roman historian and biographer Suetonius. About 115 CE he reported that "Chrestus" had fomented a riot. We do not know the date of the riot or where. Even more important we cannot be sure that "Chrestus" meant Christ. In any case Christ means "anointed one," and need not have referred to Jesus, though one is hard pressed to think of whom else Suetonius might have meant. It is equally difficult to think of a riot that Jesus had caused. If possible Suetonius may have known even less about Jesus than did Pliny and Trajan. The most cogent reference to Jesus, coming about the time of Suetonius' comments, derives from Roman historian Tacitus, perhaps the most capable intellectual of his age. Tacitus knit three historical people together, noting that Governor Pontius Pilate executed Jesus during the reign of Emperor Tiberius. This information, laconic as it is, is almost certainly correct and represents what appears to be the total information that pagans knew about Jesus. Note not only the brevity of these accounts, but also the absence of any miracles or other spectacular events. Jesus' claim to fame lay not in some supernatural realm but in the fact that for a moment he was notorious enough to face execution through the gruesome process of crucifixion. It is hard to make a dead man god.

The Problems of Translation

Translation of a popular or important work is necessary if it is to be widely known. For example, because I do not know Russian, I must rely on English translations to read the works of Russian novelist Fyodor Dostoevsky. The major works of the last 5000 years have all been translated into a number of languages, whether one specifies the Epic of Gilgamesh, Plato's dialogues, or *On the Origin of Species*. The books of the major religions have received the same treatment, so that it is not unusual to read the bible in translation. In fact, unless one can read ancient Hebrew, one cannot read the Old Testament in the original language, and unless one reads Greek, one cannot read the New Testament in the original. Translation is thus the norm for those of us without a solid grounding in some or all of the ancient languages.

Translation may appear to be a straightforward task. To translate the bible into English, one might suppose that the translator need only render the Hebrew of the Old Testament and the Greek of the New Testament into a word-for-word equivalent in English. This task is not easy to accomplish. In writing about the need for accuracy, Ron Rhodes, theologian and president of Reasoning from the Scriptures Ministries, defends the desire to "communicate to today's readers the same meaning that the original author's text conveyed to his original readers."[1] But is such an accomplishment possible or desirable? Rhodes appears to ignore the fact that the original autographs of the canonical gospels no longer exist. At best, translation of the bible means translation of later manuscripts already loaded with errors. Deference to the original authors is misplaced. Remember that they never knew Jesus and that we know nothing about them, not even their names. In such an instance, why should we grant them the status of authorities? They were simply fallible men who knew nothing by direct apprehension about the historical Jesus. Moreover, a translation is always an interpretation. It never passes undisturbed through a conduit from one language into another. The person making the translation must use his or her judgment. Translation is thus a selective process. In other words, it is never a perfect exercise.

Focusing solely on the bible, one may be surprised to learn that it was the product of translation even before church leaders finalized the canon and centuries before the life Jesus. Israel's position in the Levant drew the interest of Greece, a center of thought throughout antiquity. The earliest efforts, then, focused on the translation of the Hebrew of portions of the Old Testament into Greek. This process was initially fragmentary because the original translators selected only a few stories from the Old Testament to translate from Hebrew into Greek. In this regard, it is possible that Greek philosopher Plato read a Greek translation of the Hebrews' flight from Egypt, the central story in Genesis.[2] By no means did Plato or anyone else have a full translation of what was then the Old Testament. These translations were not literal renderings of Hebrew into Greek, because the Hebrew tradition of telling stories to illustrate a point did not coincide entirely with Greek tradition of constructing philosophical dialogues to convey meaning. Accordingly, the first translations introduced dialogues that were not part of the original Hebrews version. We will see that the problem of loose translations, of the attempt to convey more than a literal rendering of the text, as a potential stumbling block to understanding the bible through translation.

The desire to render the Old Testament into Greek produced the monumental translation of antiquity: the Septuagint. The date of this translation is uncertain and probably occurred between roughly 250 and 100 BCE, with the later date in favor among current scholars. The Septuagint satisfied an audience of Greek readers, but it ran the risk of dividing Christianity into two halves. During the High Roman Empire (roughly 200 BCE to 200 CE), no Roman could consider himself truly

---

[1] Ron Rhodes. *The Complete Guide to Bible Translations* (Eugene, OR: Harvest House Publishers, 2009) 17.
[2] Roland H. Worth, Jr. *Bible Translations: A History through Source Documents* (Jefferson, NC and London: McFarland Publishers, 1992) 3,

educated unless he read both Latin and Greek. Statesman and author Cato the Elder, statesman and orator Cicero, and Emperor Marcus Aurelius all demonstrated command of both languages. By the Late Empire, however, the Latin West had only a tenuous hold of Greek. Moreover, in the fourth century CE, linguist and scholar Jerome despaired over the many differences among the various Greek translations. He set himself the task of translating the Septuagint, in what was tantamount to a dead language in the West, into Latin, the language of Roman antiquity and medieval Europe. Jerome aimed to produce an authoritative text whose translation would not be challenged. One of Jerome's cardinal parts was the desire for meaning irrespective of a literal rendering of the bible. This freedom of translation created passages that differed from the language of the Septuagint. Moreover, because Jerome started with the Septuagint, he never wrestled with the Hebrew of the Old Testament. At least in the case of the Old Testament, Jerome did not start with the original language. His bible was a translation of a translation. The farther one stands from the original languages the greater is the probability of introducing errors into the text. Jerome's translation has been known as the Vulgate, meaning in the language of the masses. He had the aim of reaching a vast audience of literate people.

Jerome's interests in translating for meaning not a literal rendering and in widening the number of bible-literate people have served as the standards for subsequent translations. The Reformation displayed these traits in abundance. Dissatisfied with the obvious corruptions in the Catholic Church, the reformers of the Reformation sought to free the people from its tyranny by making every literate man and woman an arbiter of the bible in translation into modern European languages. One need not appeal to someone else's opinion of the bible. One could read it on one's own to form one's own judgment. Even before the Reformation of the sixteenth century, this process was in full swing. The fifteenth century produced two notable German translations of the bible so that by the time of religious reformer Martin Luther, there was nothing odd about the desire to create a new German translation of the bible. As Jerome had not done it, Luther returned to the original languages of the bible and admitted that he struggled mightily with the Hebrew of the Old Testament.

Luther was the inspiration for a wave of new translations among Protestant nations. In the seventeenth century, English king James I led the charge for a new English translation of the bible. James was no idle monarch. As early as age 10, he read a Latin translation of the bible. As a teen he translated several of the Psalms from the original Hebrew into English. James commissioned a committee of scholars to translate the bible from the original languages into English. Like Jerome and Luther, King James sought an authoritative text that would be the foundation upon which English Protestantism was built. Also like Jerome, James' intent was to steer clear of a mere literal rendering of the original Hebrew and Greek.

The King James Bible was of course not the final word in English translations of the bible, and the result has been an aggregate of bibles that differ in subtle and not so subtle ways from each other. Consider just the King James Bible, the American Standard Version and the Revised Standard Version. The first renders the fifth chapter of the gospel of Matthew in 1081 words, the second in 1056 words and the third in 1002 words.[1] In this context, consider a simple example of the choice of words in a single verse: Matt 4:19. The Revised Standard Version renders Jesus' language as "I will make you fishers of men," whereas the new Revised Standard Version renders this sentence as "I will make you fishers of people." This example is not as trifling as one might suppose. The difference is the gender-specific "men" versus the gender neutral "people." Notice that if we cling to "people" rather than "men," we affirm that Jesus wanted to recruit women as well as men to be his disciples, but is this certain? Jesus does seem to have had female followers. Consider the famous case of Mary Magdalena. She may have been a recruit, but it is no less plausible to say that she was his lover, confidante and perhaps shadow wife. Perhaps she was all of these things, but the mere word "people" does not quite capture what may have been the complexity of Jesus' thought. We are left with two translations that are not equivalent and no real guidance for which to prefer. For this reason, translations may create as many problems as they attempt to solve.

---

[1] Ibid, 117.

CHAPTER 2. THE BIRTH OF JESUS

Two of the four canonical gospels mention that Jesus' mother Mary was a virgin when she gave birth to him.[1] Although she was the mother, her fiancé Joseph was not the father. Instead, the holy spirit, a manifestation of the Jewish god Yahweh, was Jesus' father. One may note immediately that, aside from these two accounts, the rest of the New Testament is silent about Jesus' birth. There is literally not a single additional word about his birth. This silence is distressing because a miracle of this magnitude should have been widely acknowledged by the Christian sources, if it were true. Our purpose in this chapter will be to demonstrate beyond doubt that Jesus was not born of a virgin mother. Our knowledge about reproductive biology and a literary analysis demolish the claim of a virgin birth. This is an example of a larger phenomenon in which we will try, time and again, to approach an aspect of Jesus' life only to find a dead end of fabricated stories. We will see how frustrating it is to pinpoint certain knowledge about the man at the center of Western civilization.

The Virgin Birth: Reproductive Biology

Three ways—reproductive biology, logic and comparative literature—lend themselves to the treatment of the stories of Jesus' birth. I wish to begin this chapter by laying out the salient aspects of reproductive biology with the aim of applying these insights to Jesus' birth. At the outset, however, please note that only two—the gospels of Matthew and Luke—of the New Testament's 27 books contain even the most threadbare mention of Jesus' birth. The key feature on which I wish to focus is the claim in Matthew and Luke that Jesus' mother,

---

[1] Matt 1: 18-25; Luke 2: 1-14.

Mary, was a virgin at the time of conception, and during the development of the pregnancy and birth of Jesus. That is, Jesus, according to this tradition had no biological father. I wish to examine the two necessary suppositions in Jesus lore, namely that his mother was a virgin and he had no biological father in the light of reproductive biology.

At the outset, let us remember that reproduction is basic to all life. Without it a species would become extinct at the end of the first generation because it lacked to ability to produce a new generation. It is obvious to even the most cursory glance that life is abundant on earth. Reproduction is at the heart of this abundance. I am not interested in all forms of reproduction, but only in sexual reproduction. The reproduction of bacteria, for example, occurs through simple cell division and is outside our purview. When we examine sexual reproduction, we note that large numbers of plants and animals reproduce their kind through sex. If one admits that humans reproduce through sex, and that Jesus was human, one must consider him within the confines of sexual reproduction.

Here we must emphasize that sex is the mechanism for the conveyance of our genes, the great macromolecules of heredity, from one generation to another. These genes come in packages known as chromosomes. Think for example, of a packet of lifesavers. The package itself is the chromosome while each individual lifesaver is a gene. Note that these lifesavers are stacked in a linear row, exactly the arrangement of genes in a chromosome. Given life's diversity it is not surprising that different species pass on different numbers of chromosomes to their offspring. The simplest case may be the female worker bee, which receives only a single set of chromosomes from the queen bee. It is known as a haploid organism. At the other pole is durum wheat, the kind that is familiar to us in the making of pasta and noodles of all kinds. Durum wheat contains six sets of chromosomes. It is important to note that unlike the male drone, durum wheat is the norm in acquiring half its chromosomes from the father and half from the mother, if one will accept this usage to describe the patterns of inheritance in a plant. That is, a durum wheat seed has three sets of chromosomes from the mother and three from the father, the male and female reproductive structures being in the plant's flowers. Having six sets of chromosomes, durum wheat is a hexaploid. Most species of plants and animals, including humans, lie between the haploid and hexaploid states. The most numerous are those that are diploids, meaning they contain two sets of chromosomes, one from the father and one from the mother. The pea plant is an excellent example. So is the human.

This is the moment when Jesus becomes important. We have established that Jesus was human and that humans are diploids. Yet according to Matthew and Luke he violates one of the most fundamental parts of what makes one a human. If Matthew and Luke are right, Jesus must have inherited only one set of chromosomes, having obtained these from his mother, exactly as the female worker bee receives its genes only from the mother, the queen bee we have seen. But the state of having only one set of chromosomes, one may recall, is that one becomes a haploid rather than a diploid organism. If we are to take Matthew and Luke seriously, we must confess that Jesus was some kind of haploid female worker bee. He, or more accurately she, was a honeybee. But this classification contradicts the long tradition that Jesus was a human. We are stuck because the logic of reproductive biology, in the light of Matthew and Luke, demands that Jesus be a honeybee whereas the gospels demand that Jesus be human. This conflict cannot be resolved if one insists on the idea that Jesus' mother was the sole source of his hereditary material.

Let us be very clear about what Matthew and Luke demand that we believe. Matthew and Luke proposed that Joseph was not Jesus' biological father. He cannot therefore have contributed any sperm, any of his own set of chromosomes. It would be as though he were sterile. With Joseph sterile on theological grounds there would have been no sperm to unite with Mary's egg. But without sperm there can be no conception. Without conception, Jesus could not have come to exist. Without Jesus, no foundation exists for Christianity. Under these circumstances I am willing to admit that Jesus was born, that he did exist. Accordingly, Mary and Joseph must have had sex, the outcome of which was a nine-month pregnancy that led to Jesus' birth. If Joseph impregnated Mary, as must be certain, then the holy spirit or any other manifestation of god must not have impregnated Mary.

This is only proper because the holy spirit would necessarily be immaterial. Containing no physical form, the holy spirit would not have had a penis with which to deposit sperm in Mary. This being would not have had sperm in the first place because sperm is physical, tangible reality. If the holy spirit was immaterial, it could not have had any chromosomes to pass down to Jesus. The result, again, is Jesus the haploid honeybee. We see again that such an idea is itself sterile, a biological dead end where diploid organisms, including humans, are concerned. If Jesus, existed, then he was conceived and born like any other person. No appeal to the holy spirit is necessary or desirable. In fact any appeal to an immaterial father contradicts the reality of human reproduction. Either Jesus was human or a drone. There can be no middle ground, no way to bridge the reproductive chasm between these organisms.

If we can be certain that god, an immaterial being, cannot have fathered a flesh and blood Jesus, then we must opt for the obvious solution: a human father must be a parent of Jesus. The gospels, canonical and non-canonical, mention Joseph as at least a stepfather, and I am willing to pinpoint him as the biological father absent any other claimant. The necessity of a human father stems again from an understanding of reproductive biology. Consider the fact that any human male, including Jesus, must have an X and a Y chromosome. These are the sex chromosomes and the Y chromosome is a precondition for being male. Without a Y chromosome, a person will have two X chromosomes and will be a female. To state the matter another way, all women have two X chromosomes and all men have an X and Y chromosomes. Because all men necessarily have a Y chromosome, only they can pass it down to all male offspring. Because Jesus was a male, he must have inherited a Y chromosome from his father, who we stipulate to be the Joseph of the New Testament. Once more the necessities of heredity exclude god from having fathered Jesus and mandate that some man, probably Joseph, fathered Jesus. The story of the virgin birth is false from beginning to end.

The Logic of the Virgin Birth

Reproductive biology is not the only answer to the problem of a virgin birth. Simple rules of logic, which we began to apply above, disqualify such thinking. An appeal to logic requires us to understand the full import of the claim that a virgin gave birth to Jesus. First, Matthew and Luke do not disagree that Jesus had a human mother. Because he had a human mother, he too must have been human. Here one encounters the slogan that Jesus was fully human. This is not enough for Matthew and Luke. They march a step farther to claim that the holy spirit impregnated Mary. If the holy spirit is god, or one manifestation of god, then Jesus' father must have been a god. At the moment I do not wish to entangle myself in the question of whether the holy spirit was a separate god from the Jewish god Yahweh or whether these two were different manifestations of the same god. I will add only that Matthew and Luke provide no answer, leaving us with ambiguity. If we sweep this aside and posit along with Matthew and Luke that Jesus' father was a god, then it follows that Jesus was at a minimum a son of God. One is tempted to say, and here I agree, that this son of God must have partaken in the divine lineage of his father and so been god as well. Was Jesus a new god or another manifestation of Yahweh? The scriptures do not answer this question. Again we must be satisfied with ambiguity. If we do assent that Jesus was a god, then we may apply the old formula that Jesus was fully human and fully god.

This premise requires attention. Let us try to enumerate some of the qualities of a human and of a god. To start with the human attribute that should arrest our attention, a human is radically finite. This is true of other animals as well. To say that a human is radically finite, I mean, among other things, that he or she has only a partial knowledge of the world, only a partial capacity to shape events, and only a finite lifespan. This final point is worth attention. Humans have known for a very long time that death truncates every life. The Neanderthals, improperly thought primitive, appear to have been the first humans to bury the dead. They understood the radical finitude and the brevity of life and wanted through burial to memorialize the passing of one of their own. Our own species, *Homo sapiens*, appears always to have buried the dead.

To be a god is to be radically different from the lot of all humans. Rather than finite, a god must be bound by no limits. Far from possessing only partial knowledge, a god must have all knowledge. That is, it must be omniscient. The state of omniscience implies that a god can make no error. Far from possessing only a limited capacity to influence events, a god has the maximum power possible. That is there are no limits to a god's power. One must claim therefore that god is omnipotent. The third claim is perhaps the most important. Because a god is not bounded by any limit, it must be radically infinite. An infinite being must have always existed, must exist now, and exist forever into the future. That is an infinite being must extend backwards in time without reaching a beginning and extend forward in time without reaching an end. Such claims are difficult to interpret, and I will not digress to consider them here because this subject will reappear in chapter 7.

Remember, we have interpreted the birth narratives in Matthew and Luke to mean that Jesus was fully human and fully divine. Let us try to harmonize these components. Remember that a human has limited knowledge and a god has limitless knowledge. To have both qualities is to be a contradiction. A human has limited capacity to influence events whereas a god has unlimited power. Again the coupling of both represents a contradiction. Finally a human has a finite lifespan whereas a god has neither beginning nor end. Yet again these qualities cannot be reconciled. To be both fully human and fully divine is to exist as a contradiction. Jesus cannot therefore have been both human and divine. Because Jesus was born, as all humans are, he must have been a human. To be a human he must have been radically finite. He could not therefore have been a god. The story of the virgin birth must be false simply as a matter of logic. Accordingly, Jesus was never a son of god. Here expanded, these problems began to trouble us in the introduction, where necessity dictated brevity.

The virgin birth represents legend, not fact. One cannot overemphasize this fact, which is really a type of trend. Here we find ourselves trying to chase the facts about Jesus only to find legends. We enter a world of theological spin, not historical analysis. We must be on guard against this problem because it will bedevil us throughout our attempt to understand the historical Jesus. Obviously we will not conflate fact with legend as Christians have done for roughly two millennia. Fiction should be in the realm of the novelist. It should not be allowed to cloud our judgment about a person, especially one so eminent as Jesus of Nazareth.

Bethlehem and the Birth Narrative

Before we consider the literary device of the virgin birth in a larger context in antiquity, let us hold fast to Matthew and Luke in hopes of understanding the birth narrative in context. Perhaps the feature that most people remember, even those who have not read these gospels, is that Jesus was to have been born in Bethlehem. On its face this news does not seem impressive. Bethlehem is an outpost of the Jewish state and is far removed from the grandeur that was once Jerusalem. Considering its scale, Bethlehem does not merit consideration as a city or even a robust town. It is a village of little economic importance. Why then would the writers of Matthew and Luke have had an interest in it?

The answer lies in notions of kingship and nation building, if I may use a modern phrase for an ancient activity. Bethlehem came to prominence because Israel's most successful king, David, claimed the region as his home. The biblical writers took much interest in David, proclaiming him a courageous giant killer and a king of great deeds. There seems to be little doubt that Israel was at the height of prosperity during David's reign. Of course the independence of Israel gave way to a series of conquerors. Someone needed to rise to restore the glory of Israel under David. Some Jewish writers came to think that only a descendent of David could accomplish this task. To claim that Jesus was this person, Matthew and Luke thought it necessary to link him both to David and to his village of Bethlehem. It became necessary, therefore, to make Jesus an occupant of Bethlehem in the most basic way. Bethlehem would need to become the birthplace of Jesus. To the writers of Matthew and Luke, Bethlehem was not simply a village. It has mushroomed into a symbol that linked Jesus to David. Putative descendant of David, Jesus was to be a special kind of king. One's birthplace, given the right circumstances, can shape a person's identity in many ways. I was born in Rome, Italy and spent part of my childhood there. Even though I have been in the United States a long time and am an American citizen, I still identify Rome as my true home. It is inseparable with my own origins and a source of pride. Certainly the gospels of Matthew and Luke must convey something of these powerful connections between Jesus and Bethlehem.

The question becomes whether Jesus was actually born in Bethlehem. Luke in particular has important details that we may test. At the outset it is necessary to note that a long tradition places Mary and Joseph in

Nazareth, another minor village. The migration of these two, particularly of a pregnant Mary, would have been possible though arduous. Remember that in antiquity one moved from place to place on foot or with the aid of another animal, perhaps a horse, donkey, mule (a hybrid between a horse and donkey) or ox (an ox is a castrated bull). These animals pulled carts that carried people. The journey was neither fast nor pleasant but it was better than walking. The trip to Bethlehem must have been a long, sweaty business. It is also true that in antiquity most people seldom traveled outside their village, so difficult and dangerous could travel be. If what Matthew and Luke claim is true, Mary and Joseph must have been the exceptions to this rule. What would have prompted them to leave Nazareth for Bethlehem, especially while Mary was pregnant?

Luke seems to provide the answer. He claims that during Mary's pregnancy, the Roman emperor Augustus called for a worldwide census, requiring every person to return to his or her ancestral homeland, presumably to register for the payment of taxes.[1] Mary and Joseph understood their connection to Bethlehem and so went there. Mary gives birth to Jesus in Bethlehem and the link among Jesus, David and Bethlehem is secure.

These pieces seem to fit together until they receive scrutiny. First, Augustus had not called a census of the whole world, as Rome had no authority over India, China and many other places. A Roman census could have applied only to people living in the Roman Empire, which were largely the lands of the Mediterranean Basin. One might retort that Mary and Joseph, on the eastern edge of the Mediterranean Basin, fit within these parameters. As a geographic matter, this is true, but important historical facts nullify this argument. The simplest claim is that no Roman records exist that Augustus ever called a census during his reign. This is important because Augustus had a number of biographers to whom a census, had it occurred, would have been a significant event. The most damning piece of evidence comes from the author of Luke. He noted, as did Matthew, that Jesus was born during the kingship of Herod, sometimes known as Herod the Great. Herod ruled as an independent monarch of an independent state. True, as a client king of Rome, Herod likely had close ties to Roman officials. If Jesus was born during the reign of Herod, it follows that he would have been born in territory independent from Rome, as we noted earlier was true of India and China. That is, even had Augustus ordered a census and his subsequent biographers forgot about it, this census would not have applied to Herod's kingdom. With no census to obey, Mary and Joseph would have had no reason to go to Bethlehem. Even if one can fabricate some torturous reason for a Bethlehem narrative, how would Mary and Joseph have known

---

[1] Luke 2: 1-4.

that the village was their ancestral homeland? If they truly descended from David, how would they have known? Hundreds of generations must have passed between David and Mary. Who can trace their lineage over such vast time and space? Even today, with ancestry.com and various other tools, it is difficult to peer into one's lineage. I have made several attempts to trace my family as far back as I can in Italian history. So far I have managed to discover the name of my paternal great grandfather. That is, I can trace my lineage to about 1875, even with the best online support. How in antiquity could Mary and Joseph have made such a leap into the depths of their genealogy? The only sensible conclusion is that Matthew and Luke fabricated the Bethlehem narrative along with the virgin birth literary convention. It turns out that we know nothing about Jesus' birth.

This circumstance should not be surprising if one considers that Jesus was not some well-connected plutocrat. He came from humble origins and was simply a nondescript member of the masses early in life. Antiquity never records the events of ordinary people, only those of eminence. Obviously at some point in life, Jesus achieved enough notoriety to clash with Roman officials, but here one refers to the adult, the mature Jesus who must have been charismatic and capable of stirring oratory. As an infant he had none of these characteristics and so was unremarkable. The attempts to fill in the details of his infancy occurred long after his death and are no more reliable that the birth narratives of Matthew and Luke.

Even the canonical gospels do not agree about Jesus' birth. Mark and John say nothing about Jesus' birth. In fact Mark begins quite abruptly with Jesus' adulthood as if to confess that this author knew nothing about Jesus' birth and childhood, a circumstance that matches well the tendency in antiquity to ignore commoners, we have noted. John may depart even farther from the Bethlehem narrative. The author of the last canonical gospel says nothing about Bethlehem. When he links Jesus with a place of residence, Nazareth not Bethlehem comes to the fore. One might benefit from listening to Johann Sebastian Bach's St. John Passion. Even if one knows no German one can still hear with great clarity the repetition of the phrase "Jesus of Nazareth." This passion contains not a word about Bethlehem because it is true to the gospel of John not to Matthew or Luke. One comes away from this hearing fortified with the knowledge that the gospel of John tried to depict a different reality than did Matthew and Luke. The point is that all the gospels are attempts at creating reality through storytelling, not the creation of reality itself. The gospels mix theology with literature and are far removed from history.

The Larger Literary World

It is helpful to consider Matthew and Luke within a larger literary context. Our initial foray will examine these gospels within the context of the New Testament. We remarked at the beginning of this chapter that of the 27 books of the New Testament, only Matthew and Luke say a word about Jesus' birth. If Jesus really had been born in Bethlehem, with its association of kingship and prosperity, old as these ideas were, and if Jesus were really the son of god through a virgin birth, should not such information have been basic to the New Testament? Why would almost the entire New Testament omit the claims to kingship and divinity? Remember that the books of the New Testament and all other religious books for that matter, seek to make converts. These books are attempts at persuasion. If you wish to convince me that Jesus was divine, should you not tell me that he was born the son of god? The New Testament at large did not make such claims because the writers knew nothing about Jesus' birth and infancy. In this sense Matthew and Luke were the anomalies. They tried to overreach into Jesus' past, about which they knew nothing. They did so within a tradition of virgin birth stories in antiquity. That is Matthew and Luke took an ancient literary form and stitched it into their narratives of Jesus. This attempt is analogous to the American use of baseball to create stickball. Note that the new creation is inferior to its model. In the case of Jesus the birth narrative does not live up to the larger literary tradition. In this instance the birth narratives of Matthew and Luke are terse and omit many details.

Outside the New Testament are other stories of Jesus' birth. These date later than the New Testament books and probably for that reason church authorities never incorporated them into the New Testament. This does not mean that these books were inconsequential. The fact that they were copied over the centuries suggests that their place was secure in the canon, though not the church canon, of stories about Jesus. Too many accounts exist to honor each, but a handful deserves our attention. The earliest may be the so-called proto gospel of James. By early I do not mean the first century during which Jesus lived. In the case of the proto gospel, the date approaches the late second century CE, over 150 years after Jesus' death. The author may have examined the accounts in Matthew and Luke, because his account reiterates much of their narrative.[1] The proto gospel mentions that Jesus had brothers. Such an idea appears in the canonical gospels and gives rise to debate about Jesus' mother Mary. Was Mary a virgin only at the time of Jesus' conception, and had Joseph impregnated her in all other instances to

---

[1] "The Proto Gospel of James," *The Other Gospels: Accounts of Jesus from outside the New Testament*, eds. Bart D. Ehrman and Zlatko, Plese (Oxford: Oxford University Press, 2014) 18-19.

yield Jesus' brothers? If Mary were a lifelong virgin, such births would be impossible, and we have seen that Jesus' birth was a biological impossibility under the claim that Mary conceived Jesus without being intimate with a man. The proto gospel of Jesus holds to this fiction regarding the conception and birth of Jesus. Here Joseph, when he learned that Mary is pregnant, naturally suspects another man and so terms her pregnancy as evil. He believes that Mary has humiliated herself to have behaved in so immoral a way. Yet in a dream, an angel confronts Joseph and he regains his affection for Mary. The Bethlehem story takes a new direction because the proto gospel claims that Jesus was born in a cave, a view expressed in neither Matthew nor Luke. In trading one fiction for another, we do not find improvement but rather a diversity of fabrications. At Jesus' birth the sun supposedly stood still. Here may be a parallel with an Old Testament story of Jewish warrior Joshua, who asked Yahweh to make the sun stand still to lengthen the day. Both claims are wrong, chiefly because relative to the earth, the sun is stationary. The earth's rotation on its axis gives the illusion that the sun moves around the earth, but even Greek scientists like Aristarchus of Samos knew the falsity of a mobile sun relative to the earth. In truth the sun does move in traveling through our galaxy, but because it brings the rest of the solar system with it, including earth, the sun is motionless relative to earth and the other planets. According to the proto gospel, midwives examined Mary after Jesus' birth to be sure of her virginity. The method is not detailed, but one may easily imagine it even though these midwives could not have succeeded. The hymen would already have ruptured. Here is another case of erroneous details being piled atop falsehoods.

The gospel of pseudo Matthew has still more details, but they are not concentrated on Jesus' birth. This gospel dates to the mid sixth to mid seventh centuries CE and so was far too new for inclusion in the New Testament.[1] In fact church leaders finalized the canon of the New Testament in the second century CE. Pseudo Matthew is unusual in not having been written in Greek. It was apparently not a product of eastern speculations about Jesus, because it was written in Latin, the language of the western part of the Roman Empire, though by its formation Rome had already fragmented. A monk at an early monastery may have written pseudo Matthew, though as with all the accounts of Jesus, we have no information about this author or his credentials. The title "pseudo Matthew" implies that the author or an editor must have had some acquaintance with the canonical gospel of Matthew, though by this time it is not possible that anyone thought the apostle Matthew could have been alive at this late date. Pseudo Matthew

---

[1] "The Gospel of Pseudo Matthew," *The Other Gospels: Accounts of Jesus from outside the New Testament*, eds. Bart D. Ehrman and Zlatko, Plese (Oxford: Oxford University Press, 2014) 37-40.

clings to the Bethlehem story, saying that Jesus was again born in a cave and only three days later transferred to a manger. At Jesus' birth dragons came out of the case to worship Jesus. Here again distortions vie with falsehoods for the reader's attention. There are no dragons and so none could have worshipped Jesus. Stories about Jesus and dragons have even less claim on our attention than tales about pirates and buried treasure because pirates exist to the present whereas fire-breathing dragons have never existed. When fabrications of this magnitude creep into texts, one can be sure that the author had no credible knowledge of what he wrote, and so no knowledge about Jesus' birth.

The Latin infancy gospel has more information germane to Jesus' birth, but little of it is truly novel. Having been written in the mid seventh century CE it dates roughly to the time of the writing of pseudo Matthew.[1] At most a century would seem to separate them. This timing is important because it opens the possibility that the author of the Latin infancy gospel may have borrowed from pseudo Matthew and even earlier works. The gospel appears to be a kind of cut and paste theology of Jesus as matters stood in the seventh century. It is not a history of Jesus. This work is theology because of its interpretations of the role of Joseph in Jesus' life. The gospel begins with Emperor Augustus' census, exactly what one encounters in Luke. Joseph and Mary set out for Bethlehem, but they are not alone. Joseph's sons accompany them. Are these the sons of Joseph and Mary? Not if the doctrine of Mary's perpetual virginity holds true. Instead these sons are the product of Joseph's intimacy with a previous wife. No longer then should one fret over the possibility that Jesus had brothers because the relationship was statutory rather than biological. The theology of the Latin infancy gospel thus preserves Mary's virginity and the belief that Jesus was literally the son of god. In the canonical gospels, Joseph receives the briefest treatment. This infancy gospel however elevated his importance, giving him substantive speeches. He emerges here as a kind of wise man. The gospel reinterprets Jesus birth. He is not born in a manger or a cave, but in a house in Bethlehem. The Magi do not visit Jesus as the canonical gospel of Matthew claimed, but rather shepherds do in a rephrasing of Luke. As with so much else concerning Jesus, these new details confuse rather than clarify. None of the authors of these texts seem to know exactly where Jesus was born, a circumstance that is not surprising. Jesus was simply too inconsequential as an infant to have merited scrutiny. We have seen that only at the end of his life did Jesus become infamous enough to cause Roman authorities to kill him.

---

[1] "The Latin Infancy Gospels," *The Other Gospels: Accounts of Jesus from outside the New Testament*, eds. Bart D. Ehrman and Zlatko, Plese (Oxford: Oxford University Press, 2014) 58-59.

We find a similar account in the history of Joseph the Carpenter.[1] Despite the name it is not a history of Joseph or Jesus for that matter. It dates to end of the Christian period in Egypt in the late sixth and early seventh centuries. As an Egyptian text it is in the Coptic of the Gnostic texts and not the Greek of the New Testament or the Latin of similar accounts. If the author could have read only Coptic, it is difficult to understand how he could have borrowed from Greek and Latin texts, except as distilled into oral traditions. The parallels with the Latin infancy gospel and by extension with Luke merit some commentary. One again finds the Augustan census that pushed Mary, Joseph, and his sons to Bethlehem. The theological purpose it to retain the fiction of Mary's virginity and Jesus' divinity. The text itself is not entirely consistent. It claims both that Mary was a virgin and that Joseph was Jesus' father. Perhaps the author meant stepfather. There appears to be a dichotomy between the soul and body, a stance that must have derived from Plato. Again Egypt was receptive to Greek thought and there seems no doubt that Plato's ideas informed the theology of early Christianity. But again, this is just theology. There is no historical information about Jesus the man. The history of Joseph the Carpenter reported that Satan motivated King Herod to seek Jesus' death, prompting the flight to Egypt. In Egypt the toddler Jesus raised from the dead a boy who had died of snakebite. Again, one must ask why, if this miracle is true and by definition spectacular, no one reported it until the late sixth century at the earliest. The answer is that the miracle never happened just as Jesus never raised Lazarus or anyone else from the dead. By comparison imagine that someone wrote a new biography of George Washington in which the general raised a soldier from the dead during the Revolutionary War. No one would believe such a tale for the good reason that all previous biographies of Washington omit any mention of any miracles. Only three copies of the history of Joseph the Carpenter have survived to the present. Two are in Coptic and the third in Arabic. The presence of Arabic suggests the period of Muslim rule, which continues today. The use of Arabic makes clear that Muslims had an interest in the stories that surrounded Jesus. Muslims accord Jesus the status of a prophet, but they do not believe that he was god, rose from the dead, or ascended to heaven. These beliefs align with the lack of evidence for grand claims about Jesus.

We have seen that the grand miracles including raising someone from the dead, whether in Mark, John, or Joseph the Carpenter. This spectacular genre of miracle is part of the world's greatest literature. Consider Russian novelist Fyodor Dostoevsky's masterpiece *The Brothers Karamazov*. In it Jesus

---

[1] "History of Joseph the Carpenter," *The Other Gospels: Accounts of Jesus from outside the New Testament*, eds. Bart D. Ehrman and Zlatko, Plese (Oxford: Oxford University Press, 2014) 78-79.

comes back to earth, but in some ways this is not the spectacular second coming predicted in Mark and Matthew. Jesus comes quietly and yet everyone recognizes him. In one of the great scenes in this novel, Jesus raises from the dead a young girl, arresting the attention of church authorities who arrest him in the desire to kill him yet again. The leader of this movement, the Grand Inquisitor, visits Jesus in his cell and frees him with the rejoinder that he is to leave earth never to return again. In an instant Jesus is gone. What is particularly interesting is that no one supposes that Dostoevsky is recounting a series of actual events. The reader accepts this narrative as fiction because it occurs in the confines of a novel. That is no one claims another miracle in terms of a new resurrection from the dead. Somehow, and for reasons that are not entirely clear, people lose their critical faculties when they encounter the gospels. They believe miracles like the raising of Lazarus and the virgin birth without questioning them.

Part of the reason for this loss of critical acumen is the notion that the gospels and all of scripture are different from other types of prose because they are thought to be inspired by god. This is an important concept that merits scrutiny. Consider the birth narratives in Matthew and Luke as examples. The notion of divine inspiration claims that god somehow guided the writing of these stories. Because god is always truthful, these stories must be true. Such thinking is enough to cause readers not to think. They read and accept. But what does divine inspiration mean? Is it the case that god dictated the text of the gospels and other parts of scripture? This cannot be true because the gospels contain errors. When we reviewed the publication process in antiquity in the last chapter, we noted that errors accrued over time in the copying of manuscripts. There is nothing divine about the insertion of errors into a text. Could divine inspiration have worked in another, less direct way? Perhaps the men who wrote the gospels were known for their holiness and as faithful members of this emerging religion of Christianity. Perhaps people thought that the authors had a particularly intense relationship with god and so could fathom its grand designs. This is a much weaker version of divine inspiration and is no more convincing because of the limited nature of the gospels and other parts of scripture. If these writers had access to god they should have been privy to its capacity for all knowledge. Yet the reader does not find all knowledge on display. In Luke for example the Augustan census was to include the entire world. Yet nowhere in the bible does anyone mention the Americas, which have always been part of the world during the period of human habitation. The Americas were not part of the whole world because no one in the Old World knew of them until the voyages of Christopher Columbus, long after the writing of scripture. The writers of the gospels and other parts of the bible therefore had no special knowledge from god. They were completely human, exercising the wholly human endeavor to write about topics to them. We see this same impetus at work in the coverage of politics in this election season. Yet no one claims divine inspiration for the coverage of Donald Trump's campaign. The lesson is that all genres of writing, including the writings about Jesus, are human expressions of ideas and have nothing to do with presumed contact with a divine author.

Perhaps the most stunning literary parallel is between Jesus and the Greek philosopher Apollonius of Tyana, an ancient city in what was Greek territory, although today it is part of Turkey.[1] Tyana was one of the many colonies the Greeks formed throughout the Mediterranean Basin. Like Jesus, Apollonius lived in the first century CE, about one generation after Jesus. The important point is that he was part of this coalescence of ideas during the High Roman Empire. To compare Jesus with Apollonius is to compare the early thoughts with the integration of these ideas into a more or less coherent, if fanciful, whole. The first point worth attention is that Apollonius, Jesus and even Socrates appear to have been itinerant teachers, more interested in spreading their ideas by word of mouth than by leaving voluminous writings for posterity. Those who have read Matthew and Luke will recognize the birth narrative. Before Apollonius' birth, a heavenly figure (an angel in Judeo-Christian terms) appeared to his mother, announcing to her that her child would be no one ordinary but would be god. Wondrous signs, akin to the shepherds in Luke and the star of Bethlehem and Magi in Matthew accompanied Apollonius' birth. Here is the virgin birth narrative, sometime in Christian garb and at other times in Greco-Roman traditions.

The parallels do not end with the birth narrative. Apollonius, as an adult, traveled through parts of Turkey to spread "good news," exactly the meaning of the Greek term *gospel*. His concern focused less on the immediacy of physical life than on the spirituality necessary for eternal lie. Here is a focus on the afterlife that one finds also in the canonical gospels, particularly in John. Apollonius gathered disciples who came to see him as the son of God. The pagan/Judeo-Christian links are difficult to dismiss. Apollonius performed miracles, among them predicting the future, healed the sick, banished demons and raised the dead. Like Jesus, Apollonius made enemies, who persuaded the Romans to execute him. Nonetheless he rose from the dead to comfort his followers before ascending to heaven. With this sort of legendary material throughout the Greco Roman world, it is no surprise that Christianity made its principal converts among non-Jews. More to the point, how can one defend all these circumstances with Jesus, but say that pagan

---

[1] Bart D. Ehrman, *The New Testament: A Historical Introduction to the Early Christian Writings* (New York and Oxford: Oxford University Press, 2012) 32-34.

superstition polluted the false beliefs about Apollonius? The answer is that Jesus and Apollonius were clones built on the same template of legends. Logic dictates that we treat both people the same. If the stories of one are false so are those of the other. Nothing is exceptional about Jesus.

Antiquity in the Larger Perspective

The notion of a virgin birth is very old and must originate in humans' observations of nature. In temperate climates it is evident that plants of all kinds flourish in warm weather only to die at the onset of cold temperatures. But the story does not end with death. The seeds of these plants ripen and disperse in autumn to put forth new roots and shoots in spring. One could thus trace a cycle of birth, maturation, death and rebirth all over again, year after year. The ancients were not botanists and could not explain this phenomenon in scientific terms. Instead they chose myth, believing that the onset of cold weather was connected to the death of an important god. Although this god had died, he rose from the dead to bring life to a new cycle of vegetation through sex with the mother goddess the next spring. Such beliefs were common throughout large parts of the world. Our interest is in the lands that would harbor these views, and so be a foundation for the rise of the virgin birth narratives in the gospels of Matthew and Luke. Prominent among these lands were the Levant (including Syria and Palestine), Egypt, Babylon and Assyria.

The Hebrews retained this tradition in Genesis. In it, sons of god, literally gods themselves and a vestige of polytheism, lusted after human women and so had sex with them.[1] Note the important point that the offspring of this union would retain the divinity of the father. This is exactly the virgin birth that would come to center stage in the gospels of Matthew and Luke. The authors of these gospels found all the matter that they would need in Genesis.

But the Hebrews were not alone. In Sumer, in what is today southern Iraq, a king, worshipped as a god, had sex with a virgin priestess. Substitute Yahweh for the king and Mary for the virgin priestess and one has the ingredients for the story in Matthew and Luke. In fact Mary emerged as a sort of priestess in the Middle Ages, when god seemed so remote. One prayed to Mary in hopes that she would convey these prayers to her son Jesus and in that way gain the cooperation of god. Note that the idea that Mary herself had never died but continued to help faithful Christians suggests that she was more than a priestess, having been elevated to goddess. This tradition notes that Mary was not subject to death as were all humans. She must have become divine. The legends that permeated Jesus' life extend to his mother. Finally, the Egyptians thought of their pharaoh as god. With each wife

---

[1] Genesis 6: 1-2.

that he married came the birth of offspring from a divine father and human mother. Again one hardly need comment about the parallel to the gospels of Matthew and Luke. It is worth noting that Egypt was, even by the standards of antiquity, an ancient civilization and so was revered. It is not surprising that its ideas became part of the Jesus cult.

The belief about virgin births therefore did not arise in a vacuum. Jesus was part of a larger dynamic in which ancients did not hold a strict dichotomy between divinity and humanity. It was natural for gods to become men, goddesses women, and humans divine because of their exemplary lives. This transition appears to have occurred to Jesus over time. The problem was that Jesus was not noteworthy as an infant and child as well. Only during his adult ministry did Jesus rise to a notoriety that brought him attention from Roman and probably Jewish authorities. By roughly the last quarter or third of the first century CE, writers about Jesus had to construct a relationship between him and the Jewish god Yahweh. The most significant part of this new mythology about Jesus was to claim that he had risen from the dead. The resurrection will receive extensive treatment in chapter 5. Here the emphasis is on the second major solution to the god problem, namely the virgin birth.

By denying that Jesus had a biological father but rather a divine one, the biblical writers conferred divinity on Jesus from conception. We have seen that only two of the 27 New Testament books make this claim, so that it is fair to infer that the tradition of a virgin birth was not a thoroughly New Testament concept. From where, then, did it arise? The answer is in other religious traditions of the ancient Mediterranean Basin. Remember that Jesus was born at about the midpoint of the High Roman Empire, the period of maximum prosperity. With trade came ideas, so that religious ideas in Egypt, North Africa, Spain, Gaul (France), Italy, and the Levant where Jesus lived, could spread throughout the empire, largely through the intensive trade networks that Rome had established in the Republic.

Our initial focus will be on Egypt, the great early civilization of northeastern-most Africa and for millennia the dominant economic, commercial and intellectual center of the Mediterranean Basin. The Egyptians believed that several gods had been born of a divine father. The most important was Ra, the sun god. One may place Jesus in the context of Ra. Both were sources of light and wisdom. The gospel of John makes this statement very early but does not draw an immediate parallel to Ra.[1] We may make this link by examining Ra and Jesus, both born of a virgin and sources of enlightenment and light itself. Note that Egyptian religious beliefs were enormously important to the Mediterranean Basin. Both Greece and Rome

---

[1] John 1: 5.

borrowed heavily from these beliefs, and if one considers Jesus to have been a Greco Roman god of sorts, then the connection among Jesus, Greece, Rome, and Egypt seems secure. Closer examination of the gospel of John will reveal that the contrast between light and darkness may have stemmed from a reading of Plato, particularly the middle dialogue the *Republic*.[1] This book is not to be confused with the Roman Republic mentioned earlier.

Note that the Egyptians equipped their gods with the anatomy for sex. Egyptian art, some of which might be considered pornography today, displays the male gods with penises so long that the gods could easily satisfy themselves with their mouths and tongues. This anatomy made possible the impregnation of goddesses and women. By the time of Matthew and Luke, such overt sexuality was no longer necessary, but they held fast to the notion that their god, Yahweh, could and did impregnate Mary, the mother of Jesus. These gospels made sex a subject of delicate reflection and so less stark and physical than the Egyptians had thought. Note, however, that the writers of Matthew and Luke kept as close to the template of a virgin birth as the Egyptians had. We have already considered the impossibility of an immaterial god fertilizing a human woman, but this problem was far from evident in antiquity. Note that an acceptance of Jesus' birth to a virgin mother forces one to recant all the tenets of reproductive biology and genetics at large. To maintain some sort of faith is to reject the advances of the sciences over at least the last three hundred years. This stance requires a disdain or disbelief in the idea of progress, in the notion that the sciences can offer new solutions to old problems. Instead the Christian retains an atavistic grasp on very old, tenuous ideas that do not comport with the reality that the sciences have detailed. Notwithstanding the beliefs of some intellectuals, science and religion really are at odds. This book supposes that the informed reader must consider seriously the tenets of the sciences.

Back to antiquity: These Egyptian beliefs may be more closely linked to Jesus through the intermediary of Macedonian conqueror Alexander the Great. Like Jesus, Alexander the Great appears to have died in his 30s. But through his short life, he amassed conquests that have dazzled people ever since. Like Jesus, Alexander attained eminence in adulthood. The only way to reward this eminence was to place Alexander in the pantheon of gods. Greek historian Plutarch wrote a biography of Alexander that in many ways seems almost as fanciful as the stories told about Jesus. In Egypt, Alexander took on the persona of a pharaoh and god. Plutarch used the virgin birth notion to impart certain divinity to him. One night, according to Plutarch, Macedonian king Philip II found his wife having sex with a snake. A symbol

---

[1] Plato, The Republic, in The Great Dialogues of Plato (New York: New American Library, 1955) 312-316.

of divinity, the snake impregnated her. The result was the virgin birth of Alexander. This of course is a weird notion of species crossing. The ancients had no notion of what a species was, so they could envision all sorts of strange cross breedings. It is clear now that a snake and human are not inter fertile. No snake-human hybrid is possible. The stories about Alexander are just as fanciful as those told about Jesus. To reject Alexander's putative virgin birth is to reject Jesus' as well, because neither has evidence in its favor.

Another tradition, one we will see again with Hercules, is that chief god Zeus sent a lightning bolt into the vagina of Alexander's mother, bringing about a miraculous conception. In this sense, Alexander the Great and Jesus are united in deriving divinity from the moment of conception. The virgin birth destined both for greatness though tragedy befell them. Of course we are dealing with mythological circumstances that have no basis in reality. Alexander and Jesus are both myths.

An older Greek story concerns Hercules. We observed last chapter that Hercules claimed a virgin birth in which Zeus conceived him by entering Hercules' mother through the vagina from a trademark lightning bolt from the heavens. This virgin birth, like Jesus', guaranteed Hercules' divinity. What merits mention in the stories of Hercules, Alexander, and Jesus is that despite their outward similarities, moderns have dismissed Hercules and Alexander as fiction but accept Jesus as true. On a purely rational basis, there seems little reason for this dichotomy. What is there about Jesus' virgin birth that makes it more real than those of Hercules and Alexander? A consistent model would reject all three as fabrications contrary to what we know about reproductive biology. Jesus could no more claim a virgin birth than could Hercules and Alexander. These stories were part of the theology of ancient Mediterranean religions and nothing more.

Rome did not shy away from such beliefs. According to legend, a Vestal Virgin conceived Romulus, the founder of Rome. Such a woman, a virgin throughout life, as was claimed about Mary, was a source of prophecy and spiritual wisdom. The Romans upheld these women as something akin to quasi-divine beings. The penalty for violating a Vestal Virgin was death. According to this tradition, Romulus, like Jesus, had no human father but had a god for a father and a woman of great spirituality as his mother.

From just this information it is not surprising, then, that Christianity should have arisen in the Roman world because some of Christianity's ideals and stories were part of Roman antiquity. In this sense Jesus was perhaps the chief Roman god, even though he and the other Roman gods were fiction. By this point we see Jesus as the amalgam of other gods, none of whom command belief today. Why should we hold Jesus as an exception?

Even Emperor Augustus joined this movement. According to his biographer Seutonius, the god Apollo impregnated Augustus' mother Artia. The coupling of god and woman is ideal for understanding both Augustus and Jesus. Augustus lived about half a generation before Jesus, so that the ideas about Augustus were ready for infusion into this putative Jewish miracle worker. Augustus' supposed father, Apollo, was the god of light and rationality, the god who brought order to chaos and light to darkness. This is certainly the Jesus one finds in John. Jesus is light that triumphs over darkness. He is the Word that brings order to the world. He is Augustus raised to the power of infinity. The Jesus in John is a fully formed god, one worthy of worship, if only what the author of John had written was true.

The Absence of the Virgin Birth in Mark, John and Other Christian Literature

If the Mediterranean world was awash in the language of virgin births and if this notion was important to Christians, then why do only two books in the New Testament contain such a scenario? In particular why do the other two canonical gospels, Mark and John, omit any information about Jesus birth? Both Mark and John appear to provide straightforward answers. Recall that Mark was the first of the gospels. In many ways it was the simplest and least prone to exaggeration, though it has its share of miracles, which by definitions are more than hyperbole. If Mark has miracles, why does it omit the miracle of a virgin birth? The answer may be as simple as the reflection that the author of Mark did not think in terms of a virgin birth. That is the legend of a virgin birth may not have existed in Christian consciousness about 70 CE, the time when Mark was written. Only about 80 to 85 CE, the time of the gospels of Matthew and Luke, did the legend of a virgin birth, borrowed from other Mediterranean religions, coalesce into a story about Jesus. Note that at the writing of Matthew and Luke we are at least 50 years after Jesus' death, sufficient time for the attachment of a virgin birth narrative and other untrue events to his name.

At first John may be a puzzle. If the virgin birth narrative were applied to Jesus as early as 80 to 85 CE, why would it not have been part of John, written at least a decade later? Once the legend of a virgin birth had been established, why did it not carry through to John? The answer is probably that John had a different agenda than Matthew and Luke. John begins, not with the birth narrative of Matthew and Luke, but with a brief prologue. This prologue has incited controversy. It seems to differ in language and tone with the rest of John so that an editor might have added it later. When rendered in its original Greek, it becomes clear that the language renders itself to musical treatment. It seems possible therefore that the prologue was a hymn that a later editor added to the beginning of John. Of course the theological purpose of the prologue suits John well so that it is not impossible that the author of the gospel made the insertion himself. However this prologue migrated to John, its message makes clear why the author did not begin the gospel with a virgin birth. Moreover we cannot be certain that John knew of the virgin birth narrative in Matthew and Luke because he seems to have taken his material from elsewhere.

The very first verse of the prologue places the narrative at the presumed beginning of the universe.[1] This setting will become significant in a moment. At the beginning of the universe was the Word. The Word was apparently whatever language Yahweh spoke at the beginning of time. Even here we are not far from Egyptian antiquity, because the gods spoke to create the universe. This is exactly what happens of course at the beginning of Genesis so that Egyptian influences are prominent in early Judaism. The author of the prologue identifies the Word with god so that the two must be identical and by definition coequal. This Word is Jesus. Now it becomes clear why a virgin birth would not have suited John. A virgin birth would have meant that Jesus had been born in time, a point to which I wish to return. According to John Jesus was not born in time but at the beginning of time, at the first utterance from Yahweh. Despite obvious differences, remember that Matthew, Luke and John all hold to a temporal sequence. With John, however, one does not read about a birth in any human sense but of the creation of the Word. To John, Jesus is divine because he issued directly from god and was equal to god. The difference between temporal and eternal existence with receive additional treatment in chapter 6.

This prologue may have less to do with Jesus than with Greek philosophy. Greek philosopher Plato cast a dichotomy between light and darkness, just as John did in the prologue. The setting is well known to students of *The Republic*, a dialogue in which Plato places a group of men in a cave, chaining them so that they can see only one wall of the cave.[2] Behind them are a fire that they cannot see and a person who passes a series of images behind them, but they can see only shadows of these images, which through their senses they perceive as reality. This is the human condition in which the senses cannot apprehend reality. All they can manage is a shadowy, impermanent, inconstant sense of what they erroneously perceive as reality. In fact they are twice removed from reality because the fire that provides illumination is not the ultimate source of light. One must break free, pass the fire and ascend to the opening of the cave and into the sunlight, which is the ultimate source of light. This is the light to which John refers in the prologue. Even

[1] John 1: 1.
2 Plato, *The Republic*, in *The Great Dialogues of Plato*, trans. W. H. D. Rouse (New York: New American Library, 1956), 312-315.

then, the person who manages to reach the opening of the cave will need time to adjust to the light. If he descends back down the cave to tell his comrades that he has apprehended reality as it is, they may be apt to kill him for attacking what they perceive to be knowledge derived from the senses. How then does one apprehend reality? Plato give his answer in the *Phaedo*, in which the intellect seeks its own space, where apart from the body and the senses it contemplates, by reason alone, reality as it is.[1] That is the intellect alone and apart from the senses is the source of knowledge about reality. At a deep level, Plato struck a chord. All religions assume the existence of a reality beyond the senses, and Christianity we are seeing borrowed heavily from Plato's ideas in trying to understand Jesus, or, better yet, in trying to recast a man as god.

Two points demand our attention. First, if Jesus may be dated, so to speak, to the beginning of the universe, then he must have had a beginning. One must ask whether it is possible for god in the guise of Jesus to have had a beginning. Recall that if Jesus were god, he must have shared every divine attribute. I wish to select the attribute that we used in the introduction, namely the quality of being unlimited. For god to be god it cannot be bounded. We saw in the introduction that god cannot suffer death. No less important, god cannot have been born in any sense of the word. That is god cannot have had a beginning or end but must be eternal. Suppose one can regress infinitely in time. There is good reason to suppose that this is impossible. But if we grant this supposition for the moment, then one should never reach a time when god had yet to have been born because the absence of god in this regression would limit god, something logic will not allow us to do. Thus Matthew, Luke, and John, all proposing some sort of birth, inadvertently confirm that Jesus cannot have been god, but must have been human because only humans are born and die. Second the theology of the prologue creates confusion. The author juxtaposed the notion that Jesus had birth in an utterance of Yahweh with the idea that Jesus was equal to god. But birth in an utterance of Yahweh strongly implies that Jesus came after Yahweh and so cannot be equal to him, certainly not in temporal terms. We are left to the conclusion that Jesus originated on the wrong side of the divine human continuum, at least as ancients saw it. The eternal existence of Yahweh, if such a being is possible, presumes divinity. The temporal existence of Jesus presumes humanity. We are witnessing the replay of a theme in this book, namely that Jesus was human and not divine.

This view gains strength from a belief of some early Jews and Christians, who held that Yahweh had merely adopted, and not fathered, Jesus as a son.

---

1 Plato, Phaedo, in *The Great Dialogues of Plato*, trans. W. H. D. Rouse (New York: New American Library, 1956), 467-469.

This adoption occurred when John the Baptist baptized Jesus in the Jordan River. Because Jesus was adopted he could not share in Yahweh's divinity. That is Jesus was entirely human and not at all divine. In sum, Jesus was not born of a virgin; he did not exist prior to his birth, a necessary condition for divinity and an impossibility in logical terms. At the same time Jesus could not have been god because Jews believed in just one god. Were Jesus god, then Jews would need to worship two gods: Yahweh and Jesus. Clearly such an idea was not congenial to monotheism. Note that these beliefs contradict both Jesus' virgin birth and his divinity. We arrive at the common sense view that Jesus was human like the rest of us. These Jews appear to have circulated an abridgement of Matthew, one devoid of the virgin birth.

Other non-canonical accounts omit or deny the virgin birth. Written in Aramaic, the language that Jesus and his followers spoke, the gospel of the Nazarenes may have been committed to papyrus at the end of the first century CE, possibly about the time of the gospel of John.[1] It seems to have much of Matthew's events minus the birth narrative. Jews may have been the intended audience, and for them, the birth narrative was blasphemous. The gospel of Thomas is not a narrative at all, though it is worth remembering that Thomas lacks a birth narrative as well. If Jesus were truly born to Mary the virgin, should not all Christian texts contain this event? Instead only two texts, Matthew and Luke, make such a claim. The poverty of evidence dictates that we abandon this belief to the scrap heap of history. It is not history and cannot be considered such.

The Apocryphon of John merits study because of its relationship to the gospel of John, especially the prologue. The apostle John's name was attached to several documents, but he cannot have been the author because death must have claimed him before the composition of any of these documents. It is not clear whether the author of the Apocryphon of John had access to the gospel of John, though their commonalities deserve attention. In the context of the narrative of a virgin birth, both books do not entertain this possibility, presumably because it does not fit their agenda. The Apocryphon of John is a fairly cryptic documents and one must labor to glean some of its insights. The Apocryphon hugs the literary terrain of the gospel of John by suggesting that the "Father" sent Jesus to earth.[2] This belief strongly implies that if Jesus could be sent to earth and if he was born (this assumption is not certain given the laconic text), then he must have predated all these events. Jesus too must have been created at the beginning of time and matter, an inference one may draw from the text. This conviction gains strength from the Apocryphon's statement that Jesus was simultaneously father (Yahweh perhaps), mother

---

[1] Ehrman, The New Testament, 219.
[2] Apocryphon of John, eds. Michael Waldstein and Frederik Wisse (Leiden: E. J. Brill, 1995) 16.

(Mary perhaps), son, and "eternal One."[1] Now if Jesus were eternal as the text notes, then of course he must always have existed and must always exist in the future. This is a characteristic of god, who must be unbounded, not of a finite human. Far from suggesting that Jesus was born the Apocryphon of John makes clear that the god Jesus had always existed and will always exist. If Jesus has all these attributes, then he must be the "invisible One" to whom the text refers. This language is striking. As Aristotle made clear we observe matter through our sense. But because Jesus was this invisible one he must not have contained matter. He must have been immaterial. How then can one ever say that Jesus had a body? Several times the Apocryphon of John refers to Jesus as "light." Here again one finds strong parallels with not only the gospel of John but with Plato's ideas. The Apocryphon of John in short seems to be Greek philosophy, notably Platonism, turned to the service of theology. Being theology, to return to an earlier theme, the Apocryphon, like all other documents about Jesus, tells us nothing about the man Jesus. By the time of the Apocryphon, Jesus is devoid of any historical content or context. Again our search for Jesus yields nothing tangible. We are chasing a phantom.

Along these lines is the enigmatic Infancy Gospel of Thomas, not to be confused with the Gnostic gospel of Thomas. The two were written at different times and in different languages. According to the infancy gospel, Jesus was "born" before the world existed.[2] This phrase is confusing. The act of being born occurs in time and space. It is something that happens in this world and yet the authors of the infancy gospel maintain a birth before the world had come into existence. If we grant this premise as much latitude as possible, then Jesus must have been born before the existence of matter. If this is so, then Jesus must have been a purely immaterial object. But can such an object be born or is birth an attribute of solely material objects? And if Jesus was born before the existence of the world, how could he have been born in time to a human mother, as Matthew and Luke claim? The result is contradiction aplenty. Under these circumstances we must deny that Jesus could have been born before space and time.

The Infancy Gospel of Thomas makes additional claims. For example, according to it, Jesus "came from above."[3] Such language must draw on John, the author of which intended for the Word to have come from the creator god who existed in some heavenly realm separate from us.[4] In a larger sense this notion fits the ideas of Plato. Plato held that the soul predated the body.

---

[1]   Ibid., 18.
[2]   "The Infancy Gospel of Thomas," *The Other Gospels: Accounts of Jesus from outside the New Testament*, eds. Bart D. Ehrman and Zlatko, Plese (Oxford: Oxford University Press, 2014) 10.
[3]   Ibid.
[4]   John 1: 1.

Whereas the soul was infinite the body was finite. The soul thus inhabited many bodies over the course of time. When the body died it liberated the soul to return to an eternal nonphysical realm. But this soul was later reincarnated in another body to live again in a physical realm. That is, Plato believed in a perfect nonphysical realm that held all knowledge. One might define this knowledge as god.

The infancy gospel also refers to "the one" who sent Jesus.[1] This statement is not all that clear either. One might guess that "the one" must be Yahweh, the creator god. Yet when did he send Jesus to earth? The question is difficult to answer. If one supposes that Jesus was born before the existence of the world, as noted above, then he must have spent some duration, and I am uncomfortable with the word "duration" because it implies the existence of time, which cannot be if Jesus were born before time and space. We are left not knowing whether Jesus spent some interval, say in heaven, before the birth of the universe and only later was born a second time, if such is possible, to his mother Mary. This would entail two births, one immaterial and before time and one material and in time. This strikes one as nonsense. We affirm that Jesus was human. Humans are born only once, live once, and die once and for all time. Therefore Jesus cannot have been born twice. In another context we will consider the perils of multiple births as reflected in the gospel of John.

---

[1] "The Infancy Gospel of Thomas," 10.

Chapter 3. Jesus' Childhood

The first chapter having laid the foundation, the second reminded us just how poor are the sources about Jesus' birth. This perspective is amplified here, where we consider what, if anything, can be known about Jesus' childhood. Our inquiry will conclude that we can know nothing about Jesus' childhood, just as we can know almost nothing about Jesus' birth. This is not the same as arguing that Jesus did not exist (though others have entertained that idea), only that we can know almost nothing about him. Jesus is the blank slate upon which theologians have written their own allegories. These after-the-fact stories have no basis in reality, as this book attempts to show. Here the absence of reality shadows Jesus' childhood.

The New Testament

The New Testament is almost silent about Jesus' childhood. Of the 27 books of the New Testament only one, the gospel of Luke, says anything about Jesus as a child.[1] Even Luke contains very little information. According to this gospel, Jesus visited Jerusalem at age 12 with his parents. I will not rehearse the conclusions in chapter 1, but by "parents" I mean Mary and Joseph. The narrative in Luke is not especially transparent, but apparently Jesus became separated from his parents. Perhaps he snuck away. Perhaps Mary and Joseph simply lost track of him. In any events the crowd was probably large, giving Jesus an opportunity of exploring Jerusalem outside the confines of his parents' scrutiny. We do not know exactly where Luke intended Jesus to go, but the gospel tells us that his parents found

---

[1] Luke 2: 41-52.

Jesus in the temple conversing with the scholars over parts of the Hebrew bible, which we know as the Old Testament.

We must ask ourselves whether such events could have occurred. I have no problem with the thesis that Jesus and his parents may have become separated and that they were later reunited in the temple, although it is not clear that Jewish authorities would have permitted an unaccompanied boy access to the temple. The idea that he was in the midst of debate over scripture with the scholars is probably farfetched. We must ask where Jesus might have acquired knowledge of the Hebrew bible. One idea is that he may have read parts of the scriptures, but this supposition rests on the tenuous claim that Jesus knew how to read. After all he was a commoner and ordinary people did not go to school. The idea of universal education lay centuries in the future and there is no reason to suppose that Jesus had the benefit of it. If anything in the Infancy Gospel of Thomas, the subject of a later section, is correct, Jesus must have grown up helping his parents. His activities would have been practical and hands on. Under these circumstances it is hard to imagine that Jesus attended school and learned to read and possibly write, though the Infancy Gospel of Thomas claims three stints in school, though not always successfully. Overall the gospels display lots of incidents in which Jesus spoke, admonishing a disciple here and captivating an audience with a parable there. Nowhere accept for a possible example does the New Testament record an incident in which Jesus read anything. If Jesus could not read, then obviously he could not have read the scriptures. Writing is even a bigger hurdle. The fact that no texts written by Jesus have come down to the present suggests that Jesus could not write. Consider a circumstance in which Jesus wrote a letter to one of his disciples. The letter would have been treasured to such an extent that it would surely have been copied and then printed down to the present. In this case the absence of evidence is surely a denial that Jesus was literate.

Even if one were to advance the shaky claim that Jesus could read, the language is in question. Would a speaker of Aramaic, like Jesus, not have learned to read Aramaic? Yet if he could read Aramaic he cannot have read what we call the Old Testament because it is written in Hebrew. It seems difficult to believe that Jesus, if he had learned to read would have learned Hebrew rather than his native language. The Infancy Gospel of Thomas provides another possibility. When Joseph presumably sent Jesus to school, an unlikely act, the child learned the Greek alphabet. Even if one stretches this implausible story into a defense that Jesus could have read Greek, one would gain nothing by this supposition. Perhaps the author of the infancy gospel favored Greek because it was the language of the New Testament. But such a claim requires ignorance of history because Jesus died before the New

Testament was written. Knowledge of Greek could not have helped Jesus read the then non-existent New Testament. Moreover Greek would have been useless in helping Jesus read the Hebrew scriptures. To summarize, none of the sources about Jesus make a credible claim that he was literate. The fact that Jesus left no writings is strong evidence not only that he wrote nothing, but also that he could not write at all.

One alternative is left, namely that Jesus picked up stories about the Jews and their relationship to their god Yahweh through oral traditions. At first glance this idea seems plausible. Jesus must have absorbed many stories, some of them religious, simply from talking with other people. Given his adult ministry there is every reason to suppose that Jesus must have been interested in religious matters in childhood. Armed with these stories, could not Jesus have entered the temple? I agree that he could, provided again that Jewish authorities granted him admission, but could he have dazzled the scholars as Luke implies? It seems implausible that a 12-year-old boy with a smattering of stories which he could or could not recall accurately could have debated scripture on an equal footing with literate men who had dedicated their lives to the pursuit of religious knowledge. Surely these scholars would, after a few moments, have heard enough of Jesus' trivial and immature thoughts. They would have turned away from him to engage one another in the significant theological questions of the day. Therefore Luke's story about Jesus' childhood must be an exaggeration at best. That stories about Jesus as a child are absent from all other New Testament texts suggests that Luke simply fabricated the story of Jesus and the scholars. In short, the New Testament tells us nothing about Jesus' childhood.

Should this absence of evidence surprise us? Remember that Jesus was the product of humble circumstances. He was not one of the elite whose childhood would have been one of study and contemplation. In reading his *Meditations*, one gains an idea of what such a life entails from the vantage point of second-century Roman emperor Marcus Aurelius. Nothing about Jesus evinces such an upbringing. Remember too that, being a commoner, Jesus would not have attracted the notice of important people who would have been eager to record the events of his life. Ancient historians concentrated on emperors and wars. They had no interest in what we now call social history. The fact that Jesus' childhood receives so little mention in the canonical gospels is not an anomaly. It is what one would expect from the dictates of the day. Even today, with the refinement of historical methods, it is unusual to find a biography of a commoner unless that person achieved distinction at some point in his or her life. This is precisely the situation with Jesus, who became notorious only in adulthood. Now he had become worthy of scrutiny.

Outside the New Testament

If the New Testament contains no reliable information about Jesus as a child, where should one look? The answer is to a surprisingly large number of sources from antiquity and the Middle Ages. Here one witnesses the proliferation of legends. Humans often have trouble tolerating stories with ambiguities and so must fabricate information. Consider the creation story in Genesis. Remember that Yahweh warned Adam and Eve not to eat the forbidden fruit. Nowhere does Genesis specify the name of this fruit, a circumstance that drove readers to make up a name. Whether Jew, Christian, or Muslim, several alternatives have been bandied about. At one time or another the fig, banana and apple have all been proposed as the forbidden fruit. The same phenomenon repeated with Jesus. Because there is no childhood narrative, one, actually several, had to be invented. Here is a case in which literature abhors a vacuum. Our task is to scrutinize the most important of these narratives to determine whether they are any more plausible than the minute information in Luke.

The accounts about Jesus that are outside the Old and New Testaments are known as the apocrypha. Being outside the canon of putative holy books, Christians are likely to react that the apocrypha is not to be trusted. It was the work of mere men rather than the work of the Holy Spirit. This claim must be examined. It posits that the Holy Spirit, a manifestation of god, guided the composition of the books in the Old and New Testaments. Because god directed the assembly of these books, they are thought to be inspired by the Holy Spirit. We broached this subject last chapter, but here additional treatment is necessary. What does inspiration mean in this context? The answer is not clear. Some evangelical Christians believe that the Holy Spirit dictated the scriptures to men who served merely as the conduits of god's words. This would be a rather heavy-handed and one-sided approach to the construction of the bible. Another meaning may be possible. The writers of the bible may have prayed and lived honorable lives of compassion and charity and so lived in the presence of god so to speak. In such a condition they produced texts of superior spirituality than might otherwise have been possible.

Do such claims have merit? The heavy-handed approach seems particularly weak. If god dictated these texts, why are there so many errors? We have seen that the virgin birth in Bethlehem is not possible. The Augustan census did not happen. The incessant cry of miracles, which will receive more treatment in chapter 4, is highly improbable. We have just witnessed the improbability that Jesus at age 12 was a biblical scholar. But if these are all errors, how could god have dictated them? Remember god by definition is omniscient and omnipotent. Having all knowledge, every idea that emanates from it must be true. Indeed the Catholic church continues to mandate that the scriptures contain no errors because of divine inspiration. Given this tension one may only conclude that god did not dictate the bible. At the very least one must establish that god exists to make any claim of divine inspiration.

The second claim is intriguing and a bit more difficult to evaluate. A spiritual person who lived life in keeping with the precepts of Jesus life, whatever can be known of it, would seem to be more likely to produce a text faithful to Jesus than a person who had a secular, worldly outlook. An analogy might help. Any examination of the life and work of German composer Johann Sebastian Bach reveals the spirituality of his own existence. It is perhaps no surprise then that Bach was able to write music of unsurpassed spiritual depth. Yet in other ways Bach seems to defy the spiritual label. He quarreled often with employers, in one case staying away from work for months. He hated teaching and seems to have regarded many of his students as inept. A prince once jailed him in irritation at his conduct. In many ways then Bach was an ordinary man with a temper and other flaws. Yet he had the capacity of composing the most sublime music. The same must apply to the biblical writers. They were ordinary men of real literary merit. There is no need to invoke divine inspiration for what may have been a wholly human endeavor.

The concept of divine inspiration is peculiar in another way. When one thinks about it, one discovers that divine inspiration was a short-term phenomenon. God spoke, in whatever way one can imagine, to certain Hebrew and early Christian writers. Let us examine the case of early Christian writers. If one dates the earliest writings to Paul of Tarsus in the 50s CE and the last with the gospel of John and probably Revelation about 100 CE, god "spoke" to these writers over a span not longer than 50 years, the equivalent of about two generations. Thereafter god fell silent. What explains this phenomenon? Why do we consider the gospel of Mark inspired but the writings of catholic saint, Jerome merely the work of a man, however competent his scholarship? Why did god briefly intervene in human events and then just as quickly withdraw from human contact? We cannot answer these questions and must assume that god, if it exists, is inscrutable. Chapter 6 will review the terrain in the quest for belief or disbelief in god.

The notion of divine inspiration, however one tries to characterize it, is weak in other ways. Remember Quelle (Q), the unnamed, undiscovered source on which the writers of Matthew and Luke may have drawn for material. Was Q divinely inspired? If one holds that Matthew and Luke were divinely inspired and that these gospels drew from Q, then one might infer that Q must have been inspired as well. Yet if it was the word of god in some sense, why is it not extant? How could someone lose something so precious as the word of god? I suspect that had people believed in the divine inspiration of Q, they would have copied it with the care they afforded the Old and New Testaments. If they thought, however, of Q as nothing more than a piece of papyrus, then such a text would easily be lost and forgotten. If Q was uninspired then the accompanying passages in Matthew and Luke were not inspired. This would lead to the absurdity in which parts of Matthew and Luke were inspired and other parts uninspired, as though god cut off communications intermittently. Because this is not plausible it appears best to think that Matthew and Luke were not inspired. The implication must be that none of the bible is inspired. This line of inquiry tangles with one of the principal notions of Christianity, notably the idea that god was and perhaps still is at work in the church. This claim seems little better than rubbish.

If one cannot claim divine inspiration of the bible then it seems fair to treat the non-biblical sources about Jesus on an equal footing with the canonical sources. There is no reason to think that the apocrypha is somehow inferior to the canon. Both contain legends and wild distortions. Why are such distortions permissible in the canonical texts and impermissible in the apocrypha? This proviso leaves us free to ask what we can know about Jesus from the apocrypha. Like the bible, the apocrypha yields little real information about Jesus.

The Infancy Gospel of Thomas

The Infancy Gospel of Thomas is perhaps the most infamous accounts of Jesus. As we mentioned earlier it seeks to fill a gap by relating information about Jesus' childhood, an unknown period of time. Much of the material disconcerts Christians, as will become clear. Before turning to the gospel itself, some context is necessary. The gospel has many problems, perhaps the most important being time of composition and contents. Some of the material is thought to date as early as about 150 CE, but this idea is based in part on the old confusion between the Infancy Gospel of Thomas and the Gospel of Thomas.[1] Recall that the Gospel of Thomas was neither discovered before 1945 nor published before 1956. Consequently those who studied the early church authorities and their writings concluded that references to the Gospel of Thomas must actually have referred to the Infancy Gospel of Thomas, which, unlike the Gospel of Thomas, had not been lost for centuries before rediscovery. That is, the Infancy Gospel of Thomas had always been part of the corpus of quasi-Christian writings but never part of the canon.

---

[1] Infancy Gospel of Thomas, in *The Other Gospels: Accounts of Jesus from outside the New Testament*, eds. Bart D. Ehrman and Zlatko Plese (Oxford: Oxford University Press, 2014) 5.

What may have been composed about 150 CE was at best a stub of an account, and it is clear when one reads later manuscripts that the gospel was enlarged over time, though it was never very long. Thus composition may have been ongoing into the sixteenth century. This is a long span of time so that it is impossible to speak about one author, one compiler, or one editor. Numerous people undertook the writing of the Infancy Gospel of Thomas over more than a millennium.

The problems of the canonical gospels reemerge in the Infancy Gospel of Thomas. Because one cannot pinpoint a single author in a text that had multiple authors, one can say nothing about the credentials of these people aside from the fact that they were willing to import into their account all sorts of fanciful stories. Because it is impossible to pinpoint the infancy gospel to a single century, one cannot hope to build the historical context. It is as though events somehow occurred in a vacuum devoid of any natural setting. In such accounts, the nullification of a natural setting only weakens the historical element in this gospel. It is not surprising, in this context, to have little more than a series of miracles as the foundation for this gospel. In relating these miracles, one after the other in an almost cryptic way, suggests comparison with the gospel of Mark, though again the long span in which the infancy gospel was composed makes uncertain the sources that these authors used.

The contents of the gospel also trouble the reader. First, there is no one set of contents. Different manuscripts contain or omit very different stories. For example the Infancy Gospel of Thomas as translated by New Testament scholar Bart Ehrman does not include the story of Jesus the helpmate of his father Joseph.[1] I use the term father because in some parts of the Infancy Gospel Jesus seems so human that it is difficult to doubt that he had a human father. Furthermore our discussion of Jesus' birth in chapter 2 demonstrated that Jesus cannot have had a divine father and so must have had a human father. Joseph, about whom we know comparatively little is as good a candidate for fatherhood as any, we established last chapter. In what I'm calling the helpmate episode, Jesus straightens beams of wood that his father had unevenly cut. The miracle is not plausible, but it probably depicts a truth about Jesus, namely that he helped his parents when he was young. Such obedience was expected of every child. We see that even simple truths are not straightforward in the infancy gospel but are clothed in miracles that almost surely never happened. They are the product of imagination alone.

Second, the contents give clues about the time of some of the events of composition, even though the gospel was too spread out in time to pinpoint anything like a date. For example, the gospel opens with Jesus constructing

---

[1] Ibid., 7.

sparrows out of mud, which he later animates and causes to fly away. This may seem an innocuous miracle, though the choice of bird may be significant. Sparrows were popular pets in late antiquity. Other objects likewise point to late antiquity, suggesting it to be a period of composition, though of course not the only one. This fact is interesting because once we get past the early church fathers who abused the Gospel of Thomas, we find that there is no reason to suppose that the Gospel of Thomas had any connection to the Infancy Gospel of Thomas. Brushing aside these church authorities, there remains little reason to infer an early date of composition. Perhaps late antiquity, say the fifth century CE, marked the early composition of the Infancy Gospel of Jesus and not the mid second century as was once thought. Of course it is axiomatic that the later the composition of a document the greater the hyperbole, the more startling the miracles and the more unreal the text, not that there are any reliable texts about Jesus. Wherever we turn, we deal with implausibilities and impossibilities.

The lack of uniform contents makes difficult the treatment of a single Infancy Gospel of Thomas. The fact that stories were added and others omitted from manuscript to manuscript suggests strongly that the authors must have known that they were fabricating stories. There is no sense that the Infancy Gospel of Thomas was ever thought an inviolable sacred text. Compare this attitude with that accorded to Bach. One would never think to add new notes to the St. Matthew Passion or to cut out passages. Such tinkering would diminish a work of genius. The Infancy Gospel of Thomas apparently had no such defenders. It was always plastic, a work in progress. If 15 miracles did not suffice, a later author could always add more incredible stories. In this way the infancy gospel fulfilled the longing to know the most sensational events of Jesus' childhood, details that the canonical gospels did not provide.

The fiction of a single author lies in attribution to "Thomas the Israelite."[1] Such a phrase may not be enigmatic. If he were an Israelite, by definition he must have been a Jew. The canonical gospels agree that Jesus selected his disciples among Jews. One of these is thought to have been Thomas. In some accounts this Thomas was thought to be the twin brother of Jesus. Perhaps this Thomas is meant by the phrase "Thomas the Israelite." This at least seems to have been the intent of the Gospel of Thomas. Again we should avoid drawing too close a parallel between the Gospel of Thomas and the Infancy Gospel of Thomas. Yet if Jesus' twin brother were meant, such an attribution to this gospel would seem to lend authority to the contents.

---

[1] Ibid., 8.

We may feel confident that the authors must have had access to Luke because the story of Jesus in the temple, a fixture in Luke and one we encountered earlier, serves to conclude the Infancy Gospel of Thomas.[1] The infancy gospel being a late construct, there is in principle no reason why the authors of the Infancy Gospel of Thomas could not have had access to the entire canon of the New Testament and several apocryphal accounts as well. Yet if this gospel used an array of literature, why is it so short? There is no easy answer, though perhaps the fact that the infancy gospel focuses on a small slice of Jesus' life contributed to its brevity. Remember the Infancy Gospel of Thomas was not like the gospel of Luke, the latter of which attempted to use material on every aspect of Jesus life, from birth to resurrection appearance. The Infancy Gospel of Thomas is just concerned with Jesus' childhood, about which virtually nothing is known.

Other scholars have pointed to the fact that the Infancy Gospel of Thomas is no literary masterpiece. It obviously cannot have been meant for scholars and the learned layperson. It is a loose collection of anecdotes, probably meant for the masses, which had a strong desire to peer into the childhood of Jesus. The void that the canonical gospels could not satisfy, the Infancy Gospel of Thomas filled. If the masses were the intended audience, one wonders how they derived information about them. Again in an era before compulsory school, the masses were general illiterate. They likely could not have read the infancy gospel, short as it was. But its brevity may have been an advantage, for people were probably willing and eager to gather around a speaker for half an hour to hear this gospel being read. Perhaps a period of interpretation followed the reading of the gospel to reinforce its lessons. In this sense the Infancy Gospel had unique material, excepting the story of Jesus in the temple, that must have made it worth hearing, reading and retaining (depending on one's language skills). The basic premise of the gospel appears to be to demonstrate that the miraculous powers displayed in the canonical gospels extended back in time to Jesus' childhood. The years of coverage, ages 5 to 12, show that Jesus had miraculous powers from the outset. Such an argument may be a way of positing that Jesus was divine from the outset. That of course is the claim of the birth narratives, the inaccuracies of which have caught our attention. Accordingly, the Infancy Gospel of Thomas is meant to be a series of stories about a divine prodigy.

The earliest Infancy Gospel of Thomas, the stub gospel, may have been written in Greek. We have seen already that Jesus and his followers would not have known Greek so that the gospel is several generations removed from the historical Jesus. In this sense it cannot tell us anything about Jesus, only what people believed about him. In fact this may be the large truth we

---

[1] Ibid., 14.

confront in our attempt to encounter Jesus. We learned earlier about the variation in contents. The surviving Greek manuscripts narrate about nine separate stories about Jesus' childhood. Other variants exist in a variety of languages: Latin, Syriac, Ethiopian, Armenian, Georgian, Arabic, Irish and Slavonic. It is immediately clear that the Infancy Gospel of Thomas must have been well known and was geographically diverse. This is more evidence of the strong desire for knowledge about Jesus' childhood, even if this was not knowledge but fiction. In fact the Infancy Gospel of Thomas is more short story than history. Translation into Arabic is particularly significant because it demonstrates Muslim interest in Jesus' childhood. One might wonder at this interest because Muslims do not consider Jesus divine. Why would they have been interested in a collection of miracles about a person who was merely human? Jesus' status as a prophet among Muslims must account for this interest.

The gospel's popularity must have peaked in the Middle Ages, though it began to wane during the Reformation. Even at its height the Infancy Gospel of Thomas was never part of the canon, for reasons that will become obvious later. So far the emphasis of this gospel was on its theological content, which is not always easy to infer. By the seventeenth century (during the Scientific Revolution) scholars were increasingly willing to treat the gospel as a text devoid of theology. This trend continued during the Enlightenment of the eighteenth century. The Enlightenment was a period of intense interest in and practical applications of science, which was understood as an activity that benefited humans. On the other hand, the Enlightenment was intensely skeptical about religion.

Out of this period came the conviction that the Infancy Gospel of Thomas was a type of gnosticism. We encountered gnosticism in the earlier chapters. Here it is enough to point out the dualism at the core of gnosticism. Gnostics held that the world of flesh and sin was weak and evil. Only a good god could redeem humans from their evil existence. This god was Jesus. Similar ideas in docetism and Manichaeism led to the Infancy Gospel of Thomas' classification in these camps as well. Yet after the discovery of the Nag Hammadi texts in 1945, the Infancy Gospel of Thomas seems much less Gnostic than had been thought during the Scientific Revolution and Enlightenment. At the same time, the 1945 discovery shifted research away from the Infancy Gospel of Thomas and toward the Gospel of Thomas.

Some discussion of the differences between these two works should help us sort out their functions. Whatever one might think of the Infancy Gospel of Thomas, it is easy to interpret within the framework of a narrative. This style puts the infancy gospel within the context of the canonical gospels, which were also narratives. The Gospel of Thomas, however, abandoned the narrative in favor of a string of Jesus' sayings. Because this is so the Gospel of Thomas strikes the reader as more abrupt in its treatment of Jesus than does the Infancy Gospel of Jesus. Perhaps more important are the differences in content. The Gospel of Thomas makes clear that one must possess the hidden knowledge of Jesus to reach the afterlife. It is this desire for secret knowledge that makes the Gospel of Thomas a Gnostic document by definition. This notion of hidden or secret knowledge is not present, at least not intentionally, in the Infancy of Thomas. It is true that some of the miracles in the infancy gospel are not easy to grasp given the brief narrative, but there is no suggestion that one need possess secret knowledge to live eternally. That is, the infancy gospel is really not a Gnostic text. Accordingly, despite the near coincidence in title, these texts should not be conflated or confused.

Perhaps the most recent interest in the infancy gospel is to place it in the category of oral literature. This attempt indicates that this gospel was composed from oral traditions. Such an idea is not surprising given the likelihood that the canonical gospels also had some foundation of oral traditions. The oral character of the Infancy Gospel of Thomas imparts the plastic quality noted earlier. One could easily add or subtract material from a text that was fluid in the first place. The gospel has hints that it was written to augment the oral component. Among other aspects, the gospel included repetition and is brief, aiding the mind in remembering it so that the gospel must have been transmitted both orally and in writing. We have seen that the oral component was probably important in diffusing the text among the masses.

If the Infancy Gospel of Thomas cannot match the literary and philosophical content of other parts of the bible, the prose is no less serviceable than what one finds in the gospel of Mark and Revelation. Like Mark, the Infancy Gospel of Thomas seems to have a number of abrupt transitions between stories. They are not interwoven with particular skill. One might assert that the Infancy Gospel of Thomas lacks psychology depth. This flaw, if it may be characterized thus, is common to ancient literature. Plato's ability to create depth does not represent most ancient literature. Remember that even gifted writers, like French author Voltaire, did not always aim for psychological depth. *Candide* itself is too brief and abrupt to permit such treatment.

Other parallels exist in antiquity. The Infancy Gospel of Thomas resembled ancient biographies of holy people. In this sense it is hagiography. Like the infancy gospel hagiography nearly removes a person from the human sphere, so frequent and great are the miracles attributed to him or her. The literature seems to suggest that the subject of this holy biography was nearly the equal of Jesus as a miracle worker. The infancy gospel has the same message. Whatever Jesus did well in the canonical gospels, he could do at a younger age in the Infancy Gospel of Thomas. The infancy gospel also resembles the biographies of Roman historian Seutonius. Yet the gospel may be unique in focusing on a hero's childhood contrary to the interest of the classicist in concentrating on the adulthood of Alexander the Great or some other heroic figure. By the same token the Infancy Gospel of Thomas is akin to ancient fairytales, myths and legends, none of which have historical value.

Differentiation is necessary among these genres. The fairytale is perhaps the easiest to recognize because it includes fantasy figures. Obviously the fairy is a staple of this genre but so are dragons and giants. The story of Jack and the Beanstalk is a well-known fairytale. Note that the story contains two giants, the one in the sky and the bean plant itself. The stories of dragons worshiping Jesus are likewise fairytales. A myth is an unscientific or perhaps pre scientific attempt to explain how the world has come to be as it is. The creation story in Genesis is an excellent example. It explains how the universe was to have begun and how life came in stages to colonize earth. It explains how all the animals got their name and how the first woman was created. The last in this trio, the legend, may be the most maddening to track because it may at its core have a historical person. King Arthur and Robin Hood may have been historical figures, or their stories may be based on historical figures. In more modern times, we know that Babe Ruth the baseball player lived but the stories about him have a legendary quality. One supposes that he pointed a bat toward a spot in the stands. On the next pitch he hit a home run to that precise spot. This is likely a legend, a fanciful story that grew up around a historical figure. If such an "at bat" occurred, Ruth may simply have taken warm up swings, as are common in baseball, in that direction and never actually pointed to a specific spot. The problem with Jesus is that the legendary material overwhelms everything else one might like to know about him. The miracles are all legends. The birth narrative is a legend. The childhood events are legends. There is no material that may actually be factual. One is left with an elusive Jesus.

Like these genres, all of which share in common their fictitious nature, the Infancy Gospel of Thomas features a hero with unusual abilities, a series of stories to bring these abilities to life, and his conflict with the larger society. Despite parallels with ancient fairytales, myths and legends, it seems clear that the authors wanted the audience to believe in a literal rendering of the stories in the gospel. This literal intent is a strong element of any legend, particularly those that grew around Jesus. The attribution to Thomas, we have seen, must have met this criterion.

Finally, one finds parallels between the Infancy Gospel of Thomas and the canonical gospels. We have seen that the authors of the infancy gospel knew Luke. In addition the infancy gospel has a very brief prologue, akin to that of Luke. Remember that John has a prologue too, but it is much different than what one finds in the Infancy Gospel of Thomas and Luke. Like the canonical gospels, the infancy gospel focuses on biography, narrative, anecdote, miracles, speeches and some attempt at chronological presentation of information. Note, however, that John provides little chronology, and chronology is not a strength of any of the gospels. The Infancy Gospel of Thomas, like the Gospel of Thomas, recounts no death and resurrection. This omission is particularly troubling in the Gospel of Thomas. One may forgive the Infancy Gospel of Thomas because the focus is on childhood, not adult events.

The gospel raises more questions than it answers. It begins with Jesus at age five.[1] As a narrative of early events, it omits any birth narrative. This conflicts with Luke and Matthew but corresponds to the rest of the New Testament. We are nonetheless left with the question why authors who focused on the early events in Jesus' life would not have included information about his birth. The omission is perplexing. At the same time there is no real reference to space and time. The location could have been any rural area. Because about 90 percent of the people in antiquity farmed, most areas would have had abundant farmland, so the sense that Jesus lived in a rural district tells us virtually nothing. To judge from the standards of antiquity, Nazareth if one may suppose it to have been the region of Jesus' childhood, was not a prime agricultural area. The people of Nazareth must have eked out a living rather than thrived, reinforcing the conviction that Jesus was likely poor. The authors set no firm chronology except to mention Jesus' age from time to time. Unlike Luke, there is no attempt to connect Jesus to the reign of an emperor. There is certainly no mention of Bethlehem, but neither is there mention of Nazareth, the village that would have served well to link Jesus of the infancy gospel to Jesus of the canonical gospels. On the whole the Infancy Gospel of Jesus tells us little about the man. What information it contains can scarcely be reliable.

A simple way of understanding the Infancy Gospel of Thomas is to grasp the importance of the stories in it. To put the matter another way, the gospel is a series of miracles that form the backbone of the stories. In this way and with a cursory glance, Jesus does not appear to have been different from the Jesus of the canonical gospels. Yet an examination of the miracles in the infancy gospel yields significant differences to the canonical gospels. That is, a different Jesus populates the Infancy Gospel of Thomas. The first two

---

[1] Ibid., 8.

miracles that open the gospel are closely linked. In the first, Jesus creates sparrows out of mud from a pool of water.[1] We alluded to this event earlier. The key point is that Jesus behaved this way on the Sabbath, provoking ire. His father Joseph admonished him and in answer Jesus told the sparrows to fly away. He had animated inanimate matter, a miracle that appears to parallel the creation story in Genesis, in which the Jewish god Yahweh created Adam from earth and animated him by breathing the breath of life into his nostrils. The authors of the infancy gospel seem driven to making an analogy between Jesus and Yahweh, likely as a way of proclaiming Jesus' divinity. Yet the analogy festers beneath the surface of the narrative. It is never overt.

The second miracle breaks this union between the two. Still at the pond, the son of Annas the scribe is also indignant that Jesus violated the Sabbath. He puts a stick in the water to disturb Jesus. Angered, Jesus curses the boy, who dies on the spot. The child's parents complain to Joseph, asking, "What kind of child do you have who does such things?"[2] In the next section Jesus, fresh from his first murder, kills a second child for the crime of accidentally hitting him in the shoulder as he runs past Jesus. Angered again, the result is the same, as the boy collapses into a corpse. These events are enormously consequential in what they reveal about Jesus. As he piles up murders (and more are to come), he becomes something akin to a serial killer. Through the Ten Commandments, Yahweh admonished his people not to kill. Yet Jesus appears to be a temperamental killer by nature. How can he be one with Yahweh if he violates god's laws with impunity? The obvious answer is that Jesus could not have been divine to behave this way, a conclusion we reached in earlier chapters. In a larger sense, the Old Testament reveals Yahweh to have been a god of vengeance, one who destroyed cities and eradicated the people. The putative flood killed nearly everyone. Perhaps in this sense the link between the Jesus of the infancy gospel and the Yahweh of the Hebrew scriptures is very close.

Christians will protest that Jesus was divine. In an attempt to shoulder their burden, let me take on the claim of divinity, even though it is not true. At a minimum, let us try to use the word "god" with as much precision as possible. I am not after all of god's attributes. These will await chapter 7. I wish to focus on the claim that god is all-loving and wants a relationship with everyone. The claim that god is love derives directly from John, and I wish to invoke it here. Let us measure the Jesus of the infancy gospel against this criterion.

---

[1] Ibid.
[2] Ibid.

Jesus does not appear to love or to desire a relationship with anyone. To put matters succinctly: if you cross Jesus, you are dead. This murderous behavior does not square with our partial definition of god. Therefore Jesus cannot be god. If Jesus was not god, how are we to define him? Is there an analogy between Jesus and Satan? The earliest reference to Satan appears in Job.[1] I do not agree that the snake in Genesis is Satan because nowhere in the text is such a connection made. When Satan appears in Job, he, with god's consent, tortures Job with several afflictions, but he does not kill Job. Nevertheless he kills all of Job's children.[2] It seems proper to designate Satan a murderer. Yet Jesus is a murderer too. The Jesus of the Infancy Gospel of Thomas turns out to bear much more similarity to Satan than to any idealized definition of god. Is this Jesus the offspring of Satan? I will not go that far. My aim is to make clear that Jesus had neither divine nor demonic powers. He was entirely human, despite what all the puffed up stories about him say. Within the context of his childhood, Jesus may have displayed many unflattering traits: anger, selfishness and other so called sins. The Infancy Gospel of Thomas compounds matters by stating in the compass of a short narrative that Jesus was a murderer.

A small point worth noting is the vagueness of the stories in the Infancy Gospel of Thomas. The authors do not tell us how many sparrows Jesus made or which shoulder the boy hit. The absence of details suggested that no such specificity was possible or the events did not happen. Consider modern affairs as a contrast. If you took chemistry in high school, you probably remember that you had to know precisely how much calcium carbonate you were about to heat in a test tube above your Bunsen burner. If you bought a new bicycle during these years, you had to give the salesperson the exact amount of money because in the real world, details and precision matter. In the fantasy world of Jesus, such details are absent because the stories are not real. The Jesus that comes to the fore in the text about him is illusory. He is fiction and no more real than Ivan Karamazov in *The Brothers Karamazov*. In fact Ivan may be more real, because Russian novelist Fyodor Dostoevsky created him as a revealing model of great psychological depth. This is certainly not true of the Jesus we know from the ancient texts. In fact not only are details absent, but the texts change over time. We alluded to the phenomenon earlier in this chapter and will encounter it again. If the narrative is not stable, how can we trust it? If I claim to have participated in the Boston Marathon today but claim to have won it 20 years ago, through the lens of my memory, why would anyone believe me? These problems plague our search for the historical Jesus.

---

[1] Job 1: 6.
[2] Job 1: 13-2: 7.

The Infancy Gospel of Thomas includes other miracles, but we need not wade through them all. Joseph, we are told, apparently to occupy Jesus more productively, made several attempts to send him to school.[1] We will examine the particulars of some episodes. Here the critical point is that Joseph sent Jesus to school with the explicit desire that he learn to read and write. That is, Jesus had to become literate in order to be worthy of debating the scholars in the temple at Jerusalem at age 12. In his first attempt at learning, Jesus expresses interest in the secret meaning of the first letter of the alphabet, alpha or A. In other words, Jesus was learning the Greek alphabet. But Jesus spoke Aramaic, and Aramaic contained no vowels and so no alpha. Here we are very far from the historical Jesus. The probability is that this story, like the others, is untrue but was fabricated to boost Jesus' credentials. If he were truly wise, according to this line of reasoning, he must have been educated as a child, and Greek was the language of philosophy, drama, history and other serious pursuits in antiquity. No Roman person could consider himself or herself truly learned unless he or she knew Greek, but this pertains to an elite, not the sons of carpenters.

At any rate, Jesus' first teacher endures him just one day before he asks Joseph to take him back.[2] Apparently the teacher thought Jesus had outsmarted him, a circumstance that would have undermined the teacher's claim to superior knowledge.

Also, at some point, Jesus resurrected the children he killed, though we do not know the reason because Jesus' thoughts are not available to us. It is almost as though the authors of the Infancy Gospel of Thomas were trying to claim that murders do not count if Jesus retraced his step and undid the crimes. Such a rationale would not likely persuade a modern jury.

As the scene shifts, Jesus and another boy are playing atop the roof of a house. The unnamed child falls from the roof and is dead on the ground. Immediately the parents accuse Jesus of pushing their son to his demise.[3] Jesus protests his innocence, climbs to the ground and resurrects the boy so that he can tell his parents that Jesus is innocent. The astounded parents begin to glorify god and worship Jesus. Here again is the god motif. It is improper to worship a person but necessary to worship a god. Yet not all manuscripts end the story on such a fine note. In some, Jesus, having gotten the answer he wanted from the boy, kills him perhaps a second time. In fact the claim that Jesus was innocent of what would have been his third murder is unclear. The child may have told Jesus what he wanted to hear, in thanks for being restored to life. In the stories in which Jesus killed the boy again,

---

[1] Infancy Gospel of Thomas, 9-10, 12-13.
[2] Ibid., 10.
[3] Ibid., 11.

the motive may have been to silence him forever so that he could not change his story.

Yet even as a child, Jesus had a flair for the dramatic. When a crowd gathered around a man who had accidentally split open his foot with an axe, fear ran through the people that he would bleed to death before help arrived. Immediately Jesus came on the scene, healing the man.[1] The appreciative crowd worshipped Jesus. His star was on the rise. One good deed deserves others, so that Jesus used his cloak to carry water to Mary and helped his father plant wheat in a field. Jesus sowed a single seed, which upon harvest yielded enough wheat to fill 100 large bushels. Even modern agricultural techniques produce no such yields. The filling of 100 large bushels from a single wheat plant would have been impossible then and now. In fact, in antiquity it is not certain that a single wheat plant would have yielded even ten seeds, the amount one could hold in the hand not in a single bushel let alone 100. Reality aside, Jesus distributed this grain to the poor. Here one encounters a kind of literary attempt to create a Jekyll and Hyde before the genre had come into being. We encounter a Jesus capable of great malice and great compassion. Such unstable behavior is of course the mark of a human, not a god, unless of course we define god as having the elements of Satan. We reinforce again that Jesus was fully human and not at all divine.

After such feats the authors bring Jesus back to school for a second attempt. The outcome is worse. Jesus quarrels with the teacher, who strikes him in the head. Jesus responds with a curse and the man dies at once. Antiquity and the Middle Ages must have had their share of disciplinary problems. At this sign of trouble, Joseph and Mary resolve to keep Jesus inside their home lest he cause more problems. This event contributes to the Jekyll and Hyde syndrome. Yet the parents relent and place Jesus back in school for a third time. Events turn out much better and Jesus raises the teacher he had killed. Again the rule must obtain that what causes not harm cannot be a foul.

Jesus seems to have turned a corner. It appears that as he matures he comes to see the value of using his powers for good. Now comes a string of positive miracles to reassure the faithful. When his brother James suffers a bite from a venomous snake and death seems certain, Jesus heals him. Then Jesus raises from the dead a child and a construction worker, neither of whom Jesus had killed to necessitate revivification. Finally, and this miracle does not appear in all variants of the Infancy Gospel of Thomas, Jesus joins his father in the carpentry business. When Joseph cuts two beams unevenly, Jesus stretches them out to be perfectly straight and of the same length. None of these miracles is true, but by the time we get the miracles that involve

---

[1] Ibid.

Mary and Joseph, an important truth emerges, namely that Jesus must to some extent have been a dutiful son. He probably helped his parents in many ways. In this, he was not god but merely a boy like any other boy who was faithful to his parents and their well being. There is nothing miraculous about such behavior. It happens every day throughout the world. Other than this nugget the Infancy Gospel of Thomas tells us nothing about Jesus' childhood. There are no facts, just a series of miracles that never occurred. Had Jesus performed miracles as a child, the astonished Jews of Palestine would have commemorated these events. The canonical gospels would have mentioned them. But all we have is silence, the same silence that attends the birth narrative. That is both birth narrative and childhood events are fiction. Our efforts have not yielded the historical Jesus.

The Gospel of Pseudo Matthew

We encountered the gospel of pseudo Matthew in the last chapter. Recall that it makes claims about Jesus' birth. It also has material on Jesus' childhood, but much less than is in the Infancy Gospel of Jesus. One of the central events of pseudo Matthew is Mary, Joseph, and Jesus' retreat to Egypt. It might have been possible for them to have gone to Egypt because both Palestine and Egypt, being in the eastern Mediterranean, are not intolerably far apart. The occasion for this change of residence was the threat of death.[1] According to both the gospel of Matthew and pseudo Matthew, King Herod feared that Jesus might grow to become a rival for the throne. It was necessary for the brutal Herod to crush all rivals. This rationale holds fast to what is known about Herod's bloodthirsty character, a man who killed his own children when he perceived them a threat. Yet the move to Egypt was entirely fanciful. While there, pseudo Matthew claims that Jesus tamed wild animals including lions and dragons. Here is the type of material one finds in a fairytale, not in a historical document. Dragons do not exist and the lion is a savannah animal and would not likely have been in Egypt. In fact the lions and dragons that came out of their caves did so to worship Jesus. Such behavior is not plausible. Jesus even commands a stone monument to worship him. In obedience the monument falls on its knees to worship Jesus. Stone monuments are inanimate and cannot behave like humans or other animals. The author obviously felt no need to tell the truth. From beginning to end pseudo Matthew is fiction. As with the gospels including the Infancy Gospel of Thomas, we cannot find the historical Jesus in pseudo Matthew.

---

[1] Gospel of Pseudo Matthew, in *The Other Gospels: Accounts of Jesus from outside the New Testament* (Oxford: Oxford University Press, 2014) 53-54.

Emil Bock's The Childhood of Jesus

No other ancient or medieval source adds to our dubious narrative of Jesus' childhood. Given the relative silence of these sources one is unsurprised by the dearth of secondary literature. What exists does not reassure. Consider theologian Emil Bock's book *The Childhood of Jesus*. The book misleads the reader in many respects. The key violation is the almost complete absence of information about Jesus' childhood, the professed subject of the book. Of the sixteen chapters, only one attempts to reflect on the childhood of Jesus.[1] That is, just nine of 318 pages are germane to the title of the book. Even these nine pages are distressing because they are more mystical reflection than an attempt to describe Jesus' childhood. Again and again one finds, as with the gospels and apocrypha, the absence of concrete, reliable information. The chapter deals in generalities not specifics. Among its conclusions is that claim that Jesus was introspective as a child and attuned to nature. There is no evidence for or against this claim and no way to test it. It is more a non-statement than a factual claim. Bock writes that Jesus had a "boundless capacity for love." Yet if one recalls the Infancy Gospels of Thomas, one finds the opposite. Jesus was not loving. He murdered three people and possibly a fourth. Perhaps one should consider this a boundless capacity for evil. Doubtless one should fear rather than revere anyone capable of monstrous evil.

Bock must have omitted the infancy gospel as well as the gospel of Mark. Mark presents Jesus as a benevolent person, but one who nonetheless killed a fig tree by cursing it. That fig tree would have been someone's property and an important source of fruit at a time when food of any kind was not plentiful, certainly not for commoners. Remember that Palestine was no a productive region of food output. Of course one might retort that Jesus found the tree without fruit. This does not mean that the tree was unproductive. Unless a tree is flowering it will not soon produce fruit. In a food scarce environment one is tempted to describe Jesus' actions as reckless. One need only read the Roman agricultural writers to gain a sense of the importance of fig trees in the ancient Mediterranean Basin. Instead Bock ascribed Jesus' love to his divinity, but our inquiry so far has found no reason to suppose that Jesus was god. He was human like the rest of us. Bock approaches this putative love from the perspective of pseudo Matthew, recalling Jesus' ability to tame all animals and to the claim that he naturally drew animals to him. Again one finds reference to dragons. It is as though Bock knew he were perpetuating falsehoods about Jesus. Of course one finds the same language used to describe St. Francis. But the repetition of a falsehood does not make

---

[1] Bock, Emil. *The Childhood of Jesus: The Unknown Years* (Edinburgh: Floris Books, 1997) 131-138.

it true in the second iteration. We must conclude that we know nothing about Jesus' childhood. Whatever information there was may have been was lost long ago.

Miracles and Jesus' Childhood

Miracles are an essential feature of the stories about Jesus' childhood. They are important as well in the stories about Jesus' adulthood. One must consider them in this chapter and the next two. To state that a miracle has occurred is to claim that an event has violated the natural order of the universe. Consider the example of gravity. In the seventeenth century British polymath Isaac Newton described gravity as a force of attraction among all objects in the universe. It is therefore an inherent property of matter and must have existed since the formation of matter after the Big Bang. The fact that matter exists necessitates the existence of gravity. One may not therefore seek its absence. Such an absence would constitute a miracle. Suppose for example that I hold a coin in one of my hands. Our massive earth tugs on my coin and if I release it, my coin will fall to the floor. If I repeat this action every day for the rest of my life, the law of gravity dictates the same result. Imagine one day, however, that a holy man visits my home. He prays over my coin and when I release it, it flies to the ceiling. Gravity would be in absence during this action and I would be forced, barring any other explanation, to concede the occurrence of a miracle. The movie the Exorcist played upon this theme by levitating the possessed girl to the terror of audiences. In this case, however, one must suppose that Satan performed this miracle. A miracle is thus an inexplicable occurrence that violates what happens pro forma in the universe. Of course the danger is that my inability to explain an event does not automatically make it a miracle. An explanation may exist but I may be unaware of it. Someone knowledge might come along to correct me of the erroneous conclusion that some event was a miracle. The power of science, of course, lies in its capacity to explain today what appeared inexplicable yesterday. Note that science considers invalid the claim that any miracle has occurred. In this sense as well as in others, science and religion conflict.

Our subject, however, is the general nature of miracles, ultimately in reference to Jesus. The presence of miracles in ancient literature is not surprising because antiquity was a period when nature was poorly understood. Rainfall at an important period when dryness threatened crops must have seemed to the ancients a miracle. In fact many ancient societies created a number of gods to bring rain, sunshine and other events to their agrarian ways. With a primitive understanding of nature, miracles were in abundance, people believed. To connect these beliefs to Jesus, one must understand that he lived during a period in which what we might call the occult was an ordinary part of life. Miracles were not unusual, implausible events. They were part of the fabric of reality, as the ancients understood it.

As such it did not take a great leap in imagination for the Infancy Gospel of Thomas to portray Jesus as having miraculous powers as early as age five. In fact this gospel does not preclude the possibility that Jesus might have performed miracles even earlier in life. We have seen that the characteristics of these miracles are bizarre. In just a few pages, Jesus killed three and possibly four people. He demonstrated no remorse, and even though he later resurrected these dead, these actions do not appear to have absolved him from sin. Of course it is an article of faith that Jesus never sinned, but the infancy gospel does not come to this easy answer. The miracles in this gospel tell us that Jesus had power in the most limitless way: he could commit evil. Murder is judged a mortal sin, meaning that it has the capacity to set one apart from relationship with god. If we apply this claim to Jesus, we see that he must have been separate from god. If Jesus were separate from god he must not have been god but merely human. This insight has been our conviction all along. Whenever we have studied some aspect of Jesus, we have found him to be fully human and not at all divine.

Apart from this theological lesson, an important point is that none of Jesus' miracles, in fact no miracle of any kind, can be verified. Miracles are necessarily at the opposite pole from science, in which any hypothesis must be subject to testing. I can think of no way to test the claim that Jesus killed three or four people as claimed in the Infancy Gospel of Thomas. The same is true of any miracle we might wish to examine. Curiously, even in our modern era of science, many people still hanker for miracles. The Catholic Church is particularly egregious in this matter, connecting miracles to saints and former popes. The places where Mary the mother of Jesus is said to have visited as recently as the twentieth century are now holy shrines that echo the promise of miracles. For this reason people bathe in the waters at Lourdes in hopes of a miraculous cure. The Shroud of Turin was upheld as a miraculous rendering of Jesus at the moment of his resurrection until simple dating methods proved it a hoax. More putative miracles await us in the next two chapters.

CHAPTER 4. THE MINISTRY

The birth and childhood narratives, examined in earlier chapter, proved to contain little if any actual information, none of it being reliable or of historical value. The historian continues his or her quest for Jesus by turning to his adulthood. For ease of treatment, Jesus' adulthood may be divided into the period of his ministry and his passion. One might suppose that we are finally on firm ground because the canonical gospels concern his adulthood. Indeed Mark confines his treatment solely to Jesus' adulthood, and except for the mysterious prologue, John has no interest in anything but the man's adulthood. Everything concrete from John concerns Jesus the man-god. Two basic questions confront us at this point. What does this material about Jesus' adulthood (and in this chapter I wish to focus on his ministry) tell us about the historical figure, and is any of it reliable? These questions will guide us through this chapter.

John the Baptist and Jesus

Before one tries to probe Jesus as an adult, one must confront another important character in the canonical gospels, John the Baptist. This man was never the focus of the gospels but rather served to exalt Jesus. Note that, in Mark, John the Baptist is the first character one encounters.[1] Yet even if one reads the gospels page by page, the writers do not provide much information about this John. He is somewhat a shadowy figure and one cannot be certain that he existed. He may easily be a literary device that served as a gateway to Jesus. Because of our uncertainty, let us brush aside the question of John the Baptist's existence. In

---

[1] Mark 1: 4.

any case it is easier to see the relationship between John and Jesus as a series of contrivances.

What then do we learn from John the Baptist? We learn many things. At the outset I wish to emphasize John the Baptist, literary convention or person, as a figure who represented one strand of Jewish thought in the first century CE. In this context I return to apocalypticism. Remember that some Jews thought that god would soon end the current age of injustice and suffering. He would condemn the wicked to hell and invite the righteous into heaven. Remember that these events were not years or decades away. Humanity was on the cusp of a cataclysm. John the Baptist serves as the mouthpiece for these ideas.[1] It is his voice that one hears in the opening verses of Mark, announcing the arrival of the end times. Who would usher in these last events? To Mark, Jesus would fulfill this message. John the Baptist thus prepared the ground for Jesus' arrival at this critical juncture in history. John the Baptist in fact is a trial balloon for Jesus' ideas, if we are right to lump both John the Baptist and Jesus as apocalyptic preachers. John delivers the opening salvo and Jesus piles on his own apocalypticism. John must have been a prelude to what Jesus hoped to accomplish. Therein lies John's purpose. It is not necessary that he existed, only that he transmitted a message that Jesus would later amplify. Because all the attention is on Jesus, little need be said about John, who may have been, we have seen, merely a literary device.

Within the apocalyptic hopes that John the Baptist raised, if he really existed, Jesus emerged very much as the savior. In fact both Mark and Matthew expend considerable energy convincing the reader that Jesus is the ultimately apocalyptic preacher. The Jesus of these gospels announces that some of his listeners will not die before the arrival of the kingdom of god. We noted the brevity of human life in antiquity. Two considerations must emerge from this insight. First because people did not live long, the end of the world must have been very near according to Jesus or the gospel writers. The more remarkable fact is that Mark and Matthew continued to put such language in Jesus' mouth even after his followers must have been dead. Remember that Matthew was written no earlier than 80 CE. Jesus' followers, to have still been alive, must have reached their 70s or 80s. Remember that ¾ of all people were dead before age 45 in antiquity. Jesus or the gospel writers were wrong to foretell an early end of times. It would seem strange for Mark and Matthew to repeat such an error, presumably on Jesus' behalf. In short Jesus must have been wrong to predict the end of times.

The probability of error has an important consequence. As we have several times already, let us invite Christians to join us. They will not swerve from

---

[1] Mark 1: 1-8.

their conviction that Jesus was god. Let us examine this claim anew. Much relies on the definition of god. We need not trot out a long list of attributes. Instead we will focus on the notion of omniscience. To be omniscient is to know everything. There are no limits to knowledge for an all-knowing being. Such a being would be remarkable. He or she would examine the stock market to foresee what the winning stocks would be in six months. Investing in these stocks he or she would become fabulously wealthy. Such a person could predict the behavior of a slot machine and clean out a casino without breaking a sweat. In other words omniscience is power.

With these conditions at hand, if Jesus were god, he would need to be omniscient. That is, Jesus would need to know when the world would end. He would not make a false prediction, giving rise to false hopes. He would know the truth and act accordingly. Because he did not, because he made an error, Jesus cannot have been god. He was a man, fallible like the rest of us. Perhaps he absorbed John the Baptist's rhetoric without any critical appraisal of what was and was not possible during his life. Jesus' insights must have been limited. Again, one cannot place limits on god but Jesus had limits and so was not god. The failure of Jesus' predictions therefore point to the failure of the god hypothesis, namely the hypothesis that Jesus was god. I use the term "hypothesis" because every hypothesis must be testable. That is, one must find a way to determine whether a hypothesis if false. We have done just by falsifying again and again the claim that Jesus is god.

To clarify our position about the definition of a hypothesis, we must be able to devise a test capable of falsifying it. We cannot however conclusively prove a hypothesis. Consider again the example of a coin. Gravity predicts that every time I drop a coin it will fall to the ground. At no time will it ascend to the heavens. The "every time" requirement, however, is impossible to fulfill. There is no way that I or anyone else can drop this coin an infinite number of times because the human lifespan is always finite, a law that holds for everyone. Because infinity is beyond our grasp, we can never state conclusively that the gravity between two objects always pulls them together. For this reason we cannot construct a foolproof demonstration that Jesus is god. We have seen, however, that we can falsify this claim. This is not a matter of hoodwinking the reader through a series of words, but of laying bare Jesus as he actually was. Note that strictly speaking we should use the past tense to refer to Jesus because he is dead. Being no longer alive he cannot be said to exist now.

Put another way, there is no solution to this problem except to deny Jesus' divinity. The gospel of John, however, tried to save face. Remember that John may have been written as late as 100 CE, 70 years after Jesus' death. By then no follower could have been alive. Rather than racket up apocalyptic talk,

John simply abandons the idea. The Jesus in this gospel did not predict the end of the world. John therefore retains the illusion that Jesus never made an error, that he was perfect, and that he by definition was god. By now we have had our fill of divinity claims. When will Christians adopt a more realistic appraisal of the man?

The apocalyptic strand of Jesus' though and subsequent claims of divinity and humanity are not the only insights that flow from an encounter with John the Baptist. The central encounter between John the Baptist and Jesus is John's baptism of Jesus.[1] This is the moment that begins Jesus' ministry, but did it happen? There are good reasons for skepticism. First, if Jesus were god, why would he need baptism of any kind by anyone? Why would John have baptized Jesus rather than prostrated himself in worship? Jesus should have baptized John not the other way around. The dynamic is wrong because Jesus should have baptized the entire crowd that gathered around him and anyone else because Jesus alone was divine. The story makes sense only if Jesus were fully human and not divine. Here is a further argument against Jesus' divinity if more ammunition should be necessary. That is, the baptism of Jesus is an implicit demonstration of his humanity.

Jesus' baptism faces another challenge. The church has made clear that the purpose of baptism is to wash away original sin. I must backtrack a moment. A literal interpretation of the creation story in Genesis supposes that Adam and Eve disobeyed god by eating the forbidden fruit.[2] This disobedience was sin and had consequences. Adam and Eve were no longer permitted in the Garden of Eden. They had to work for their food and they were no longer immortal. This first sin that caused so much strife was known as original sin. Every person, being a literal descendent of Adam and Eve, received this sin at conception. Baptism was thus necessary to cleanse a person of this sin. But if Jesus was baptized, he must have had this original sin and so needed cleansing. Yet if Jesus were god he should not have needed cleansing because he was perfect. A god cannot sin. Hence Jesus cannot have committed or inherited any sin. But because he was baptized he must have needed the original sin cleansed from him, which is to say that he must have been human rather than divine. At every turn we are able to debunk the god hypothesis. We invite Christians to examine these issues critically, as we have.

Christians may have opted for baptism as a way of persuading converts to undergo baptism. If so the baptism episode must have been added well after the events that actually happened. In fact the first century CE Roman world was awash in baptisms. The mystery cults that were so popular then featured baptism as a rite of initiation. The cult of Mithras mandated

---

[1] Mark 1: 9-11.
[2] Genesis 3: 1-24.

baptism for example.[1] Mithras was an important god, probably stemming from Zoroastrianism, a Persian (Iranian) religion. Many features join Zoroastrianism and Christianity because Christianity borrowed from this earlier religion. In fact Mithras became a kind of proto Jesus in his spread throughout the Roman Empire. He was the god of light. Read the gospel of John, just the prologue, to grasp the importance of light in understanding Jesus. Being the god of light, Mithras was the winter solstice god, marking the triumph of light over darkness. It is this triumph that we celebrate when we commemorate December 25 as Jesus' birthday when we have no idea when Jesus was born. Like Jesus, Mithras was a resurrection god. Because baptism was important for this god it became important for Jesus and for all Christians who came after him.

An important question follows. If we know details about Mithras and see the parallels between he and Jesus, how can we be confident that what we read in the gospels concerns the historical Jesus and not the Jesus propped up to be like Mithras, a popular competitor god? In short we cannot know. Borrowings from foreign religions must obscure our understanding of Jesus. If we claim that Mithras was a false god, why is Jesus better? Why should we be more confident in our ability to know anything substantive about Jesus when we assert that competing claims about Mithras are lies? It is not easy to account for the fact that most of us are atheists in every respect except that concerning Jesus or Buddha or some such figure. If we disbelieve in Mithras, Isis, Osiris, and many other gods, if we consign them all to the garbage heap of history, why do we think Jesus alone worthy of worship? I suspect that the inertia of history leads us like sheep to follow a 2000-year-old dead man and to worship him as god. Because we cannot live apart from history; we are stuck with its contents, irrational though they may be.

The Temptation

We noted in our examination of Jesus and John the Baptist the uncovering of a possible piece of historical information, namely that Jesus might have been an apocalyptic prophet. This is the one piece of possible datum that our search for the historical Jesus may have yielded after fruitless searches through Jesus' birth and childhood. The canonical gospels record a second major event in Jesus ministry. We learn from the synoptics that after his baptism, Jesus went into the "wilderness" for a period of fasting.[2] The synoptics tabulate this period at 40 days. This long duration makes imperative an understanding of the term "fast." If by fasting we mean

---

[1] Bart D. Ehrman, *The New Testament: Accounts of Jesus from outside the New Testament* (Oxford: Oxford University Press, 2014) 44.
[2] Mark 1: 12-13.

abstinence from food and water, then we must dismiss the story as fiction. In a warm region like Palestine, one should drink about a gallon of water per day. If Jesus drank nothing, he would have died within a week and perhaps sooner. If one defines fasting to include the drinking of water, then the issue becomes food. Had Jesus eaten nothing, he might have lasted longer. Keep in mind, though, that in the pre modern era, the only way for Jesus to have accomplished anything would have been through sweaty, taxing manual effort. At a minimum he would have needed 2000 calories per day and the actual figure may have been larger. Without food, Jesus likely would have perished in two or three weeks, well short of the 40-day threshold. The only way that Jesus might have fasted for such a period would have been that he fasted during the day but took a meal after dusk. This remains a practice among Jews and Muslims and was the only way that Jesus could have survived such a long fast.

Yet even then, the actual duration cannot be known because the play with numbers within the gospels conformed to a kind of code. The number 40 is not random but appears elsewhere in the Hebrew scriptures. The famous example regards the flood. Genesis states that rain deluged earth 40 days and nights.[1] It is not an accident, then, that the gospel writers put Jesus' fast at 40 days. It marks a way of keeping continuity between these new writings and the established Hebrew bible. Put simply, the 40-day fast is a literary convention and not a literal span of time. If Jesus did fast, we have no idea how long. In fact other stories of Jesus confirm his penchant for plucking seeds from wheat plants and eating them on the Sabbath. Such behavior was prohibited but Jesus must have eaten regardless of Mosaic laws because he was hungry. This does not sound like a man prone to fasting. Which is the real Jesus, the one who fasted 40 days or the man who could not suppress his quest for food during a single day, namely the Sabbath?

Perhaps the gospel writers meant to portray Jesus as weak at the end of the fast and so vulnerable to temptation. One might imagine Jesus capable of hallucinations at the end of an ordeal, and in this state he may have hallucinated about an encounter with Satan. Keep in mind that by hallucination we mean the perception of something that does not present itself to the senses. If I claim to have seen a unicorn, I must be lying or hallucinating because such a creature does not exist. Such a state of mind is common among psychotics, but one need not think Jesus had broken with reality as a precondition to mental illness. I do not posit that Jesus was ever mentally ill, though this is the opinion of a historian not a psychiatrist. Something much more innocuous was at work. Imagine that whatever happened during the fast, Jesus emerged weak and tired. Imagine any modern person in the same state,

[1] Genesis 7: 12.

say at night, when sleep beckons and weaknesses and faulty perceptions rule the hour. In such a condition it is easy to perceive that a shadow darkens or elongates or that a sinister figure materializes in the night air. These are not oddities. Many people have had such experiences. My ex wife for example claimed to perceive a ghost in a forested area through which she drove at night. So compelling was this sensation that she never again drove this road at night. Even during the day she did not wish to go near the dense growth of trees.

Under such circumstance, it is not difficult to posit that Jesus was susceptible to hallucinating about the appearance of Satan. If this episode was not a hallucination, it either happened or the gospel writers fabricated it. At this juncture we need information about Satan.

Recall that Satan appears to have been the creation of the writer or writers of Job. "Satan" simply means "adversary." In this sense Satan was god's adversary, working against its designs. We see this behavior in the opening of Job whereby god permits Satan essentially to torture an upright man and kill his children. Because god grants permission for such horrible treatment, it as well as Satan bears responsibility for inflicting misery. In fact part of this torture includes, we have seen, the massacre of Job's children, a murderous act in which god and Satan are culpable. God and Satan thus appear similar in their actions. If Satan were an evil murderer, can we withhold this judgment from god? If Jesus was god, was he, too, evil? Such a question is unnecessary if we resign ourselves to the obvious fact that Jesus was nothing more than human. Of course many humans are evil, and this disposition appears to apply to Jesus, at least in cursing the fig tree and killing people in the Infancy Gospel of Thomas, we have seen.

If we retain the lesson from Job in our examination, it must be clear that Satan, if he appeared before Jesus, did so with god's permission. We do not know the nature of these temptations. The standard model in the synoptics is of temptations that allow Jesus to quote passages from the Hebrew bible. Here, as with the number 40 and the putative appearance of Satan, such a narrative functions to strengthen the connection between Jesus and the Hebrew scriptures. In this guise, Satan appears to be a literary device to serve the larger purpose of imputing a relationship between Yahweh, the god of the Hebrew bible, and Jesus. Such linkages build a case for the claim that Jesus was the son of god.

No less important the connection between Yahweh and Jesus affirms the basic tenet that Jesus was Jewish. It is not at all clear from the gospels that Jesus sought to create a new religion. He may have been intent on reinforcing the chief principles of Judaism. It may be then that Jesus was not a Christian but a Jew intent on having his deeds and utterances conform to Judaism as he understood it. Here is a case of a fallible man making judgments about what did or did not conform to Judaism at its purest. Ultimately of course Judaism rejected Jesus as god and so one tends to see him today through the lens of Christianity. This is a modern view and does not appear to pertain to the historical Jesus, what little can be known of him.

If one wishes to maintain that a literal Satan tempted Jesus, some other mechanism must have been at work. In an earlier publication I tentatively put forth the notion that we may be mistaken to assume Satan to be equivalent to some evil god. I suggested that it might be more realistic to suggest that Satan was a beautiful woman who visited Jesus.[1] In no way do I attempt to claim that women are evil. I simply meant to convey something of the carnal relationship that might have consumed the two. Such a union was not evil, though it transgressed the human perception of what it meant for Jesus to have had an active libido. Every man and woman has surely felt tempted in such a way, and because Jesus was human, he must have been subject to the same yearnings and desires. This woman, if she existed, must have been different from Mary Magdalene, because in the gospel of Philip, Jesus does not attempt to hide his relationship with Mary. The canonical gospels, it is obvious, are different. They wish to portray Jesus as a chaste person, almost an ascetic. Some will discount my claim by pointing to Jesus' putative condemnation of lust. Remember, though, that the gospel writers put such language in Jesus' mouth. We have no idea what he really said, given the passage of decades after his death before the extant writings were composed. The idea of a puritanical Jesus strikes me as fiction. He was a young man in the prime of adulthood. Luke put the age at which Jesus began his ministry at 30 years old. Ask any 30-year-old man how often he thinks of sex. The frequency of these occurrences might make you blush. The gospel of Philip, a Gnostic text mentioned above, claims that Jesus frequently kissed Mary Magdalene on the lips. Under these circumstances it seems reasonable to infer that Mary Magdalene was Jesus' lover. Maybe, as an alternative to the Satan hypothesis, Mary was the woman who appeared to Jesus in the wilderness, though I have serious doubts. We simply do not know.

If the attempt to humanize Satan in order to make sense of the temptation narrative is repugnant, then we must suppose that the episode never happened. This line of thought is in keeping with the difficulty of knowing whether Satan exists. Over the centuries a cottage industry developed to blame Satan for all the ills in the world. To Satan gathered an army of followers (demons) who made humans miserable. These ideas are part of popular culture in which a movie like "the Exorcist," retains staying power in the imagination to this day. The Catholic Church continues to promote

---

[1] Christopher Cumo, "The Temptation," *Swallow* magazine (2007) 11-13.

the idea that demons may possess a person, requiring exorcism. Despite all this talk, it is difficult to point to a shred of existence that pinpoints Satan anywhere in the universe. Without concrete evidence it seems better to disbelieve than to believe in Satan. If Satan does not exist, then no encounter could have occurred between this literary figure and Jesus. Accordingly the temptation narrative may be one of the weakest elements in the New Testament. Satan is as much literary device in the gospels as he is in Fyodor Dostoevky's *The Brothers Karamazov*. Satan changes with the times because of our perceptions not because he ever existed.

Nevertheless, whether Satan existed or not, he performed an important service to humans by making the world more intelligible. A cursory glance at the world reveals terrible misfortunes. Hurricanes are capable of killing hundreds and even thousands of people. Earthquakes are to be feared for the same reason. Mosquitoes of several species carry terrible pathogens. Anopheles mosquitoes continue to transmit malaria to people throughout the tropics with the awful truth that they kill children at very young ages with the result that the children never had a chance to reach their parents. They differ from you and me only in the misfortune of their geography and poverty. When the mariner Christopher Columbus and his followers came in wave after wave of ships to the Americas, they spread diseases, malaria among them, that almost extirpated the Amerindians who had lived in the New World millennia before European contact. Europeans then initiated the slave trade to the Americas, unleashing savagery and death onto million of Africans.

Our list could be much longer, but at some point we must ask why there is so much evil in the world. If god is loving, why is the world such a mess? Because love and evil cannot commingle, some explanation is necessary. Herein lies the function of Satan. If we can ascribe all the evil in the world to Satan, god is off the hook. There is no reason to blame god for Satan's malice toward us. The problem with this explanation, even if one feels it necessary to posit the existence of Satan, is the difficulty we encountered in Job. Remember that god granted Satan permission to torture Job and kill his children and so is complicit in the evils that circulate throughout this book. Despite all our attempts, it is never really possible to grant god clemency for all the suffering in this tortured world.

A Ministry of Miracles

Perhaps the outstanding feature of the canonical gospels is the profusion of miracles. Chapter 2 began our exploration into the nature of miracles. In the gospels, the term "miracle" is roughly synonymous with inexplicable act of magic. In this sense a miracle occurs beyond the bounds of human conceptualization. That it violates the laws of nature means nothing to believers because this is exactly what they expect. A miracle is a manifestation of shock and awe and can never be subject to the bounds of logic. Miracles triumph in the human imagination because they defy all applications of reason. They are outside the bounds of the known and the knowable. Nothing more needs be said in their defense. With these comments out of the way, further commentary may benefit our analysis. Perhaps the most salient point about these miracles is not to pinpoint any one or two, but to establish their prevalence throughout Jesus' ministry. It should strike us immediately that Jesus' miracles appear to be an anomaly. We do not know anyone in modern times who performs miracle after miracle almost as though he or she were a virtuoso. Who goes from town to town expelling demons, curing all sorts of ailments including blindness, whose power may be tapped simply by touching his or her garments, and who can even raise the dead? These powers are astonishing, particularly the last one. We know death, and not merely a near death experience, to be irreversible. How can someone revivify a corpse?

We will examine a small number of miracles to bring home the point. Here it is enough to note that Jesus seems to have existed at a singular moment in history, a time when literally anything was possible. This Jesus is inseparable from notions of divinity. We have already noted that god must be a limitless being. That is we cannot place barriers on what he can know or do. If Jesus were this limitless being he could raise the dead, even though I, being limited, cannot reanimate my favorite Venus flytrap. Jesus' miracles are thus a device of persuasion. If one assents to the claim that Jesus went from one miracle to the next, then one cannot deny him divinity because only a god can do such things. By contrast a human is impotent. This argument, if one takes it at face value, is almost too persuasive. Because humans cannot do miracle and Jesus did, it is easy to conclude that Jesus was fully divine but not human. Here is the Manichaean claim that Jesus only seemed to be human when in fact he was 100 percent god.

It is not surprising, given this line of thought, that Jesus' miraculous powers were on full display in John, the canonical gospel that makes the boldest claims about Jesus' miracles. Even though it was the last canonical gospel to be written I wish to begin with it. At its best, the gospel of John, like the synoptics, uses simple but powerful language to create tension and drama. Perhaps it was this text that pushed Johann Sebastian Bach to such heights of emotive and spiritual expression in his St. John Passion. Even a quick read of the gospel of John reveals the author to have been a skillful prose stylist. The author was at the apex of his powers, I believe, in describing the raising of Lazarus.[1] Much of the text builds the drama to dizzying heights whereas the miracle itself occurs swiftly. This is the kind of treatment that one might have expected from Greek dramatist Sophocles, so pivotal is the episode. The author or authors of John, writing in Greek, may have read the great Greek dramas and so have gained skill in describing the raising of Lazarus so convincingly.

We need not recount every verse in John, though the reader should consult the text to appreciate the quality of the prose. One must observe that Jesus learns of Lazarus' sickness but does not immediately go to his aid. While he waits, Lazarus dies and the news travels to Jesus. Only then does he set out for Bethany, the place of Lazarus' burial. The author makes explicit the fact that Jesus knew that Lazarus was now dead. One might infer that Jesus undertook the journey to Bethany to conquer that which cannot be vanquished, death. When Jesus arrives in Bethany he learns twice that Lazarus has been in the tomb four days. It is clear that the author wishes the reader to know that Lazarus is not asleep or in a trance, but as dead as a corpse can be. Jesus feels great anguish and at one point cries, so great is his grief. His emotions do not derail his purpose. Following instructions to remove the stone in front of the entrance to the tomb, Jesus enters as though he is a hero who has descended to the underworld to save the damned. He calls Lazarus in a loud voice and the dead man, now alive, exits the tomb with Jesus.

What does this monumental story tell us about Jesus? In short it tells us little about Jesus the man and much about the perception of Jesus as god. This human divine duality has beset us from the beginning of our inquiry. How can a mere human revivify a man who has been dead four days? Such an action must by definition be impossible. Between one and three days after death the organs are in the process of decay. By the fourth day, blood begins to bloat the body and to drain from the mouth, ears, and nose. By this stage it is clear that the corpse is beyond repair. All the wonders of modern medicine cannot save it. Yet in primitive conditions Jesus managed the impossible. This claim of arguably the greatest miracle in Jesus' ministry defies all we can come to believe about the irreversibility of death. Keep in mind that the Jews did not embalm the dead. Even the Egyptians had followed this practice only for the elites, and Lazarus was a humble man. In fact, it is just as well that no one embalmed Lazarus because the organs would have been removed. How, for example, can one live without a brain or kidneys or liver? Embalming would have made the raising of Lazarus even more improbable. But in the conditions of the eastern Mediterranean Basin, heat would have hastened

---

[1] John 11: 1-44.

the process of decay. Despite all the advances of science and medicine, it is not possible to raise a decayed corpse.

What then are we to think about this story? The obvious answer is that it never happened. Jesus never raised Lazarus or anyone else from the dead. Instead the author of the gospel of John appears to use this miracle to provide Jewish leaders with a reason for wanting to kill Jesus. The claim is that Jewish authorities feared that a vigorous Jesus, hell bent on pursuing his ministry, might cause the Romans to intervene in Jewish affairs. This reason makes little sense. Even the gospel of John tells us that the Jewish homeland was already under Roman control through the auspices of the Roman governor Pontius Pilate. Pilate and other governors were almost always ex military officers accustomed to giving orders and wielding power. In *The Prince*, Italian author Niccolò Machiavelli relates what he learned from studying Roman history: the Romans confronted trouble while it was distant, long before it could invade Italy. Accordingly when problems arose in the Roman Levant, Pontius Pilate crushed them. The idea that the Jews still had some independence does not square with Roman governance. Even if the rationale for killing Jesus is nonsense, there is no doubt that the author of John used it as a device for building drama and bringing Jesus face to face with the specter of death.

In a larger sense the juxtaposition of Jesus the miracle worker and popular opposition to him makes no sense. If Jesus really cured the sick and raised the dead, all who saw him would have converted to his way of life. It is hard to believe that even Jewish officials would have withheld their admiration. Even today, a person like Barack Obama remains popular and draws huge crowds even though he has performed no miracles. His list of accomplishments is not long. Would not the unity behind Jesus have been all the stronger, given his extra abilities? Jesus should have been exponentially more popular than Barack Obama is today. In sum the raising of Lazarus was a literary device to place the hero of the gospel in peril. It served to heighten tension and deepen the drama. It says much about the author's talents and nothing about Jesus. If it would be ridicule to crucify President Obama for his lack of achievements, why does it make sense to have crucified Jesus given the most stupendous record of working miracles known to history, or so Christians claim?

Other miracles are curious as well. One of the most enigmatic puts Jesus in the familiar role of exorcist. The synoptics, Mark, Matthew and Luke, all record it. Jesus approaches a man possessed by many demons, intending to cleanse the man. The simplest act would have been to exorcize the demons and press forward. Yet there is more to the story because the demons ask

Jesus if they may enter a herd of nearby pigs.[1] Jesus grants the request and the possessed pigs rush into the adjoining body of water, where they drown. This story should raise eyebrows. Why would a powerful miracle worker like Jesus fulfill the request of evil spirits? Was not Jesus the champion of goodness and punisher of evil? The result is an economic catastrophe for at least one person and probably a family. The pig has long been an important domestic animal. Roman writers make clear that pork was the favorite meat in the Roman Empire. True Jews did not eat pork, so two possibilities exist. First a Jewish family may have raised pigs to feed the Romans in the area. Second a non-Jew may have kept the pigs partly for home use and partly for the market. In either case it seems clear that Jesus circulated among the masses, who had little money. The family that owned the pigs likely had an enormous investment in them. The pigs would have been the family's chief and perhaps only source of income. With a single stroke, however, Jesus allowed demons to destroy this investment. Jesus thus perpetrated an evil again a presumably hardworking family. One must ask again whether a god can do evil. The standard answer is that god cannot do evil. Yet Jesus appears to have done just this to a poor family of stockmen. How then can Jesus be divine? By our rules of evidence he cannot have been god. He was a human apparently capable of evil as presented in the synoptic gospels and the Infancy Gospel of Thomas.

This story and all the others involving demons are troubling for another reason. Even into modernity medicine was frequently at a loss to explain an illness. In this context demons were a convenient scapegoat. If Jesus really thought he were curing people possessed by demons, he may in reality have tried to cure people with epilepsy and other maladies far more serious than the presumed medical competence that Jesus had. We cannot know what really happened at these exorcisms. There is no reason to suppose that they accomplished any good. If Jesus truly set himself apart as a physician of sorts, he cannot have had legitimate medical skills and training. The Jesus of demonic possessions must have been an imposter. It is better to think that these exorcisms never occurred.

This is not the end of the miraculous stories that circulate throughout the canonical gospels. In fact the story of Lazarus is not the only resurrection account. Mark seems to provide the first instance of such a miracle.[2] Like the raising of Lazarus, Mark's account is skilful in its ability to combine two miracles in a single episode. According to Mark, a Jewish authority named Jarius approaches Jesus with the request that he accompany Jarius home where his daughter is near death. Word spread instantly and a large crowd

---

[1] See for example, Luke 8: 24-33.
[2] Mark 5: 21-43.

gathered around Jesus as he walked. In the crowd was a woman who had suffered from excessive bleeding over the years. She believed that Jesus was a miracle worker and approached Jesus with the intent of touching his cloak, secure in the belief that this gesture alone would cure her. She was correct, though when she touched Jesus' garment from behind, he became aware of a discharge of power. Jesus asked the person to come forward. She did, professing her faith in him. Jesus upheld her as a model of faith.

At that moment a servant comes to Jarius and Jesus to say that Jarius' daughter has died. Jesus persists and in a curious utterance claims that she is not dead but merely asleep. Remember that in the raising of Lazarus, the gospel of John has Jesus state plainly that Lazarus is dead. Although Jesus raises the girl, a certain ambiguity remains. Was she dead or merely asleep? Moreover she was not entombed for one moment, let alone four days as the gospel of John claims about Lazarus. The raising of Jarius' daughter thus appears to have been a minor miracle compared to the full-blown triumph of the raising of Lazarus in John. One must remember that John, the last of the canonical gospels, the one written about 70 years after Jesus' death, is the culmination of the miracle tradition. In John Jesus appears to have been at the peak of his powers. Only Jesus, the god of the grandest designs, can reach the colossal heights of miraculous power. In John, Jesus has reached the apex of divinity. Nothing appears to be impossible for him.

These variations in our understanding of Jesus, at least as presented in the canonical gospels and apocrypha merit commentary. To an extent variability should be expected. Consider again nineteenth-century Russian novelist Fyodor Dostoevsky. His novels were so vast in their insights that they invite a wide spectrum of opinions. The psychologist wishes to plump Dostoevsky's acuity as a psychologist, the philosopher Friedrich Nietzsche being perhaps the first to grasp the potency of his psychological insights. The theologian struggles to reconcile the deep piety and atheistic despair that one finds within a few pages of one another in The Brothers Karamazov or some other novel. The philosopher emphasizes Dostoevsky's contributions as a forerunner to existentialism. One man united in his life these diverse perspectives.

Does Jesus fit this mold? In many ways Jesus breaks the mold. In The Infancy Gospel of Thomas, Jesus is a murderous child. He is both good and evil, contradiction though this is. In the synoptics a tinge of evil remains in the killing of a fig tree and an entire herd of pigs. This is apparently Jesus the anti agrarian miracle worker. At his worst, Jesus' miracles carry an aura of uncertainty. Did he raise Jarius' daughter from the dead or merely awaken her from a deep sleep? And if this miracle really occurred, should we not know her name? By the time of the gospel of John all ambiguities and evil have vanished. Jesus is conspicuous in his powers, weeping over Lazarus one moment and raising him from the dead the next, after four days interment. I find it difficult to resolve all these Jesuses into a single historical figure. Rather what one finds is a series of legends that preach many conflicting stories about Jesus, who by the time of the gospels and the apocrypha is no longer a historical person. Again we see that we cannot trust the gospels or apocrypha to tell us any concrete, reliable information about Jesus. He remains inscrutable.

My contention is that Jesus never performed any miracles at anytime. He was merely human and could not have brought about the impossible time and time again. He did not raise Lazarus or Jarius' daughter from the dead. He did not ruin the livelihood of livestock raisers and kill fig trees with a curse. Blind people did not receive their sight from Jesus. He never walked on water or calmed a storm. He was human, all too human, to borrow from German philosopher Friedrich Nietzsche. One must imagine that Jesus had charisma and rigorous ethical standards, but such characteristics did not make him a miracle worker. What happened instead is that by the writing of the gospels legendary material had wiped away any trace of the man who was now proclaimed god. The gospel of John in notorious in this respect because it is the last of the canonical gospels, the one in which hyperbole and the most boundless and groundless exaggerations reached a crescendo of false claims. The miracles credited to Jesus never occurred and tell us nothing about Jesus. The historian's quest must continue as he or she plans to apply this reasoning to the claims that Jesus rose from the dead. Chapter 5 holds the key to these arguments.

In this spirit we must broaden our inquiry. Consider for example the fact that the miracle laden canonical gospels do not speak authoritatively. Across the chasm of chapters in this book, we retrieve the gospel of Thomas, noting that it records not a single miracle, not one. Why the silence? If the gospel's author wished to communicate Jesus' divinity, why did he omit every single miracle recorded elsewhere? There is no convincing rationale here. If Lazarus really rose from the dead, Thomas should have shouted this miracle from the rooftop. If one claims that the gospel of Thomas did not have as its purpose the recording of miracles, then let us consider Mark, Matthew and Luke. These gospels profess many miracles; yet not one gospel records the grandeur of the Lazarus miracle. How can this be? Why would Mark, Matthew and Luke have omitted the most spectacular miracle of Jesus' ministry? Why does Mark claim that Jesus raised a young girl from the dead but not Lazarus? The synoptics inexplicably omitted Jesus at the virtuoso heights of miracle working. The only explanation that makes sense is that Mark, Matthew and Luke did not record the raising of Lazarus because it never happened. Jesus never raised anyone from the dead, including Jarius' daughter as well. Jesus never performed any miracles because he was human to the core and humans cannot perform miracles. Every magic trick after all is an illusion. In the same way, Jesus was, by the time the gospels were written, an illusion.

Jesus as Communicator

The gospels do not quite agree on how Jesus presented his message to people. The synoptic gospels suggest that Jesus told pithy parables to convey his message. In John, however, Jesus has advanced beyond the parable to giving extended speeches about his divinity. These two modes are not at all equivalent. To this extent they provide different Jesuses, two people who appear to have understood themselves in different ways and who had different messages to convey. This recognition is a bit troubling. One should expect a more or less uniform perception of Jesus, who after all was one man. Having voiced my skepticism, it is true that complex people may elicit many different perspectives from others. We have considered the example of Fyodor Dostoevsky, and Friedrich Nietzsche provides a similar revelation. He has had many biographers who have stressed different aspects of his thought. This is to be expected because Nietzsche's ideas cannot be understood in isolation. The attempt to do so conveys only a fragment of his thought. Nietzsche, skilful a writer as he was, is difficult to interpret, even when one has tried to grasp the totality of his ideas. To an extent this must have been true of Jesus. He may have been a man of sufficient complexity to have created the divide between the synoptics and John.

Let us descend beneath the surface. Consider first the parables that are the backbone of the synoptic gospels. Mark makes clear that these parables often confused people.[1] In this context they hindered rather than hastened communication. Why would Jesus have adopted a style of communication that baffled his listeners, at least according to Mark? This notion of Jesus does not readily correspond with the later chapters in Mark, when Jesus is firmly an apocalyptic preacher.[2] No one seems to have misunderstood Jesus in this context. The world was about to end and many of Jesus' followers would be alive to witness this event. Here Mark abandons parables in favor of a Jesus who spoke directly to his audience. What is unclear is why Jesus moved from confounding his audience through an artful dance of parable to the plain speaking apocalyptic that everyone seems to have understood. Was not Jesus an apocalyptic preacher all along and if so, why was it necessary to

---

[1] Mark 4: 10-12.
[2] Mark 13: 3-36.

a man with an urgent message to have dabbled in parables that Mark claims did not convince the masses or even some of the apostles?

What then should we make of the parables? It seems evident, at least to some extent, that the parables were confusing because they were contradictory. Let me begin with the parable of Lazarus and the rich man.[1] This parable has no relationship to Lazarus the man who Jesus supposedly raised from the dead in John. This is the synoptic Lazarus, a rich man on the margins of whose estate lived a very poor, homeless man who lived a life of misery. Jesus made clear in this parable, if it is really germane to him, that Lazarus lived every day in luxury and undertook not a single action to help the poor man. The men die, the poor man finding himself in heaven and the rich man in hell. Lazarus now begs the poor man for help, but the patriarch Abraham of the Hebrew scriptures will not permit such actions. Lazarus had never helped the poor man in life, so in the afterworld Lazarus would not receive help as part of his punishment. The parable is interesting at least partly because Abraham appears in it. Here may be an attempt of the gospel writers to connect Jesus with an important figure in Jewish lore. Perhaps the attempt was to strengthen the memory that Jesus had been a Jew throughout his life. The parable may therefore have had the aim of convincing Jews to take a fresh look at the Jewish roots of Jesus.

In addition the parable displays at least an implicit hostility toward the acquisition of wealth. One finds this view strengthened in Jesus' claim that a rich person can as easily enter heaven as a camel can pass through the eye of a needle. This passage has been interpreted in many ways, but again the impetus is on the suspicion of wealth. To be wealthy is to imperil one's soul, if we are to allow the gospel writers to use a Platonic term in a purely theological context. These views seem complementary, but the problem is that the synoptic gospels claim other teachings about wealth. Among the most compelling is what one might call the parable of the coins, where Jesus speaks of the fate of three men. Each has received coins of varying value with the charge that he invest this money. The notion of investment by itself contradicts the putative teachings against wealth. By its nature, investment seeks to increase wealth, and this is the action of the first two men. They received the most money, invested it, and could show a profit on the king's return. The third man, the one who received the least money, did not know what to do and so he buried the coins to make sure he didn't lose the money. Upon the king's return the man could show no profits on the money over which he had charge. The king grows furious at this news.[2]

---

[1] Luke 16: 19-31.
[2] Luke 19: 11-27.

If we are to interpret this parable in a meaningful way we must concede the supremacy of the profit motive, the engine that drives capitalism. Was Jesus a proto capitalist about 1700 years ahead of Scottish economist Adam Smith? If Jesus advocated the profit motive, by default he advocated an unequal distribution of wealth, exactly what occurred in the parable of the coins. In other words, Jesus was advocating the concentration of immense wealth in few hands and the impoverishment of the masses. Jesus was advocating a world of Lazaruses and poor, homeless men. In other words we have arrived at a contradiction. It seems that Jesus could not have preached both parables. At least one must be fiction. Perhaps both are untrue. We learned in the first chapter that we cannot be confident that we know anything about what Jesus said. Long after his death, the gospel writers added legendary material and did not attempt to be historically accurate. The result is not comforting. Through the gospels a number of Jesuses emerge with a number of different beliefs. We have seen that some are contradictory. Two options exist: Jesus contradicted himself or Jesus never contradicted himself. A god cannot contradict itself, so that if Jesus were god one must cling to the notion that he never uttered a contradiction. Accordingly some of the parables must be false. Alternatively Jesus was merely human. Humans contradict themselves all the time so that these contradictory parables may stand scrutiny. What is the person who claims the accuracy of the canonical gospels to do? He or she cannot maintain the inerrancy of the gospels and at the same time the divinity of Jesus. The simplest solution is to claim that Jesus was fully human and so subject to all kinds of errors. One obvious error, which will receive more treatment, is Jesus' prediction of the world's end in the very near future. About 2000 years after his death, the world still has not ended. There is no sign of an end times and the intervention of god in human affairs to right all wrongs.

Consider again the comparison with Plato. Remember that Plato depicted his mentor Socrates in a number of ways. The Socrates of the early dialogues is an intense questioner, a man who is wise because he knows the full extent of his ignorance. By the middle dialogues, the *Meno*, *Phaedo* and *Republic* for example, Socrates is no longer ignorant. He answers his own questions in remarkable detail and power. How can Socrates be the same two people? This is possible only because Plato made Socrates a largely fictional character who is the mouthpiece for Plato's ideas. The same must be true of the gospels, whose writers used Jesus to express their own ideas. In this sense Jesus was a literary construct rather than a historical figure.

The parables are only part of the story of Jesus' ministry. By the time one gets to the gospel of John the parables have shrunk in number, having been replaced by long speeches that are often called discourses. These discourses, in the sharpest terms, seek to define Jesus as god. If the synoptics imply divinity, John makes this idea explicit and at length. Many of these speeches remain memorable, but it is a single phrase that seems to have galvanized evangelical Christians. The author of John puts into Jesus' mouth the enigmatic claim that one must be "born again."[1] I confess that the phrase appears virtually meaningless, but evangelicals would disagree. For them Jesus instructed listeners of the need for a new birth. The first birth was purely biological, the coupling of the sperm and egg. The second or new birth must be spiritual rather than biological. It must include a transcendent moment when one realizes that Jesus has saved him or her from damnation. The person is now on a trajectory to enter heaven. Without this new birth and acceptance of Jesus as the savior, one cannot hope to enter heaven. The theology is simple but distressingly popular. This interpretation seems wildly inaccurate. Remember that the author of John did not write the gospel until 60 years after Jesus' death, and perhaps even later. Such an elapse of time must make the retrieval of Jesus' words virtually impossible. By John there is no hope of knowing what Jesus said or did. He has by now become pure legend. To the specific point of a spiritual birth, it is pure conjecture. All the evidence from modern science and medicine points to the fact that humans are purely physical and biological beings. To be blunt there is no spiritual component to us. We do not have immaterial souls. Such views are very ancient and primitive and have no place in modernity. They are the vestigial organs of spirituality and do not deserve serious consideration in a world that after many millennia cannot find a shred of evidence for the existence of the soul. There is nothing, in other words, that can be reborn spiritually. In fact we cannot be reborn in any sense because the trajectory of life takes us inexorably from birth to death. There are no detours along the way, at least none of enduring importance.

Consider the skeptics' position. Doubt has been a feature of religious thought at least since the Middle Ages. During the late twelfth and early thirteenth centuries, Holy Roman Emperor Frederick II was an infamous skeptic. He decided to test the notion of a soul in a cruel way, having a man weighed and then sealed in a coffin, where he suffocated. Upon death, Frederick supposed that the man, if he had a soul, yielded it to the afterlife. The weight of the corpse should thus be less than the weight of the live man. The implication was that the soul had a material component that, when removed from the body, caused a loss in mass reflected in lost weight. But this materialistic notion does not square with the Platonic and Christian idea that the soul was immaterial. Accordingly its loss would not

---

[1] John 3: 3-5.

register any loss in weight, exactly what Frederick discovered. If Frederick's experiment was not satisfactory, a more modern thought experiment should help. Let us ground this experiment in the rise of evolutionary biology in the nineteenth and twentieth centuries. One of the important insights, anticipated by French naturalist Comte de Buffon, is that all life must have a single origin. This origin must have been very simple. That is, the earliest life can have been nothing more complicated than a single molecule about to replicate itself. All the diversity of life issued from this simple beginning. One must ask whether this molecule had a soul. The idea seems peculiar and it is difficult to imagine that a group of carbon molecules had an immaterial soul. If it did not, where in the long trek from molecule to humanity did we acquire a soul and how did this happen? This question is insoluble. The principle of parsimony mandates that we shave off unnecessary entities, in this case unnecessary ideas. The soul is such an idea. In short, the idea of being born again is nonsense and the idea that Jesus said so has not the slightest evidence of support.

Other discourses in John point to Jesus as the "way" to the father. Presumably Jesus is the intermediary between humans and Yahweh. But in fact John wishes us to believe that Jesus is equal to Yahweh. That is, Jesus is every bit as much god as Yahweh is. Again we face the tiresome problem of Jesus being human and somehow divine too. In fact the emphasis in John is on Jesus as god. There is comparatively little effort to humanize him. The problem that this line of thought cannot surmount is that even in John, Jesus dies. Chapter 5 will examine this problem in more detail. Here it is enough to ask whether it is possible to kill a god. We know that it is possible to kill a human.

An Odd Ministry

The canonical gospels fail to resolve a central tension in Jesus' ministry. Page after page describes Jesus in astonishing terms. He wins disciples simply by calling them. There is no need to convince. These men, and surely women, follow Jesus without question. We have seen that Jesus performed miracle after dazzling miracle. He spoke of the present and immediate future in riveting terms. John the Baptist felt entirely inferior to him. These actions should have won Jesus' great renown. If people today say that he was god, why were his contemporaries, who must have known him firsthand, less sure? It is perverse to realize that Jesus appears to have been more influential centuries after his death than he was during his life. Why did not contemporaries recognize his astonishing qualities? The gospels suggest that Jesus made enemies during his life. This is surprising news. Mother Theresa was beloved worldwide, and Jesus must have been so much more spectacular, if we can trust the gospels. We have seen that Jesus' parables are thought to have confused people, and his miracles alarmed authorities. These surmises seem to be weak attempts to explain why the Romans executed such a great man. In other words, the ministry is crafted in such a way to propel Jesus toward his Passion. If this were the intent of the ministry narrative, then the information serves a pedagogical purpose whether true or not. One may reduce the ministry to its essence: Jesus began a ministry about age 30, incurred the animus of the Romans and died on the cross. This death, of course, is part of the Passion and not ministry, but we see in this summation what must have happened during the ministry. Note that we do not surmise much because we cannot know what Jesus said or did during his ministry. The elapsed time and the contradictions mar our ability to know anything about Jesus during this time. Whereas the absence of information about the birth narrative and childhood meant that we can know nothing about Jesus during these times, the apparent abundance of information about Jesus' ministry is illusory. We simply do not know anything more about Jesus during his ministry than during his birth and childhood.

Ministry and Anti Semitism

In large measure, the Christians' centuries-long dislike of the Jews stems from the belief that the Jews were responsible for killing Jesus. This is a serious crime if one considers that Jesus was god, making the Jews god killers. Because of this circumstance, chapter 5 will link these ideas with the crucifixion of Jesus. But because one may find this sentiment in the accounts of Jesus' ministry, one must begin the investigation into anti Semitism here. There are several references to anti Semitism in the canonical gospels. We need not reiterate every instance but instead examine a parable. According to the gospel writers Jesus told his followers of a king who wished to celebrate a wedding by inviting many eminent guests, but they did not come. Instead the king ordered his servants to recruit anyone they could find in the countryside to attend the wedding and reception.[1] In this way he filled the hall and presumably had a fine time. This parable is interpreted in a standard formula. The eminent guests, the people the king most wanted to invite were the Jews, but they did not come. That is, the Jews rejected Jesus' message, leading him to recruit newcomers among the non-Jewish population. The Jews had turned their back on Jesus and so were unworthy of the kingdom of god. The non-Jews, however, responding to Jesus' vision, proved themselves capable followers and worthy of the kingdom of god.

But could Jesus actually have said as much? Remember that Jesus was a devout Jew. The same appears true of John the Baptist, of Mary Magdalene,

---

[1] Luke 14: 15-24.

and the twelve apostles. In short, everyone Jesus favored was a Jew. Why then would Jesus have gone out of his way to criticize his people? The question is particularly pertinent because it is difficult to believe that Jesus intended to found a new religion. He seems instead to have wanted to purify Judaism. Another episode will hammer home this point. One might try to argue that Jesus recruited non-Jews, but this is not true. Even Paul of Tarsus was a Jew. Of course Jesus never tried to recruit Paul. Paul chose this sect of Judaism even though he never knew Jesus.

It seems then, as in so many other cases, that the gospel writers put anti Semitism within Jesus' mouth even though he never said such words. Why would such distortions be necessary? The answer lies partly in the religious lives of the Romans. It is a truism to say that the Romans were polytheistic. They had their own gods and as they spread throughout the Mediterranean Basin they absorbed other gods. By way of the Greeks the Romans absorbed many of the Egyptian gods. The example is apt. Both the Greeks and Romans esteemed Egypt as an old, wise, successful civilization. Whatever could be learned from Egypt was thought to benefit Greece and Rome. That is, the Romans esteemed old, revered gods. A long established religion was necessarily a good religion. This formula applied to Judaism precisely because it was an old, venerated religion. Yahweh was thus part of the Roman pantheon of gods, though his worship was probably confined to the Jews. In the first century CE, however, the emergence of a sect of Judaism began to cause problems. When it became clear to the Romans that Jews no longer considered these people part of their religion, Rome became suspicious. Being a novelty, this newcomer could not claim the protection of an ancient god. Instead these new people claimed to worship a god guilty of treason against Rome. They ate his flesh and drank his blood. It might go too far to claim that Rome feared change, but like most ancient peoples, the Romans were not fond of innovations. The new religion of Christianity counted as such an innovation. The manner of worship, as outlined above, offended the Roman sense of what constituted proper religious behavior. In short now that Christianity was exposed it was vulnerable.

Who deserved blame for this state of affairs? Christians answered that the Jews were responsible because they rejected Christianity as a viable form of Judaism. The writers of the gospels were part of this new Christian movement, and so it is no surprise that they tried to shift blame to the Jews for the difficulties Christians now suffered. It became necessary even to interpret Jesus as critical of the Jews. These words issued from religious and political realities that had nothing to do with Jesus the man. Therefore such parables tell us nothing about Jesus. Again we are at a loss to understand the real Jesus.

Perhaps the most significant action that led to Jesus' arrest, the occurrence that sparked the events of the passion, was Jesus' aggressive actions at the temple in Jerusalem. The act was probably not an instance of anti Semitism but of condemnation of Jewish authorities. It was an event when Jesus challenged Jewish leaders, to his detriment. The gospels claim that during Passover Jesus entered the temple, the holiest site in Judaism, and attacked the salesmen in it. The gospel writers tell us that this event sealed Jesus' fate.

Did it happen? This question is not easy to answer. The actions suit a vision of Jesus as a righteous man filled with reverence for the proper worship of Yahweh and protection for the poor. His affinity to the poor probably caused him to be suspicious of the wealthy. His charisma and his sense of propriety may have pushed him to this action. It is hard to say, therefore, that the gospel writers exaggerated Jesus' behavior. There must have been reason to execute Jesus, and this event might have provoked such a reaction against him. It is possible then that here is an important clue to Jesus the historical figure. If so, we might conclude that Jesus may have been an apocalyptic prophet who created a disturbance at the temple in Jerusalem. This is scant information, but it is better than nothing.

Chapter 5. Death and Resurrection

The focal points of the canonical gospels are Jesus' death and resurrection. In fact these events, more than any others, define what a Christian believes. The events leading to Jesus' death are known as the Passion and are among the most hallowed in Christianity. In 1724, German composer Johann Sebastian Bach, under tremendous deadline pressure to produce a passion, chose the gospel of John because its passion was the shortest. The result is the tumultuous St. John Passion. In it Bach conveys the savagery of crucifixion in a way that no other art has. Three years later came the St. Matthew Passion, regarded by many musicologists as the finest passion every conceived. The music alternates between the sublime and the tempestuous. It encompasses all human emotions. Perhaps no other music has equaled this outpouring by Bach. It seems clear that Bach must have taken these events at face value as though they all happened. It is fair today to ask whether Bach's faith suffices any longer even if his music remains supreme.

The Last Supper

The Last Supper ushers in the Passion and deserves immediate attention.[1] The Last Supper provides the context for one of Italian polymath Leonardo da Vinci's masterpieces. Unfortunately the paint has not preserved well, but even now it remains one of the world's great art treasures and one of the archetypal works of the Italian Renaissance. Leonardo rendered the scene imaginatively, as imagination is all that is left to us. He focuses on a Passover meal that Jesus is to have celebrated with his disciples. The meal has a long tradition in Jewish lore. It

---

[1] See for example, Mark 14: 22-31.

is to commemorate the Jews' freedom from Egypt. It marked the moment when the Jews set out in earnest for their own homeland. No longer were they to suffer the caprices of the pharaohs.

Passover was thus one of the critical events in the lives of Jews, including those of Jesus and his disciples. Notice that the Last Supper, then, is a purely Jewish event, affirming the identity of Jesus and the men around him. It was an event that must have built solidarity for a Jewish minority in a Roman world. The canonical gospels tell us that Jesus and his men had a simple meal of bread and wine. The bread must have been unleavened, as this was the Jewish tradition. It was likely made of wheat, which has sufficient gluten to make it stick together. Wheat was one of the earliest edible plants to have been cultivated in that region of the world so that a meal of bread was a metaphor for a food that played a role in creating the first civilizations. Wine was also an important food (beverage). Almost since the beginning of wine making, grapes were the essential fermented fruit. For many reasons that need not detain us now, wine was the principal beverage in the Roman world. If one wished to drink water, it was almost always consumed in wine so that the water diluted the alcohol to prevent severe drunkenness. The alcohol in turn killed the microbes in the water, making it safe to drink.

The components of the Passover meal were thus dietary staples in the Roman Mediterranean world. There is no surprise, then, that Jesus and his disciples would have consumed bread and wine, assuming the event occurred. Otherwise it is not surprising that the gospel writers conceived a meal with bread and wine. Were the event retold today, perhaps Jesus and his disciples would eat a Big Mac and drink a vanilla milkshake. My point is that context is everything. If we cannot know with certainty whether Jesus and his disciples shared this meal close to his death, we can at least feel comfortable that the food and beverage must have been proper in that time and place. The surprise comes in Jesus' treatment of these foods. The canonical gospels say that Jesus claimed that the bread was his body so that the disciples, in eating it, were consuming Jesus. Similarly, the wine was Jesus' blood. This reading suggests a stylization of cannibalism. Yet the act of eating the bread and drinking the wine could not have been a mechanism for consuming Jesus because he remained in their midst during the Last Supper. What may be at issue are the mystery cults, which as we have seen shaped religious practices in the Mediterranean Basin. Several of these cults, notably the one devoted to Mithras, celebrated ritual meals of bread and wine. In fact Mithras is to have created a large receptacle of wine that never diminished despite numerous attempts to drink it all.

Mithras' wine miracle has an obvious parallel in John's gospel. A brief detour is necessary. According to John, Jesus' first miracle occurred at the behest of his mother. Attending a wedding, Jesus, Mary and the other guests must have enjoyed themselves to the point that they drank all the wine. At Mary's intercession, Jesus turned large containers of water into wine. This was wine of exceptional quality and there is no record that the guests exhausted this new source, a strong hint of Mithras' influence. The suggestion that it is possible to convert water into wine defies basic biology. Water alone will not suffice. One must have a source of sugar—grapes satisfy this criterion—and microbes to convert this sugar into alcohol. That is the microbes eat the sugar and excrete alcohol much as humans drink water and excrete urine. Because these elements were not present to Jesus, he cannot have created wine out of essentially nothing. The story is merely a twist on the legends about Mithras.

The Last Supper is thus one part Jewish lore and a second part mystery cult. Jesus and his disciples may have gathered for a meal, but the body and blood imagery is a legendary addition to this meal. Yet Christians have had difficulty pursuing a path away from a literal interpretation of the canonical texts. In the thirteenth century Italian Dominican friar Thomas Aquinas, a saint in the Catholic Church, attempted to marry Last Supper lore to philosophy. The key to this blend was an understanding of Greek philosopher Aristotle, the most accomplished student of Greek philosopher Plato. We need not consider his ideas in detail, but we must define "substance" and "appearance." The substance of an object was the definition of what it was. Bread, for example, was the ground seeds of wheat plants, usually combined with yeast to cause the bread to rise. Technically rye seeds are just as good in making bread, but humans seem to have preferred wheat for millennia. The appearance of bread is all the external qualities: taste, texture, and other elements apparent to the senses. In the case of the Last Supper, however, Jesus miraculously kept the appearance of wheat unaltered while changing its substance to his body. This is a shocking claim that inverts Aristotle's logic that made the disciples Jesus' eaters. Of course this explanation is difficult to grasp in literal terms. How is it possible to eat a person's body apart from an act of cannibalism? Perhaps the solution is to claim a symbolic consumption of Jesus' body and blood. Some Protestant denominations hold to this symbolism in the certainty that Jesus did not intend to promote cannibalism. Perhaps a better solution is to discard all talk of consumption of a body and blood. Yet the Catholic Church is unable to make this concession. Even today, there is a point in the Mass when someone rings a bell to alert worshippers that Jesus, still alive in heaven, has changed the communion wafer into Jesus' body and the wine into Jesus' blood, exactly as Aquinas proposed.

In contrast to church dogmas, I favor a conservative approach, one that employs Ockham's razor. English philosopher William Ockham claimed that the simplest explanation that covered all the facts should be preferred as the most likely explanation.[1] Cumbersome explanations that trotted out all the bells and whistles were just rhetoric and unlike to depict events as they really occurred. One must take a razor, then, to shave off all unnecessary elements in an explanation. In the case of the Last Supper, the razor is easy to employ to shave off what does not make sense. The simplest explanation is that Jesus and his disciples ate bread and drank wine. The idea of transformation of these foods is unnecessary and surely hyperbole. The responsible reader will shave off these elements as fanciful. All along we have attempted to employ Ockham's razor to the stories about Jesus.

Another element of the Last Supper deserves attention. The canonical gospels claim that Jesus used this gathering to predict his betrayal and death. He seems to have known that his disciple Judas would betray him. Consequently over the millennia Christians have hated Judas, but this is not the claim in the non-canonical gospel of Judas.[2] In this gospel Judas is Jesus' closest confidant. Jesus teaches him elements of the secret wisdom that other disciples do not hear. Jesus convinces Judas to surrender him to Jewish and Roman authorities. Judas, then, is no betrayer, but a loyal follower of Jesus. Judas in this case possessed the secret knowledge that is at the heart of Gnosticism.

Obviously this tradition deviates from the canonical gospels, which heap blame on Judas, who in distress is said to commit suicide. Leonardo's Last Supper fulfills this belief. He partitioned the disciples in four groups of three. Leonardo captures the moment when Jesus announces that someone will betray him. At this moment Leonardo isolates Judas to emphasize his guilt. The Last Supper, perhaps most significantly propels Jesus toward death. That is its significance and all other details are scarcely relevant. Whether Jesus made such statements is unclear. As a literary device the Last Supper must lay the foundation for death, but in literal terms the meal, using Ockham's razor, may have been nothing more than a meal of bread and wine devoid of larger theological issues. The gospel writers added these issues decades after Jesus' death when a theology of Jesus began to form in the fledgling Christian communities in the Mediterranean Basin.

---

[1] William C. Placher. *A History of Christian Theology: An Introduction* (Philadelphia: Westminster Press, 1983) 165-168.

[2] Bart D. Ehrman, *The New Testament: A Historical Introduction to the Early Christian Writings* (New York and Oxford: Oxford University Press, 2012) 232-234.

Arrest and Trial

After the Last Supper, the scene shifts to a garden known as Gethsemane, where Jesus retired with his disciples to pray.[1] The atmosphere is tense and fear seems to be the dominant emotion. My initial focus will be on Jesus. The most curious claim about him occurs in Luke, where Jesus is in such distress that he sweats blood. Is such an action possible? Ordinarily sweating is a physiological attempt to dissipate heat. Having evolved as a relatively hairless type of ape in the tropics of Africa, humans evolved a dense network of sweat glands to secrete water. This water contains the heat in the body and upon evaporation the heat leaves the surface of the skin, providing modest cooling. Note from this description that the sweat glands release water and not blood. That is the evolutionary function of sweat glands is to release water not blood. There is good reason for this distinction. The blood vessels, whether arteries, veins or capillaries, carry blood, which is not available to the sweat glands. For the body to sweat blood would require a violation of the normal state of affairs. The blood vessels would need to rupture to disperse blood and that blood would need to invade the sweat glands, which would then secrete blood and not water or perhaps a mixture of blood and water. One may not be able to say that such an improbable event is impossible, but it is so implausible that a responsible account of Jesus in the garden should defend basic physiology by stating that Jesus sweated water and not blood. The claim that one may subvert basic biology is not credible, given that Jesus, like the rest of us, was human.

Tensions rise in Gethsemane. Peter is eager to demonstrate his loyalty to Jesus, but Jesus tells him that he will deny him thrice. Other disciples fall asleep repeatedly, exasperating Jesus. Jesus seems to have nowhere to turn for solace. In this isolated state, Jesus, at the instigation of Judas, faces arrest. A disciple intervenes at the last minute to slice off the ear of a servant of an arresting official. Jesus responds by restoring the ear in form and function.[2] This rapid sequence of events breaks down upon analysis. Where had the disciple gotten a sword? Being a disciple, he was surely poor and probably could not have afforded to arm himself in any way. Even if he had a sword, why would he have struck the servant? Should not the arresting official have received the blow, and not merely to an ear but to the neck or head to ensure death? After all this, even if we assume that a servant lost his ear, how could Jesus have reaffixed it? He would have needed to realign all blood vessels in the ear to those in the head. Otherwise the ear would become gangrene for lack of blood. Not only would it be a miracle to put the ear back on; there is

---

[1] See for example, Luke 22: 39-46.
[2] Luke 22: 50-51.

no logic in the story as it stands. It is more of the same rubbish that we have encountered throughout the gospels.

From Jesus' arrest to his execution, the gospel writers insert material that is not easy to interpret. From the outset there appear to be two authorities claiming control of Jesus' fate. Jewish and Roman authorities may have participated in his arrest, but why would Jewish participation have been necessary? The Romans, under the governorship of Pontius Pilate, controlled the region and Jesus' fate. The presence of Jewish authorities, if they were there, appears to be another case of an unnecessary entity that Ockham's razor would do well to excise. Nonetheless, the canonical gospels insist that Jesus went from his arrest to trial by the Sanhedrin, a group of Jewish authorities.[1] Again, such information is surprising given that the Romans held unfettered access to the force of law. Members of the Sanhedrin might have had close ties to Roman authorities and perhaps the two groups shared information and formed judgments, but the Sanhedrin could not have told the Romans what to do. Pontius Pilate was in control of Jesus' fate from the outset.

No less important were the Roman attitudes to the Jews. It is clear that Pontius Pilate disliked Jews. When he came to take control of Judea, Pilate set up standards with the image of Emperor Tiberius. The Jews regarded this display, in Jerusalem no less, as pagan idolatry. Conflict embroiled the Jews and Romans with many Jews dead from Roman attack. At other times Pilate killed Jews simply for worshipping Yahweh. This contempt of the Jews must have led the Romans to disregard Jewish sentiments. Whatever the Sanhedrin felt about Jesus, the Romans surely would not have cared. On the other hand if the Sanhedrin had the power of life and death over Jesus, there never would have been the need for Pilate to judge Jesus guilty of treason. Two verdicts make no sense, and because we know that Pilate was in charge, Ockham's razor must shave off the Sanhedrin conviction of Jesus. That is, it never happened.

If fact, the canonical gospels focus on Pontius Pilate in a curious way. Time and time again, Pilate appears to be the man of reason.[2] He is reluctant to condemn Jesus as he tries to free him in place of a notorious criminal. Pilate claims that he will torture Jesus to appease Jewish authorities and then release him. Pilate claims in Luke that Jesus is innocent. In a dramatic flourish, Pilate washes his hand in water, saying that he will not be guilty of Jesus' death. How has the man who disliked Jews come to the defense of one of its apocalyptic preachers? Skepticism is warranted. Elsewhere Pilate is described as a cruel man. Remember that the governors of provinces,

---

[1] Luke 22: 66-71.
[2] Luke 23: 1-5.

including Judea, were successful military officers. They were used to command. They did not cater to the will of subordinates. Pilate was a dictator within Judea and would never have had the temperament, training and aptitude to listen to his underlings. His way of solving problems was to kill people. Pontius Pilate and no one else condemned Jesus to death. It is hard to imagine that the Sanhedrin had even the slightest influence on Pilate.

Bereft of the Sanhedrin, Pontius Pilate acted quickly in condemning Jesus to death. There is no certainty even that Pilate and Jesus met. A report from an accuser might have sufficed for Pilate to execute Jesus, sight unseen. The canonical gospels, however, insist that the two met. I have noted the reasons for skepticism about how Pilate behaved toward Jesus given his animus toward the Jews. If they met, Pilate likely had needed but a moment to condemn the powerless king of the Jews to death. There is no reason to suppose an elaborate scene. From Pilate's condemnation, events moved swiftly as Jesus suffered among the cruelest forms of execution. The canonical gospels note that Jesus was exposed, likely in the sun, with few clothes. Because the Romans practiced crucifixion, it is necessary to seek their records of it. Remember here the importance of eyewitness accounts in our attempt to learn about Jesus. There are no historical records of Jesus' death, so we must find knowledgeable Romans who wrote about crucifixion. These records are scattered and one might think surprisingly minimal in their details. The surprise may be unwarranted. Consider a modern example. How many Americans know which states favor a particular method of execution? What are the details of killing someone by lethal injection? Do any American death row inmates still suffer hanging as the means of execution? How many people did the United States execute in 2015? The fact is that we are all busy with our own lives and pay scant if any attention to the unfortunates who fall victim to a capital sentence.

In this respect it is not surprising that the Romans wrote so little about crucifixion.[1] To begin with, crucifixion applied to the undesirables, poor people who had no alternative but to suffer the ultimate penalty. For the elites, about whom we have information, the expectation was that they would save face and demonstrate courage by killing themselves before the state took their lives. For the elites, the favored method was to cause oneself to bleed to death. Thus Emperor Nero, with the help of a slave, stabbed himself to death. Elites who could not muster sufficient courage disgraced themselves. Emperor Claudius' third wife, Messalina, was by all accounts a gorgeous woman of unbridled sexuality. An affair with a powerful Senator led her to plot Claudius' murder. The plan discovered, Messalina faced

---

[1] Bart D. Ehrman, *How Jesus Became God: The Exultation of a Jewish Preacher from Galilee* (New York: Harper One, 2014) 156-160.

death. When she could not bring herself to slash herself, soldiers executed her. When Claudius learned of her end, he apparently said nothing about her, ordering more wine instead.

With crucifixion for the masses, then, the Romans paid little attention to its details. The Romans seemed to have used it as a means of terrorizing the poor as if to say: do not behave in such a way or you will suffer the greatest torture and death. This rationale must have guided the Romans in crushing the slave rebellion led by slave and gladiator Spartacus. The Romans crucified participants all along the Appian Way, for miles. Jesus must have suffered the same fate because he was poor and probably also because he was Jewish, a member of a religion that Pilate despised. It appears that Jesus never had the option of taking his own life — the poor were offered no such luxury, if one may use that term.

The death of Jesus as a criminal by a brutal means of torture must have shocked those who knew him. Such an event could not be the random outcome of bloody Roman policies but rather had to have some transcendent meaning. This meaning was not apparent to Jesus' followers but was only constructed by people who had never known Jesus. The principal architects of this meaning were Paul of Tarsus and Augustine of Hippo. Under their guidance, Jesus' death gained meaning as an act to expiate our sins. This theology — and not history or reality of any kind — began at the beginning the Old Testament with the Garden of Eden in the opening chapters of Genesis. To bible literalists, the first two humans were a man and woman named Adam and Eve respectively. They communed with god in the garden in a state of innocence, so the theology goes. Regrettably they chose to disobey god by eating the fruit from the tree of knowledge of good and evil. This act was the first sin and so was named original sin. Augustine insisted that sex passed this sin from parent to offspring generation after generation. How could one get rid of the sin of disobedience? The answer was that humans could not eradicate this sin on their own. They needed divine intervention. This intervention came in the form of Jesus' willingness to die for our sins and so to rid humanity of the evils of original sin.

This rationale might seem persuasive to some but it crumbles under scrutiny. Many problems arise almost immediately. For example, is it possible to speak of a first pair of humans? Evolutionary biology suggests that we, like all organisms, have evolved from simple self-replicating molecules over billions of years. Where in this long trek from molecules to modern humans did the first humans appear? Could the early members of our genus somehow qualify? How about *Homo erectus* or Neanderthals? Neanderthals appear to have been the first people to express religious beliefs. Did they not merit consideration? Were not Neanderthals Adam and Eve? Bible literalists would reject this claim because the authors of the creation story must have had in mind modern humans. Then we must locate the first anatomically modern humans about 200,000 years ago. But scientists have been unable to accomplish this feat. Exactly where does one draw the line between anatomically modern humans and other archaic peoples? The truth is we have no idea and so must reject the claim of a first man and woman. If the creation story falls, then the claim of original sin is equally untrue, so why would Jesus need to die for a sin that did not exist?

Equally troubling is the notion of sacrifice. If Yahweh demanded that Jesus die by crucifixion, as the canonical gospels suggest, then he must have demanded this death as a form of human sacrifice. One ridicules the Maya and Aztecs of pre Columbian America for such practices, but somehow it is appropriate to have demanded the death of Jesus as a form of human sacrifice. Why was such behavior illegitimate for the peoples of Mesoamerica and Central America but perfectly rational from the perspective of Christians? The answer is that we cannot have a double standard. If human sacrifice was cruel in the Americas, then it was equally cruel to demand such a sacrifice from Jesus. With the notions of original sin and human sacrifice rebutted, one is left with a meaningless death. The Romans crucified him as a criminal, but we can never hope to understand the ultimate rationale of this decision. The mythmaking of the gospels, Paul and Augustine are no help. They merely perpetuate falsity.

Archaeologists have found few artifacts from a crucifixion. The find of a nail is important because it confirms that the Romans nailed their victims to the cross. These nails are uncommon. Apparently the Romans who observed a crucifixion took the nails back when nothing more than a skeleton was left on the cross. These nails were apparently tokens of good luck. The standard thought that two nails secured the arms of Jesus, one through each palm, is likely incorrect. Jesus' body would have pulled on the hands, tearing the flesh from them. It's more likely the arms were secured by piercing each wrist with a nail. This is exactly what the Shroud of Turin depicts, but we now know that to be a forgery. Nonetheless the perpetrator had solid knowledge of the anatomical requirements of crucifixion. A third nail would have secured the feet, one atop the other. The fact that none of us has endured such a fate makes it impossible to gauge the agony of such torture and death. One must conclude that Jesus suffered excruciating pain.

Undoubtedly the Romans devised crucifixion to prolong one's agony. Jesus would not have died immediately but must have been conscious for some time, hours perhaps. What did Jesus do during this time? One account holds that Jesus was crucified beside two other men.[1] One mocked him but

---

[1] Luke 23: 39-41.

the other defended Jesus, whereupon he told the criminal that upon death he too would enter heaven. The other synoptic gospels stick to this formula of two men crucified along with Jesus.[1] It is a contradiction, however, to imagine Jesus alone in the sense that no family or disciples were brave enough to witness his death. Strictly speaking, both scenarios cannot be true, and it seems impossible to judge between them. In still another account Jesus prayed for the Romans who crucified him, saying that they did not know what they were doing.

In another version, Jesus tells the apostle John to take his mother Mary home and to care for her after Jesus' death.[2] Of course there was no real evidence that John or Mary or both attended the crucifixion. For Mary to be present, she would have had to journey from Nazareth to Jerusalem. In an era before telecommunications, how would she have learned the fate of her son and made her way to Jerusalem? Could she have arrived in time, given the short interval between Pilate's condemnation and Jesus' execution? One also wonders whether she would have had to courage to witness the excruciating death of her son. She likely would have fainted on the spot. From these considerations one must conclude that although Jesus was crucified, the details we read surrounding his death are fictional.

The most spectacular claim comes from the Coptic apocalypse of Peter. The atmosphere is surreal in its attempt to make a theological point. One encounters the case of three Jesuses.[3] The scene is the crucifixion. The first Jesus is nailed to the cross. A second Jesus joins the apostle Peter in the crowd watching the execution, and a third Jesus floats above the cross and laughs at having tricked the Romans. The lesson, told by the Jesus in the crowd, is that the Romans had succeeded only in crucifying the body of Jesus. The soul, hovering above these events, was safe from all defilement. Because the physical world was the work of an evil god, all things physical must be evil. Accordingly it was proper to crucify a body. But the soul was part of the pure and perfect spiritual realm and was not subject to death by any means. Hence Jesus' soul, the real Jesus, never died.

This text is often pigeonholed in the category of Gnosticism, but a larger context is necessary. The idea of a pure and perfect immaterial realm and of the soul itself derives from Plato's idea. The dualism between an evil physical world and a good spiritual realm is at least as old as Zoroastrianism, an influential Persian (Iranian) religion. The mixing of these elements in the story of Jesus' torture and death suggests that the gospel authors added these ideas to what must originally have been a simple and stark narrative of Jesus' end. The story in the gospel of Peter is a fabrication based on a single

---

[1] See for example, Matt 27: 33-44.
[2] John 19: 25-27.
[3] Ehrman, *The New Testament*, 231.

piece of evidence. The canonical gospels agree that Peter denied Jesus three times and fled from his side. Fearing arrest, he did not witness Jesus' death as this gospel claims. The entire story has no merit beyond asserting a crude theology. It is not history and provides no insight into Jesus the historical figure.

It is not possible to know how long Jesus survived on the cross. One passage suggests that he might not have survived as long as the Romans expected.[1] After some hours, it was apparently a Roman practice (though Roman literary sources do not confirm it), for the executioner to break the legs of the survivors. The rationale is simple. The survivors had held onto life by pushing up with their legs to relieve the torso. If stretched too far the torso would inhibit a person's ability to breathe and so cause death through suffocation. Breaking the legs would thus hasten suffocation. Yet when the executioner came to break Jesus' legs, he found Jesus already dead. Perhaps this is an authentic rendering of Jesus' end. The depictions of him in art almost always suggest an emaciated man who probably could not have long survived the rigors of crucifixion. Yet one must be cautious. These artistic renderings are not grounded in eyewitness accounts but in the prevailing lore about Jesus. Whatever else one might think about art, it does an excellent job revealing prevailing attitudes and practices.

Yet nowhere in any of the accounts about Jesus is there a description of his appearance, making it very difficult to know what he looked like. Our best clue is geography. Jesus lived in the Mediterranean Basin. We have a good idea of what Mediterranean people looked like from the death masks found in the Fayyum Desert in Mediterranean Egypt. Judging from them, it seems probable that Jesus was dark haired with dark eyes. His skin was likely olive and he probably tanned easily. The traditional beard we know stems from the art of Byzantium. The earliest depictions of Jesus show a clean-shaven man. As a Mediterranean man, Jesus was likely slightly built. He was certainly no hyper-muscled bodybuilder. Being small and not rugged, Jesus might have died comparatively quickly, but so should every other crucified person in this region. The Romans were themselves Mediterranean people and should not have expressed surprise at the swiftness of Jesus' death, at least according to the canonical gospels.

Here controversy ensues about what happened to Jesus' body after his death. The canonical gospels relate that a member of the Sanhedrin, Joseph of Arimathea, requested to bury Jesus in the tomb that Joseph had reserved for himself.[2] We return to an earlier problem. The Sanhedrin had condemned Jesus to death by a unanimous vote. If this is true, and we have already stirred

[1] John 19: 31-34.
[2] Mark 15: 42-44.

up grounds for doubt, why would a man who voted to condemn Jesus now turn full circle and wish to honor him with burial in a fine stone tomb? The Joseph story is contradictory, highly implausible and was added to the Jesus' narrative to advance the claim that Jesus was buried.

This claim did not reflect a historical event. Why was this detail essential? The answer lies first in Mark. The author of this gospel had to have Jesus buried so that others could search for his tomb three days later. According to Mark, Mary Magdalene and another woman came to this tomb on Easter Sunday to anoint Jesus' body with oils and spices.[1] The language is correct because an anointing must by definition involve the use of oil, almost certainly olive oil, to rub upon some part of the body. This practice was widespread throughout the ancient Mediterranean world.

When they reached the tomb, Jesus was not present according to Mark. Instead Mary and her companion saw a man who told them that Jesus had risen from the dead. At this critical juncture, Mark ends. That is, no additional material appears in the earliest manuscripts of Mark. Mary and her companion do not actually see a resurrected Jesus. In fact no one does.

Later manuscripts, however, contain extra verses, written by someone else and much later, describing Jesus' appearance to others. Despite enormous grounds for doubting this late material, the Council of Trent in the sixteenth century affirmed that this text was also divinely inspired. This decision is not easy to understand. If the holy spirit inspired the gospel of Mark, as the Church held, why would not the holy spirit have hewn Mark from a single block of divinity? Why did the holy spirit come in two apparent flashes of insight separated by centuries? The only plausible answer is to shave off the extraneous entity of the holy spirit. There is no such instance of divine inspiration. No part of Mark, early or late was inspired. In fact no holy writings are inspired. Ordinary people struggling with large questions wrote the gospels and other theological writings. The information about Jesus' torture and death thus comes from people trying to understand Jesus in a religious context. They were not concerned with historical accuracy.

Do not forget that the story about Joseph of Arimathea and Jesus' tomb is necessary to persuade one that Jesus rose from the dead. What would happen if this entire story were shown to be implausible? What would happen if Jesus had no tomb and had never been buried? This possibility is not farfetched but rather is likely to be true. We must return to the practice of crucifixion. Here Roman sources make an important contribution to our knowledge. The Romans made the practice of crucifixion more terrible by denying burial to the victim.[2] Instead he was left to rot on the cross. Of

---

[1] Mark 16: 1-8.
[2] Ehrman, *How Jesus Became God*, 156-158.

course birds and predatory mammals, dogs for example, chewed the corpse to rob it of flesh, leaving only bones. Under these circumstances, why would Pontius Pilate have given Joseph of Arimathea Jesus' body? Both Joseph and Jesus were Jews, people Pilate hated. He would not have honored Joseph's request. Joseph and Jesus were not even kin. Even had Pilate been favorably disposed, why would he have released Jesus' body to a virtual stranger? In fact the canonical gospels make no attempt to link Joseph and Jesus by blood or even familiarity. For all we know Jesus never knew Joseph. Rather Joseph of Arimathea was a literary device that Mark employed to make it seem reasonable that Jesus would have been buried. Remember, burial was necessary for Mary Magdalene and her attendants to find Jesus missing from his tomb three days later.

The gospel of John, apparently to avert trouble, concocts another issue. Jesus body had to be removed from the cross because it would have been improper to leave it derelict on the Sabbath.[1] Here we see the same fiction that Pontius Pilate somehow would have been sympathetic to Jewish concerns. In fact in the canonical gospel Jews are in charge of the crucifixion and burial not any Roman authority. Such a claim cannot receive serious attention. If anything Pontius Pilate would have burned the memory of crucifixion into the Jews by letting the corpses rot on the Sabbath. Pilate would have made no concessions on this point. There is no plausible way to infer that Pontius Pilate would have acted with the slightest interest in preserving Jewish law or sentiments. Jesus rotted on the cross, Sabbath or no Sabbath.

For a moment let us try to take Mark's account seriously. Imagine that Jesus really was buried three days. During this time, as we saw with Lazarus, Jesus' corpse would have begun to decay so that resurrection would not have been possible, either for Lazarus or Jesus. Let us put aside these medical and scientific concerns for a brief interval. Let us suppose that Jesus was buried three days. What occurred to him during this time? The obvious answer is microbial decay, but we will suspend this thought to benefit the canonical gospels. The fourth century Nicene Creed, though it is not a canonical document, is nonetheless a terse statement about what many Christians believed. The creed states that Jesus was buried and then rose from the dead. But what happened between these two events? A variant of the Nicene Creed, still used in some Orthodox churches, states that between burial and resurrection, Jesus descended into hell. The popular story says that Jesus went to hell to rescue, Adam, Eve, and many other exemplary figures of the Old Testament. This line of thought is puzzling. If Jesus were really dead and nothing more than a corpse, how could he have gone anywhere? We can save face only by supposing Plato's dichotomy between body and soul.

---

[1] John 20: 38-40.

Under this line of thought Jesus' physical body had died, but the immortal soul (remember that in the *Phaedo* Plato sought to prove in four ways that the soul is immortal) can never be killed. This soul was the essence of Jesus and could have gone where it wished during this interval.

Note however that to maintain this fiction, one must subscribe to two types of death. As a rule, Christians assume that only humans have souls. Let us consider a mosquito then. Imagine that a female mosquito, the only kind that can bite, buzzes around your body, settling finally on your right arm. You act quickly to crush it with your left hand. In an instant she had gone from life to the totality of death. This is a death without mitigating circumstances. Nothing survives death in this case. One does not know whether mosquitoes have consciousness and memories. Likely they do not, but if such mental states are possible, then death has extirpated them. This issue is more acute when one considers the death of a human. If we put aside the notion of a soul, then the death of the body is the final end. Neither consciousness nor memories survive. The person, cremated or committed to the ground, is no more. This is certainly the lesson of atheism.

The second type of death is best understood as only partial death. True the body succumbs to whatever malady ails it, but this is not really the end. The soul persists as Plato and Christians claim. It has your consciousness and memories and is the real you, at least according to Christians. Plato denied these extra circumstances, but our focus will be on Christian beliefs. Death as Christians define it, is really liberation of the soul from the body, an idea in keeping with Plato's thought. For the righteous the soul, upon liberation, goes to heaven. Evil souls rot in hell. For the Nicene Creed to claim that Jesus descended into hell, it must invoke this second kind of death, which we define as partial. In the entire tenure of humans on earth, no one has amassed evidence for this type of death, which requires the presence of a soul. Because the soul has never been shown to exist, Ockham's razor must shave it off any description of reality. Humans therefore do not have souls. Thus Jesus, being human, never had a soul. When he died then he should have been dead in the first sense to which we have referred in this section.

How then could Jesus have risen from the dead? Perhaps our only alternative is to consider Jewish notions of death and resurrection in accordance with the fact that Jesus and his followers were Jewish. The writers of the canonical gospels must therefore have had a Jewish conception of death and resurrection. This is not to say that the writers saw themselves as a new type of religious advocate for a new type of religion. It is possible that at least some of them must have considered themselves more strenuous in their Jewish faith than were the Jews who denied Jesus divinity. At the outset let us consider Jewish notions of death. The important point is the lack of uniformity in beliefs. Not all Jews believed in an afterlife. Both Ecclesiastes and Job powerfully describe the fleeting nature of life. Ecclesiastes notes that a time comes for all of us to die. There is not much sense of an afterlife in either book. In fact, Job presents a belief in shoal, a bleak afterworld far inferior to what the dead had known in life.[1] If one wishes to consider this an afterlife, such a belief is fine so long as one stipulates the undesirability of it. Some of the prophets whose writings form parts of the Old Testament move beyond these considerations to write about the resurrection of the body.[2]

This was the specialty of New Testament enthusiast Paul of Tarsus, whose letters form part of the New Testament. Paul was a Jew who believed in the resurrection of the body. Although Paul was arguably the founder of Christianity, his notion of resurrection differs from what many Christians believe today. The reigning belief is a hybrid of early Christian and Platonic ideas. But the Jews who believed in resurrection broke from this formula. In fact Jewish thought likely predated Platonism by several centuries and so never would have considered the alternative of duality between body and soul. The doctrine of the resurrection of the body states the semi permanent nature of death. When one dies all mental and physical activity ceases. One no longer exists at the time of death. The flesh decays to leave only the bones. About a year after a Jew's death, the kin dug up the bones to place them in an ossuary for preservation. It is these bones that Yahweh will resurrect at the end of time, clothing them in flesh so that the newly restored people will be recognized. Note that Jesus lived in an era of apocalyptic thought and was likely an apocalyptic preacher. Such notions would have been important to him and his followers. Because Jesus seems to have believed that the end of the world was approaching, he must have believed that the final resurrection was at hand. This thinking permeated Paul's letters and the gospels of Mark, Luke and Matthew. For these reasons Jesus, if the canonical gospels are right, must have risen bodily from the dead. Luke emphasizes this point by having Jesus appear to his disciples. They fear him a ghost, but Jesus answers by eating a piece of fish. Can a ghost or spirit have a mouth with which to chew a piece of fish? Obviously not, proving that Jesus must have been resurrected as body and not merely as spirit.

But did Jesus rise from the dead? We have already come upon serious objections. Jesus was likely never buried but rather left on the cross to rot. If there was no burial there was no resurrection. Remember that the resurrection stories come from people who were not eyewitnesses to the event. Most of all in this context one would wish to have Mary Magdalene's account of the empty tomb, as Mark claims her to have been the first to hear

---

[1] Job 7: 1-21.
[2] Daniel 12: 1-13.

the news that Jesus rose from the dead. Yet Mary Magdalene left nothing. True, a gospel of Mary Magdalene exists, but Mary cannot have been alive at the time of composition. The absence of a document from Mary Magdalene must be odd. If the gospel of Philip is any guide, Mary Magdalene must have been Jesus' lover. The fact that Mark announces her as the discoverer of the empty tomb suggests that Mary had special status within the early Christian community. The possibility that Mary was Jesus' lover and confidant would have given her exulted status. It should have been imperative therefore that an early Christian would have interviewed Mary about what she saw and recorded this information for transmission down the generations. An authentic account from Mary or someone who knew her should have been prized. Christian communities should have lovingly copied it to ensure its survival. The fact that these obvious steps did not occur strongly indicates that Mary Magdalene saw nothing. In fact she never visited any tomb because Jesus was left to rot on the cross. Mark had fabricated the story from beginning to end.

The canonical gospels state further that Jesus appeared to his discipline, possibly for days after his resurrection. Yet these same gospels murmur about doubts. Apostle Thomas was a doubter according to John.[1] If Jesus had really appeared to the disciples, why would anyone have doubted the events? The example of Thomas hammers home this point. Jesus finally confronted him, inviting Thomas to probe the wounds of crucifixion. Confronted by Jesus, Thomas relinquished his doubts. The same should have been true of everyone else. Note however that this episode between Jesus and Thomas allows John to warn against unbelief. Why would unbelief have been a problem if Jesus really rose from the dead? The answer is that Jesus did not rise from the dead. Had he been resurrected, the gospel of Thomas surely would have mentioned it. What other evidence would have given Thomas a better opportunity to prove that Jesus was god? The resurrection was arguably the greatest miracle in humans' tenure on earth. Yet Thomas is silent. Thomas' silence makes no sense unless one concludes that Jesus never rose from the dead.

How then did people come to believe in Jesus' resurrection? They became believers because other people told them that Jesus had risen from the dead. The foundation of these stories may go back to a handful of Jesus' original followers. Remember our earlier discussion about hallucinations. Now couple this discussion with Mary Magdalene's mental state after Jesus' death. If she had been Jesus' lover and confidant, his death must have caused her inordinate grief. During such episodes the senses may not record events accurately. One of my aunts was a beautiful and vibrant woman. When her mother-in-law, my paternal grandmother, died, she told me that she felt

---

[1] John 20: 24-25.

the spirit of this woman pass her on its way out the window. I asked her repeatedly whether grief might have caused this sensation. All her life my aunt maintained the accuracy of her perceptions. If my aunt had a hallucination that day, as may be the sensible conclusion, could not Mary Magdalene have suffered a similar illusion at feeling similar grief? The apostle Peter and Paul of Tarsus seem to have preached the resurrection. Paul admitted that he had a vision. More likely, he had a hallucination. Peter likely did as well. All that is necessary is a bit of momentum to give life to an implausible story.

Remember that Mary, Paul and Peter did not live in an era of science and medicine. Mainstream medicine has shown us that a chasm exists between life and death. But in antiquity the boundary must have been more permeable. In fact the story of the death and resurrection of a god is part of the mythology of western Asia and the Mediterranean Basin. Consider Isis and Osiris. Isis the goddess and Osiris the god were more than Egyptian deities. They were siblings and husband and wife. Perhaps their analogues were Mary Magdalene and Jesus. Like Jesus, Osiris had enemies, the most powerful of whom killed Osiris, chopped him into minute pieces, and deposited these remains in the Nile River of Egypt. Here was a death and burial that is not far removed from the events claimed about Jesus. As Mary Magdalene came in search of Jesus, Isis came to find her brother and husband. She recovered all Osiris' parts and put him back together. Osiris was now the god of resurrection, exactly the status claimed for Jesus. And if Mary did not revive Jesus, she at least must have been the first person to attest to his resurrection, according to Christian lore. Note that Osiris was the god of the last judgment, exactly the position Jesus is to fill at the end of times. Note also that the story of Isis and Osiris was inordinately popular throughout the Mediterranean world. It was thus one of the cults of the Roman Empire. It must have been easy to co-opt parts of this story, claiming them true for Jesus. One may protest that the story of Osiris is superstition but the claims about Jesus are fact. But this is merely an assertion. What evidence proves that Jesus rose from the dead but Osiris did not? Why are outlandish beliefs about Jesus more acceptable than those about Osiris? Here we encounter a puzzlement of history. Osiris has died, only to remain in a distant, forlorn past. But Jesus survives as the god of Christians. In this context it is important to remember that the quest for the resurrected Jesus has always been a fact free enterprise.

Isis and Osiris are not the only models for Jesus the religious construct. Earlier we encountered Mithras, a Persian god that became important in the Mediterranean Basin before, during and after Jesus' life. Mithras celebrated a last supper, was executed, and rose from the dead. In this context Jesus was Mithras. The two underwent very similar Passions. Other examples may be given, but the point is that an attribute of a god was to die and then rise from the dead. This is the template that the canonical gospel writers used in constructing Jesus. This is the construction of Jesus the legend rather than Jesus the man. Important historical figures often come with baggage.

Consider George Washington. Victorious Revolutionary War general and first president of the United States, George Washington is at the top of the roster of America's great historical figure. Because of his status, writers have added legends to make him greater still. Consider the story of the cherry tree. According to legend, Washington chopped down the tree. When his father returned home he questioned George about this mishap. Rather than try to justify himself or blame others, the son admitted his culpability. Yet the story is almost certainly false. George Washington was the son of a Virginia slave owner, and Washington would own slaves in turn, facts that are often absent from our historical memory of the first president. The son of a well connected and prosperous slave owner would not have performed any labor but would have delegated these duties to a slave. In other words, George Washington would not have chopped down a cherry tree. He would have ordered a slave to do the work. Beyond this reasoning, it is hard to imagine that anyone in an agrarian setting would cut down any fruit tree that was still productive, and there is no indication that the tree was dead or dying. Why then do we tolerate such a falsehood? We tolerate this lie because it reinforces what we claim to know about George Washington and America at large. For example, by telling the truth Washington reminds us that we are a nation of laws and open and honest debate. One may doubt the truth of this statement, but it remains part of our collective consciousness.

The same is true of Jesus. The gospel writers constructed him to fit the Mediterranean model of gods that died and rose from the dead. Jesus was the answer to the cults of Isis and Osiris and Mithras. Like George Washington, Jesus told the truth about his status through the resurrection, which the gospel writers have him predict before his death. Such attempts at prediction were worthless because they were put in Jesus' mouth after and not before his death. In this sense the gospels are little more than a composite of fictional anecdotes about a man the Romans killed, as they had probably killed many other false prophets. I doubt that anyone would remember Jesus today but for the fact that a handful of people believed erroneously that he rose from the dead.

It remains to challenge a few odd ideas. The first is the claim that Mary Magdalene encountered an empty tomb because, unknown to her, some disciples stole the body from the grave. The idea that some disciples perpetrated a hoax to make it appear that Jesus rose from the dead makes little sense. First, we have seen that Jesus likely rotted on the cross rather than being buried. Second, this scenario seems to require a second burial. Where was this burial and why is it not a holy shrine? Had Jesus' disciples reburied him and then forgotten the location? Had they reburied Jesus and told no one of the location? This type of tortuous reasoning seems very implausible.

A second oddity cannot be ignored given the force of parapsychology in the modern world. The near death experience (NDE) is now a fixture of popular culture. The idea is that some trauma—a car accident, a great fall, or a bungled surgery—brings the body to the point of death. By all modern instruments, the physician cannot detect any sign of life in the person. He or she has no pulse, no brain activity, and none of the other indicators of life. Sometime later, usually after a few minutes have elapsed, the person revives, either through the assistance of a physician or through some unknown physical process. Afterwards the person may claim that between the moment of putative death and reanimation, he or she experienced a number of events that seem to have a religious motif. The person approaches a pure white light, encounters a being thought to be Jesus, and is told to return to life because death is not yet at hand. It is not my purpose to critique these stories but to show that Jesus did not have a NDE. The problem is the claim that Jesus was entombed for three days. We know that this claim is unlikely, but if we grant it for the moment, it seems clear that Jesus was not clinically dead for three days only to revive and leave the tomb before the approach of Mary Magdalene. Even if one grants this implausible scenario, would not the revived Jesus have lingered around the tomb in the hopes of seeing his confidante and lover? Instead we are to believe that Jesus left the scene so that Mary Magdalene would perceive an empty tomb, as Mark tells us. In that case where did Jesus go? If he simply revived after a NDE, how was it possible for him to have walked through locked doors after his putative resurrection, as the other canonicals claim?

It is much more likely that none of these events occurred. The Romans executed Jesus, leaving him on the cross, as was their practice. Jesus died and so could not have revived. He was not buried and did not rise on the third day as the Nicene Creed claims. Instead a few of his followers, grief stricken, imagined his appearance in what we now term a hallucination. These followers spread their message, keeping alive the memory of Jesus. Making converts, this movement grew until it was the dominant religion in the Late Roman Empire. All this activity drew sustenance from a series of fictions. These fictions grew over time. For example, Mark holds that Mary Magdalene encountered one man at the empty tomb. Matthew holds that one angel appeared. Luke puts the figure at two men whereas John avers that two angels appeared. Why can these accounts not agree? The answer is because everyone constructed his own fiction. These stories are a microcosm of the entire gospels, full of illusions as they are. The fascinating point is that Christians continue to believe this rubbish. Somehow the will to believe is stronger than the will to know.

Yet does another possibility exist for the life of Jesus, the resurrection and the prospect of eternal life for us all? Possibly, but the flurry of ideas in the 1980s strike me as speculative. Worse, an American scientist, Frank Tipler, abandoned the Scientific Method in proposing them in what amounts to a grand thought experiment. Tipler's interest lies in the power of computing. We know the computer to be a device for the storage and retrieval of information. This capacity is finite but is growing rapidly according to Moore's law, which states that memory and processing speed double every 18 months. This prediction has largely held true. It should be the case that computers will come to store exponentially huge amounts of information. Perhaps these supercomputers of the future will store the entire mental states of a person from birth to death.[1] Perhaps a computer can in a sense revivify a deceased person inside a computer. As long as the computer exists, so will the person. If one can posit, and this must be a difficult conjecture to uphold, that the computer is eternal, then so will be the person. Of course even more powerful and fast computers should store the mental states of not just one person but perhaps all 7 billion people who exist now, everyone who came before them, and everyone who will come afterwards. That is computers of sufficient power will revivify everyone who has ever lived. Even more powerful computers should be able to create the mental states of people who never lived so that the whole gamut possibilities should be realized on a computer.

Among all these people, the computer should resurrect the mental states of Jesus. One should be able to trace his development from egg and sperm to death by crucifixion. If the computer can perpetuate these mental states, Jesus is a sense will be raised from the dead. Such ideas sound like fantasy. How exactly will we know Jesus among the billions of people in the computer? Will he perform miracles to convince us? Will it be meaningful to say that Jesus is divine if he is just like the rest of us in occupying memory in a computer? If I find myself centuries from now in a computer I will have as much claim to resurrection as can Jesus, so that there is nothing special about him. Rather than god, Jesus becomes subservient to the computer that holds all his thoughts and memories.

Further, there has been no demonstration that such events are possible for a computer. This is wishful thinking in search of a death proof strategy, a desire to perpetuate ourselves in the implacable face of death. Culture after culture has attempted to brush aside death as some phantasm. This is the attempt of physics and computer science to do the same, dressing up modern terminology for an audience of science enthusiasts. This diversion is no proof

---

[1] Frank J. Tipler, *The Physics of Immortality: Modern Cosmology, God and the Resurrection of the Dead* (New York: Doubleday, 1994) 128.

that Jesus rose from the dead and that we will as well. It is fantasy attired in the language of science.

Jesus, Hell and Heaven

If one makes the safe assumption that someone named Jesus lived in first century CE Roman Palestine, then two events are certain: his birth and death. We have already demonstrated that the narrative surrounding his birth is false. We have worked to demonstrate the falsity of the events surrounding his death. Here I wish to focus on the three days that the canonical gospels say elapsed between his death and resurrection. We are familiar with those variants of the Nicene Creed that tell us that Jesus, while entombed, descended into hell. This claim demands that one believe in a literal place of great and perhaps unending torment. The gospels say that Jesus compared hell to a burning trash heap, so that one has the idea of hapless victims being eternally tortured by fire.

Yet having examined the gospels, we know that they tell us virtually nothing about Jesus. We cannot know that he said anything about hell, though the belief in hell would correspond to the world view of an apocalyptic preacher who wanted to usher in the end of time, the last judgment and the consignment of the evil to hell and the just to heaven. It may be, then, that Jesus believed in hell. If we are to take this belief seriously, we must be able to locate hell. In other words, if it exists, it must be possible to fix its geographical location. Imagine, for example, that I claim to be a lifelong resident of Ohio. In fact I am not, but let us suppose so nonetheless. You would be right to question my claim, were I unable to tell you anything about the state's geography. Worse, imagine that I told you that Tennessee is north of Ohio and North Dakota is east of Ohio. You would have the strongest possible grounds for suspecting that I know nothing about Ohio's geography and possibly nothing about U.S. geography. My failure to locate Ohio expresses the full extent of my ignorance.

In dealing with hell, a similar situation arises. If it really exists, I must be able to pinpoint its location. Is such a task achievable? Let us start with the gospels. Note that none locates hell as a geographical place. The Nicene Creed attempts partly to remedy this problem by mentioning that Jesus descended into hell. He must therefore have gone downward to find hell. Immediately we come upon uncertainty. We know that the gospels claim that Jesus rose bodily from the dead. Does this mean that he descended bodily into hell? Maybe not. Maybe the ghost or soul of Jesus descended into hell, not his body. The problem is that the gospels have no clear conception of the soul. It was Plato, not the gospel writers, who took pains to describe it. The gospel authors give us Jesus as an animated body, nothing less and nothing more. It seems that we must insist that Jesus descended bodily into hell. Does this mean that hell is somewhere beneath the surface of earth? Did Jesus' body somehow bore its way through the extensive rocks that must have separated earth's surface from hell? Was Jesus a human drill? Obviously not. Did Jesus find a series of subterranean passages to hell? We do not know. We do not even know where hell was to have been. Was it in earth's core, a naturally hot place? Was it somehow through earth and somewhere in space? Immediately we encounter problems. If Jesus were a body, he would have needed oxygen to survive. Would there have been oxygen in earth's core? We know there is no oxygen in space, so Jesus could not have visited a hell in space. The fact remains that we cannot pinpoint hell and have every reason accordingly to doubt its existence.

The same is true of Jesus' putative ascension into heaven. If Jesus really rose into heaven, it must be somewhere above us, but where? Again, Jesus could not have reached heaven in the sky unless he had some source of oxygen. Heaven cannot therefore have been located in space. Could heaven have been in the upper atmosphere? The oxygen there is minimal and Jesus did not have an oxygen tank such as the climbers of Mount Everest do to make up for the lack of oxygen. Oxygen tanks had not been invented in Jesus' day. For that matter, how was Jesus able to rise, no less than in a cloud, to heaven? A cloud cannot support any weight, so how could have supported Jesus? One might claim that Jesus was not heavy. After all, he was a Mediterranean man, and Mediterranean peoples tend to be small. Plus Jesus was likely poor and simply could not have afforded a robust diet. He may well have been emaciated, as some artwork depicts. In an environment where food is plentiful, as in the United States, the weight of men tends to approach 200 pounds. All these men of course were not diminutive Mediterranean peoples. Jesus was, so let's estimate his weight at about 120 pounds. What cloud could have lifted 120 pounds into heaven? The answer is that Jesus never ascended into heaven.

Mark, the earliest gospel, does not mention the ascension. The story was a later add-on with no basis in fact. Jesus did not ascend into heaven because heaven does not exist. It is part of the wishful thinking of people who understandably are afraid of death and need to comfort themselves with the thought of bliss in the afterworld. Speculation about death is natural for an event about which we know virtually nothing. It seems probable that life is finite and death the end, a portal to oblivion, to an eternal night from which no one is rescued. Jesus is as surely dead as I will be one day. We will both cease to exist in the most fundamental way possible, losing everything we hold dear. We may overcome many tragedies, but death is not one of them.

Chapter 6. Theologians and One Scientist Take the Offensive

Theology has long staked out a claim of superiority over other fields of knowledge. Here I wish to examine the claims of two theologians and one scientist acting as a theologian. I do not intend simply to present their views. Where necessary I challenge these views on the basis of what this book reveals about Jesus, and god for that matter. It is important to remember that all the world's basic religions are ancient, arising before there was knowledge about the sciences. In such a context fertile imaginations created gods of the most extraordinary abilities. Jesus was thought to be such a god. We have repeatedly rejected this characterization. Jesus was man alone.

Wolfhart Pannenberg and Richard Swinburne

Yet even today theologians have not bent to the reality of god's death or that Jesus was not god. German theologian Wolfhart Pannenberg will not compromise on these points but insists that one may know that god exists and the Jesus was god.[1] British theologian Richard Swinburne is less dogmatic, asserting that it is moderately probable that god exists and that Jesus was god.[2] Obviously these claims are not identical.

Let us entertain Swinburne's position first. One must note that Swinburne writes not of certainties but of probabilities. In this sense he is a theologian of the physicists because modern physics, especially quantum mechanics does not speak of certainties. For example one may propose the existence of an electron in a region of an atom without daring to guess exactly where it is. One must settle,

---

[1] Wolfhart Pannenberg, *Jesus—God and Man* (Philadelphia: Westminster Press, 1977) 19.
[2] Richard Swinburne, *Was Jesus God?* (Oxford: Oxford University Press, 2008) 5.

instead, for probabilities. One may point to the electron not in a precise location but in a cloud of probability. This is the best the physicist may hope to do. Swinburne applies this analogy to god, but is even less precise. What after all does he mean by "moderate probability?" I assume that a probable event has more than a 50 percent chance of occurring, but how much more? Is moderate probability 2/3, for example? It is difficult to believe that it could be any larger. The difficulty is the term "moderate" because I have no way of quantifying the word. Imagine for example that I have undertaken a 20 miles bicycle ride and at 10 miles claim moderate fatigue. Does this statement suppose that I will be too tired to finish the ride or that I will finish in a state of exhaustion? There is no way to know, so that it would never occur to me to speak of moderate fatigue while I'm cycling. The more one inspects Swinburne's language, the more empty it becomes. At its core, then, Swinburne's claim becomes meaningless. That is, this claim tells me nothing about god and Jesus.

There is no ambiguity in Pannenberg's claim that we can know that god exists and that Jesus was god. The claim of knowledge is a claim of certitude. No one quarrels over the definition of a triangle because this definition resides in the realm of certainty. Simply by appealing to the definition of a triangle I can be certain of my knowledge of it. This seems to be Pannenberg's objective: to remove all doubt about god and Jesus. But we have already dismissed the accounts about Jesus because of their implausibility. We have tested the sources, examined the virgin birth, other putative miracles, and Jesus' resurrection to conclude that none of these events occurred. Pannenberg is pursuing an illusion by claiming certitude for events that never happened. As a theologian, Pannenberg may have no training in the methods of history such that he erroneously purports that a theological statement is historical reality. This is a dangerous leap because history and theology are different disciplines. The claim for example that Jesus was god is a theological statement, not a statement about the reality of Jesus' humanity. If this book does nothing more, it should absolve one from the temptation to believe that theology attempts to describe reality. It does not.

Yet Pannenberg, once down the slippery slope, issues other untenable claims. He notes that god's most supreme revelation was Jesus and that to speak about Jesus is to speak about god because the two are coequal.[1] Let us begin with the first claim. We cannot prove god's existence so to speak about its revelation is an uncertain proposition and cannot be stated as a fact. I cannot speak for all 7 billion people on earth, but I know in my lifetime I have never experienced anything like god's intervention in my life or in the

---

[1] Pannenberg, *Jesus*, 19.

lives of the people I know. This may be because god does not exist and so intervention is impossible. God may exist but concerns itself only with the maintenance of natural laws. In this case god does not intervene in the lives of humans or mosquitoes or what have you. Even if one bends over backwards in support of Pannenberg, why is it necessary that Jesus is the supreme revelation? Were the plagues that god is said to have unleashed on Egypt not powerful revelations or the bestowing of the Ten Commandments on Moses, or any of a number of events? The claim that Jesus was the supreme revelation depends wholly on the belief that Jesus was god, that he rose from the dead, and that he will come again at the end of the world to judge all humanity. Here one encounters Pannenberg's second claim and the implications of it. The problem is that Jesus was human and not god, as this book has stressed. Jesus did not rise from the dead and there is no reason to suppose that he will return at the end of time to judge us all. Pannenberg's statements are nothing more than improbable assertions. Under such circumstances, Pannenberg should defend rather than merely state assertions.

Pannenberg is particularly bold in linking history and theology in asserting that the statement that Jesus was god is a historical fact. This kind of conflation is dangerous because it is more than a linking of history and theology. It is a conflation of the two and an attempt to set up theology as an arbiter of what happened in the past. Nothing could be farther from the truth. I have attempted to argue repeatedly. History has its own methodology, its own way of testing the past to try to determine what actually happened. Theology has none of these tools. We have seen that Christian theology depends on the canonical gospels, which were not historical documents but instead legendary accounts. Christian theology, then, is built on falsehood rather than truth. I am not claiming that history can pinpoint exactly what happened at every juncture in the past. To take up a topic of Civil War buffs, I do not think any historian has adequately explained why Union general George B. McClellan did not attacked the forces of Confederate general Robert E. Lee at Antietam, Maryland, immediately upon learning that Lee had divided his forces. However, even if history cannot solve every problem in the interpretation of the past, it can lay down rules about how one ought to examine and interpret the past. One certain lesson is that legends can never suffice for facts. As we have seen, the problem is that Jesus exists to us only in the form of legends. Such material can never be the basis of theology, however daring it may wish to be.

Having set forth these ideas, Pannenberg is perhaps most brazen in insisting that one can know the historical Jesus. I have committed myself in this book to testing this claim. Remember that our starting point, the canonical gospels, were written decades after Jesus' death and by men who were not eyewitnesses to his life. If we lack eyewitness testimony, we can have no chance of knowing Jesus the man. The sources do not allow us to find such knowledge. I argue that we may know a few broad facts about Jesus, but certainly nothing as bold as the gospels claim. Above all else, we can establish that Jesus was not god and did not rise from the dead. He performed no miracles and achieved notoriety only through his crucifixion. Most of what we can know about Jesus, then, comes in the form of negations. This type of knowledge parallels that of Greek philosopher Socrates as told by his pupil Plato in the *Apology*. Remember that Socrates was wise because he was conscious of how little he knew. We seek that same wisdom in our attempt to show just how little it is possible to know about Jesus. In this sense we seek to provide a corrective to all the treatises of theology written over the centuries. It is time to tell the truth.

Along these lines, Pannenberg believes that one may seek the historical Jesus in sources earlier than the canonical gospels.[1] This kind of thinking glosses over the reality that such documents do not presently exist. One might infer their existence but one cannot hold them in one's hand. This point is central to chapter 1. In our case we may attempt to go back to Q. Remember that Q was thought to be a source from which Matthew and Luke borrowed, in addition to borrowing from Mark, the earliest gospels. But because Mark did not borrow from Q it is thought that Q must have been written after Mark and so cannot be the pre gospel document that Pannenberg had in mind. In fact, there is no evidence of any kind that any document predated Mark. It is difficult to think of what Pannenberg might have had in mind. It is obvious, however, why Pannenberg would favor the existence of such texts because the earlier in time one gets to Jesus the greater should be the probability of finding real historical information. Maybe Pannenberg has in mind Paul's letter, but they are not historical. We recall that Paul never knew Jesus and so cannot have written a historical account of him. Furthermore the information that Paul provides about Jesus, notably his resurrection, is not historical information but rather theological. Again one must guard against conflating the two.

In this regard, Pannenberg claims the New Testament as a collection of historical sources. The canonical gospels, part of the New Testament, are not historical sources and neither is the rest of the New Testament. Not a single book in the New Testament is an eyewitness account about Jesus. The attempt to read the entire New Testament confers on the reader only a small amount of information about Jesus, mostly in the form of negations. We learn what Jesus was not rather than who he was.

---

[1] Ibid., 24.

Pannenberg must be immune from criticism because he even ventures so far to claim that we can know that Jesus rose from the dead.[1] I showed in chapter 5 that we can know that Jesus never rose from the dead. One can scarcely draw a sharper contrast between two positions. The reader may draw his or her own conclusions after having examined the evidence in this book.

Pannenberg is perhaps more cautious and consistent, given his belief that Jesus was divine, in asserting that Jesus must have preexisted his birth. This sounds contradictory, but it must be true if Jesus were god. Consider the opinion that Jesus came into existence only at his birth, or perhaps earlier at conception. This would be proper for a human but not a god. Remember that one may not limit god in any way, a position that Richard Swinburne affirms. To say that Jesus is god and came into existence at some moment in time is to limit god in a radical way by constraining him in time. That is, were Jesus god, he must have existed for eternity. The prologue to the gospel of John says as much but even in this instance, we have seen the difficulties of positing the eternal existence of anything. We will not repeat these arguments here, but it seems clear that the very eternity that is a necessary quality of god cannot exist so that god cannot exist and Jesus cannot be god but merely a man.

This caution dissipates in Pannenberg's claim that the "incarnation" was a historical event. By incarnation he means that Jesus the god was born at a moment in time. This moment was the inception of god as man. When we say that Jesus was born we return to the earlier problem that only two canonical gospels mention Jesus birth and that both claim that Mary was a virgin at the time of Jesus' birth. We must confront this problem anew given Swinburne's insistence that god could have performed this miracle in a variety of ways, notably by doubling the chromosomes in Mary's unfertilized egg.[2] Remember that Mary's egg must have been haploid, containing half the number of chromosome necessary to any diploid organism, humans in this case. That is Jesus must have contained two and not one set of chromosomes in each cell. The miraculous doubling of the chromosomes in Mary's egg seems to solve all problems in one great feat of genetics. Indeed chromosomes do on occasion double part of their length, an instance known as a mutation. The result of a mutation is almost always deleterious so that the cell with the elongated or shortened chromosome will die in most cases. Here, though, Swinburne proposes the complete doubling of every chromosome in Mary's egg. There is no evidence that such a large mutation has ever occurred. Let us bend over backwards to consider Swinburne's proposal. Each human egg has 23 chromosomes so that at doubling Mary's egg would have had 46

---

[1] Ibid., 53.
[2] Swinburne, *Was Jesus God?* 50.

chromosomes, arranged in 23 pairs, the number in the somatic cells of any human. The problem is that this organism will contain two X chromosomes because every woman, Mary included, can pass down to her offspring only an X chromosome. Doubling the X will give us two X chromosomes. That person will always be a woman. But if Jesus resulted from this doubling, how could he have been a man? He could not have unless more miracles occurred. First god would have doubled the first 22 chromosomes. Coming to the 23rd chromosome, the sex chromosome, god cannot have doubled the X chromosome. Rather it must have held the chromosome constant while creating a Y chromosome out of nothing, and then pairing the two. The resulting baby will have an X and a Y sex chromosome and so will necessarily be a boy. These miracles would have been necessary to create Jesus. Considered in this light, the virgin birth appears to be as impossible as ever.

Pannenberg makes a second attempt to prove Jesus' divinity, claiming that the resurrection demonstrates this fact. Of course there are no facts here, just suppositions. The basic problem with Pannenberg's approach is that neither he nor anyone else has demonstrated the reality of the resurrection. It is a claim made about Jesus and written decades after his death. Even were one willing to grant Pannenberg's assertion that Jesus rose from the dead, we would still have a problem determining what such a resurrection proves. The claim that it proves Jesus' divinity is premature when one considers the possibility that god might have chosen to resurrect a person from the dead. No one, for example, claims that Lazarus was divine because Jesus raised him from the dead after four days in the tomb (according to the gospel of John). If Lazarus could rise from the dead, as was claimed, and remain human, why could Jesus not rise from the dead and remain human? The talk about post resurrection miracles and an ascension to heaven are just more legendary material about Jesus. Faced with inaccuracies at every turn, the sensible reader will conclude that Jesus never rose from the dead, as last chapter made clear, and was never god, Pannenberg's claims notwithstanding.

A related matter is the conclusion that Jesus was the son of god. The son of a human must be human and the son of god must be divine. From the point of view of the virgin birth legend, we determined that, on the basis of reproductive biology, Jesus must have had a human father. In this context we conclude that Joseph, not god, was Jesus' father. The notion of Jesus as the son of god, repeated in the canonical gospels, can be little more than a linguistic device. Perhaps it means that Jesus was faithful to god in a way that a son is faithful to a father. This statement is an analogy not a literal claim that Jesus was the actual son of god. To take this phrase literally is to stir up all sorts of trouble. As the son of god, Jesus must have been distinct from god as a son is distinct from his father. But if we insist that Jesus was a distinct god than at least two gods must exist. Indeed one finds in scripture claims that the father was greater than Jesus. Could Jesus somehow have been a lesser god? Is it possible for one god to be greater and another lesser? The answer must be no because god must be unlimited. As an unlimited being god must partake in perfection and it is not possible to be perfect to a lesser degree. One must be perfect, period. So the retreat to polytheism must be false on logical grounds. We arrive at the same conclusion: Jesus cannot have been the son of god.

The claim that Jesus was the Messiah is, however, a separate issue. The term messiah is Jewish, not Christian. The longing for a messiah takes up surprisingly little space in the Hebrew scriptures. The notion of a messiah, however, lends itself to apocalyptic thought. We have already established that Jesus was likely an apocalyptic preacher, so that the notion of a messiah likely resonated with him and probably with John the Baptist as well. The Messiah was assumed to be a figure, likely a military hero, who would come at the end of the world to rescue Jews from Roman persecution and right all wrongs. It is natural that apocalyptic Jews, Jesus among them, saw the world in stark terms of justice and injustice. In this context, the effort to depict Jesus as the Messiah seems strange. He was not a military savior. He did not free the Jews from Roman oppression. He did not usher in the end of the world. In fact if Jesus believed himself the Messiah, he must have been incorrect. Some Jews still await a savior 2000 years after Jesus' grisly death.

If Jesus was not the Messiah, he must nonetheless have been unconventional. Some sayings attributed to him appear to be counterfactual. His Sermon on the Mount in the gospel of Matthew contains blessings to the poor and claims that the world belongs to the meek.[1] Nothing could be farther from reality. The poor and meek live miserable lives and are constantly at the mercy of the elites. One may pray all one likes, but the poor and meek remain downtrodden. Jesus may have foreseen this tragedy given the claim that the world will always have poor people. The impetus for social justice ended in Jesus' crucifixion. There is nothing divine about such a turn of events. Jesus, being only human, could not protect the poor any more than he could protect himself from cruelty.

Nonetheless, Christians have turned away from these inconvenient facts. The claim that Jesus was god is inseparable from the notion that he was infallible or incapable of error. It is self evident that a perfect being, namely god, cannot err. Thus Catholics claim that Jesus must have been infallible in his choice of Peter as what would be the first pope.[2] All subsequent popes

---

[1] Matt 5: 3-10.
[2] Pannenberg, *Jesus*, 58.

must be infallible by virtue of their descent from Peter. There are of course many popes who did not display edifying conduct so that the notion of papal infallibility is false. Yet even today, Catholics believe that the pope is infallible when he speaks about matters of faith. This also is wishful thinking.

The emphasis on Jesus' divinity does not square comfortably with Pannenberg's claim that Jesus may not have expected to rise from the dead.[1] Once more, if Jesus were divine he would have been omniscient. Having all knowledge, he would have possessed a complete accounting of past, present and future events so that if Jesus had been divine he would have predicted his resurrection. He cannot have doubted this event. On the other hand, were Jesus merely human, he would not have known of his own impending resurrection. The desire to have Jesus as both god and man is senseless. We trod this path earlier. As a reminder we need to recall that god is unlimited and man limited, god perfect and man imperfect. The two cannot go together.

Inexplicably Pannenberg claimed that the resurrection ushered in the "end of history."[2] This cannot be true in a world, 2000 years after Jesus' death, in which humans continue to make history. In fact the resurrection, if Pannenberg believed it happened, has ended nothing. Time has not ended because we continue to move forward through it. Space has not ended because we continue to be surrounded by it. The world has not ended but we continue to be enmeshed in its events. True we live in a more technologically sophisticated world than the one Jesus inhabited, but this is perhaps one of the few meaningful differences between his time and ours.

One of the worst problems facing Pannenberg and his colleagues is the failure of apocalypticism. An apocalyptic message as well as an end-of-history message states that the world must soon end. Jesus must have expected this end during the lifetime of his followers. The fact that he was wrong alone disproves the claim of divinity. According to the gospels of Mark and Matthew and the book of Revelation, Jesus was to come in glory at the end of time to usher in a new age of justice for the righteous and punishment for the wicked. Revelation claims that god, in ushering in this new age, will transform the world into something humans have never experienced. Why have these glorious events never happened? The answer seems to be because Jesus was wrong to predict the immediate end of the world. Because he was wrong, Mark, Matthew, and Revelation have perpetuated this error. This error continues to haunt us. I once dated a woman who confessed that she had prepared for the end of the world on January 1, 2000, and was shocked when nothing out of the ordinary

---

[1] Ibid., 66.
[2] Ibid.

happened. Even 2000 years after Jesus' death, she was powerless to avoid the same error that so many people have made.

But other errors abound. For example Pannenberg believes that one can know what Jesus actually said. The only sources of what Jesus might have said come from the accounts of his life, both canonical and non-canonical. We have noted earlier that these accounts were written decades after Jesus' death and cannot hope to be a transcript of his parables or speeches depending on whether one consults the synoptics or the gospel of John. Of course by John we read long speeches by Jesus. These cannot have been memorized in the 60 or 70 years after Jesus' death. During these decades his words would have been forgotten and not memorized. The only tenable conclusion is that we have no idea what Jesus said during his life. The principal problem, we have seen, is that Jesus wrote nothing about his own life. The absence of such a document demonstrates that we cannot know Jesus' actually words.

Pannenberg compounds this error by using Paul's letters as evidence about Jesus.[1] This line of thought is inaccurate because Paul never knew Jesus. Paul therefore was never an eyewitness to Jesus' life. Given this distance between Jesus and Paul, one cannot rely on Paul for expert testimony about Jesus. At most, Paul was no more than an observer or spectator who must have known a little about the apostles but nothing about Jesus. For example consider that someone who has never met me would inquire about me to my father. Because my father and I share almost nothing in common, my father could not give this spectator an adequate account of my life. To be sure, my father could recite my date of birth and so my age, but he could provide nothing substantive about me.

In one sense, though, Pannenberg is able to use Paul's letters to reveal one nugget about the resurrection. Keep in mind that Paul wrote his letters before the authors of the canonical gospels wrote their texts. As a rule, what appears in both Paul and the gospels may elicit some confidence. For example, Christians claim, Paul and the gospels mention the resurrection. This reasoning might be sound in another universe but we must remember that Paul says almost nothing about the resurrection other than that it happened. But because Paul never knew Jesus, he had no grounds for claiming the resurrection. In fact the gospel writers never knew Jesus and so cannot have known whether Jesus rose from the dead. The only people, then, who attested to the resurrection never knew Jesus. Is this evidence or absence of evidence? Remember Mary Magdalene, a key figure in the gospel of Mark, never wrote a word about the resurrection. She is the one person who should have had much to say about the events surrounding Jesus' death and putative resurrection; yet she remained silent. Her silence may mean that she

---

[1] Ibid., 72.

never witnessed anything out of the ordinary and so was silent because she had no news to share with anyone. Instead the story of Jesus' resurrection was left to men who had never known Jesus. How reliable can they have been? Nonetheless Pannenberg counts on Paul for a crucial piece of evidence, obtained from his silence. Pannenberg notes that Paul never mentioned any appearances of Jesus to his followers after his resurrection. To Pannenberg, this silence means that these appearances never occurred.[1] But if the canonical gospels made up this information, how are we to know that the accounts are not largely fabricated? By this I mean that the virgin birth was a fabrication, as was the story in the temple, as was the raising of Lazarus, as was Jesus' resurrection. Pannenberg is right, but he did not go far enough. All the stories about Jesus are almost surely legends. This circumstances stem from the fact that the accounts about Jesus are theological and not historical.

If Paul did not have access to resurrection legends, they must have grown in number after his letters were more or less complete. Remember that the gospel of Mark did not initially contain resurrection stories. The earliest manuscript says only that Mary Magdalene, in searching for Jesus' tomb encountered a man who told her that Jesus had risen from the grave. This type of secondhand testimony, if it is even testimony, is not the same as a resurrection appearance, whereby the risen Jesus confronts his followers anew. Such stories appear only in the gospels of Matthew, Luke and John. The earliest are Matthew and Luke with both written about 80 to 85 CE. If we date the end of Paul's letters about 60 CE, with his death not long thereafter, then these legends must have gained a foothold in the minds of Christians over the next 20 to 25 years. This is ample time for audacious stories to arise. Once Christians were in the midst of legend making each subsequent legend must have been easier to construct. With the passage of sufficient time, the authors of Matthew, Luke and John must have had innumerable legends to incorporate in their Jesus stories. The fact that they did so does not mean that these stories were true. It means only that the authors were opportunists who plucked whatever fruit was ripe on the legend tree.

Among the items that Paul does not mention is the notion of the empty tomb. This omission is curious because it is the foundation of Mark's resurrection account. Since Mark contains no resurrections stories, the basis of faith in the resurrection rests on the claim that Jesus was buried in a tomb, that Mary Magdalene knew the existence of this grave, at that she approached it on Sunday only to find it empty. A man at the tomb told Mary that Jesus had risen from the dead. Without the story of the empty tomb, there is no resurrection account in Mark. That is, the empty tomb was so

---

[1] Ibid., 89.

important that had it existed, Paul probably should have known about it. The fact that he did not suggests that the story was nothing more than a literary device. Jesus was never buried we have seen because Pontius Pilate left him to rot on the cross. Without burial, the gospel stories fall apart.

Perhaps Pannenberg's weakness is his reliance on revelation, that is, the word of god. Embedded in this notion is the claim that god somehow transferred his ideas to the biblical writers. This transfer of information must mean that the bible is devoid of error. There are many problems in this view. First, it implies that over a period of a few thousand years god spoke to humans in a way that it no longer does. We know of no book, written say in 2010, that is now part of the Hebrew and Christian scriptures. Why do we not have a cottage industry of new biblical texts? We do not apparently because god no longer reveals its ideas to humans. This idea of transmission now but silence thereafter makes no sense.

Second, if god transmitted its ideas to humans, the bible should contain no errors. One may consider several examples, but one should suffice. God must be omniscient and so must contain all knowledge. How could such a god display in the bible such limited geographical knowledge? The god of the bible knew only Africa, Asia, and Europe. God apparently did not know of the existence of the Americas, Australia, and Oceania. In fact god's knowledge of Asia does not seem to have included Southeast Asia. Indonesia, Malaysia and others part of this area receive no mention in the bible. This is understandable once one realizes that humans alone wrote the bible. The people of Palestine simply did not have any knowledge of many of the world's landmasses. This led to compound errors. The writers of the bible knew nothing about corn or the Venus flytrap or a number of other species because they did not know about the Americas. Ignorance tends to multiply, a circumstance common to humans but unknown to gods.

Even though Pannenberg must have had moments of doubt, he remains steadfast that Jesus truly rose from the dead. He tries to turn the tables on the old theological arguments by invoking modern physics.[1] Perhaps his crucial insight is that physicists do not know the laws of nature with certitude. In the absence of certitude one must accept the possibility that a vastly implausible event must occur given sufficient time. Because the laws of nature are imperfectly known, it is impossible to say categorically that such and such an event cannot occur, again opening the door to the resurrection. Because all of this is so, history can neither affirm nor deny the resurrection.

Perhaps this is Pannenberg's finest moment. The linkage to physics and the laws of nature is clever, but is it correct? First, it is true that physicists do not have a precise accounting of the laws of nature, but this does not mean

---

[1] Ibid., 98.

that new developments will not clarify matters. It is interesting to note that in 1904 no one anticipated the groundbreaking discoveries that German physicist and Nobel laureate Albert Einstein made between 1905 and 1916. At every turn during these years Einstein astonished his colleagues and the larger public hungry for a scientist-celebrity. The point is that it is not possible to predict the twists and turns of modern physics. The statement that physicists cannot define precisely the laws of nature today tells us nothing about tomorrow's developments. In other words Pannenberg may be right today but wrong tomorrow.

Second the claim that the resurrection is impossible to deny in the face of a contingent universe is difficult to evaluate. The key is to determine whether the universe is truly contingent. Pannenberg appears to be correct today, but again physicists are good at pulling very large rabbits out of hats that no one knew existed. All bets are off about what may happen tomorrow. If, however, and this is a huge if, Pannenberg is right than the resurrection must be possible. But any possible event must occur only with the passage of infinite time. Our universe gives us only finite time in which case one cannot say that the resurrection must have occurred. Even if one is adamant in favor of the resurrection, where does one stop? Does the resurrection of Jesus mean that Lazarus also rose from the dead? Was Jesus' mother really a virgin? Is it possible that during Jesus' short life innumerable miracles occurred and since then not a single miracle? Of course Christians will point to saints as the performers of miracles, but no miracle is plausible. They are all devoid of evidence. The miracle that Pannenberg cares most about—the raising of Jesus from the dead—is no more plausible than any other miracle. Deconstructed they appear to be nothing more momentous than fanciful assertions.

Third a theologian (a non historian) can claim that history can neither affirm nor deny the resurrection. Contrary to this belief the historian is bound to make a judgment. Remember that Jesus left no account of his life and his followers were silent too. That is, no eyewitness testimony exists about any part of Jesus life. In the absence of evidence the historian must deny the resurrection. The resurrection cannot have occurred. Otherwise a deluge of eyewitness accounts would be available. No one who actually witnessed the resurrection could have restrained him or herself. Eyewitness would have written these remarkable accounts on papyrus and shouted this miracle from the rooftops. But none of this happened because Jesus did not rise from the dead.

Why do such accounts not exist? Pannenberg seems to suggest that they do not because ordinary people would not have been able to fathom such a miracle. Only the visionary can understand such a reality. I do not know how to critique this assertion in detail. Instead I will take the example of Paul, who himself claimed to be a visionary. Yet this is a dangerous claim, for what Paul perceived as a vision might have been illusory. Simply put he may have had a hallucination. Science has never uncovered someone who has had a legitimate vision, but there are plenty of examples, of hallucinations. Indeed hallucinations sometimes occur when one suffer from a psychotic break with the past. If Paul was psychotic, and it is not possible to know today, then readers should be careful how they interpret him. I suspect that Jesus' death occasioned hallucinations from his grieving followers but no visions.

Richard Swinburne

A celebrated theologian and writer, Swinburne is in many ways traditional in his beliefs. His universe is one in which god is unlimited and humans have free will. I contend that these traits cannot coexist. First, consider the notion that god is unlimited. Literally, then, I cannot limit in any way any of a number of traits. For purposes of illustration, let me take the trait of knowledge. If god is unlimited, its knowledge must be complete in every way. Second let me consider the notion of free will. Imagine that I am thinking of going to law school. For reasons of interest, location and affordability, suppose I am considering both Ohio State University and Pennsylvania State University. Imagine that I am having difficulty deciding the right course of action. I switch repeatedly between Ohio State and Penn State. It is obvious that my anguish must stem from my position as an agent of free will struggling to make the right decision. But if one returns to god with the conviction that it knows everything, then he will know that I will be a law student at Ohio State a year from now. Because god knows everything, this knowledge is certain. No matter what I might think, the hidden hand pushes me inexorably to Ohio State. My conviction that I have free will turns out to be an illusion, even though I am never quite able to grasp this fact. If god exists, its omniscience is necessarily unlimited. Therefore humans lack free will.

Suppose on the other hand that you wish to press me into admitting that we have free will. This would not be a helpful concession. If we have free will, we seem nonetheless bent on evil. One always points to Nazism and the Holocaust but there are many other examples of genocide throughout history. In fact, one might label the twentieth century as the century of mass murder. Portraying itself as the land of liberty, the United States has been guilty of forcibly sterilizing women, depriving them of their reproductive right. Their offense was poverty and a poor education. Racism has had a long and tortuous history in the United States, and yet Americans claim to be somehow exceptional. Is the United States really a beacon of morality?

We can easily test the proposition that free will, supposing it to exist, tends toward evil with a small example. Imagine that you are on an unfamiliar stretch of highway. Suddenly you recognize your exit ahead. Unfortunately you are a lane removed from the exit and so must activate your turn signal in hopes of entering the correct lane prior to your exit. We all know what happens. The lane is clogged with traffic. No driver will allow you to enter the lane and you miss the exit. This type of scenario happens many times a day every day, proving the basic selfishness of almost all humans. We think nothing about such behavior because we almost all do it. What people call free will is a program toward selfishness and other manifestations of evil. Perhaps this behavior is an evolutionary adaptation to harsh surroundings. Throughout much of human history resources of all kinds, especially food, were scarcely. Humans had to be evil to take possession of food at the expense of others. In other words evolution seems to have programmed us to behave in ways that benefit oneself, one's kin and no one else. If this is free will it is very weak against the biological forces that have shaped us. It is hard to have much sympathy for Swinburne's optimism for free will.

Swinburne is sensitive to the issue of evil, noting that "God cannot always do the best action."[1] This means I guess that god cannot maximize the well being of all people. Certainly the world is evidence of this fact. In general terms, the world's plutocrats monopolize wealth while condemning the masses to poverty and despair. This is nothing new. The Roman Empire built its grandeur on the backs of poor farmers and craftspeople. Our own society is not immune from this effect. The United States has more billionaires than any other country. In effect America is the wealthiest nation in history; yet poverty abounds. Economists admit that the gap between the rich and poor is expanding in the United States, as we enter a new Gilded Age. Governments slash funds to public education, including state colleges and universities. As tuition rises, it prices Americans out of the pool of applicants. How can people succeed without a quality education? Notice that rising tuition does not affect the plutocrats. They will continue to attend the best, most expensive schools. They will perpetuate their elitism.

Most troubling is Swinburne's insistence that god cannot ensure the best for everyone. Why not? If god is unlimited, as he insists, it can at least in principle ensure any outcome it wishes. If god does not act to maximize our collective welfare, it must be because god chooses not to act or chooses to act in a manner contrary to our interests. This seems to be the message of the book of Job. Remember that god allows Satan to torture Job and kill his children. As an enabler, god is a partner in murder and torture. Had god had any backbone, it would have resisted Satan's request for permission

---

[1] Swinburne, *Was Jesus God?* 10.

to commit these atrocities. The god of Job is truly unlimited because it is capable of unlimited good and evil. Perhaps these characteristics are what Swinburne means by the assertion that god is unlimited. Perhaps it is better to have no god at all rather than a god of both good and evil. Perhaps atheism is preferable to a theism of messy results.

Yet Swinburne persists, claiming that "God has the right to impose on some of us bad things."[1] This is a shocking statement and can only come, one suspects, from an intellectual who has led a cushy life of privilege. It is clear that evil occurs to many people. Swinburne does not attempt to assuage our grief but to justify evil by deriving it from god. Here perhaps is the closest one can get to an affirmation that god is evil. At the same time Swinburne claims that "God is love." Within the context of evil this statement is nonsense. It is terrible theology that does not correspond to reality. Assume that you are full of love. Would you, had you sufficient power, consent to the death of even one two month old infant from malaria? Yet this is exactly the world we inhabit. If god is love, where do we see this love on display? The contentions that god is capable of evil and love do not correspond in any way. Swinburne has set up a contradiction, one that he does not resolve. Are we to worship a god of contractions?

Another suspect claim is Swinburne's assertion that god is eternal. We have dealt with this problem elsewhere. Here I seek only to remind the reader that the claim that god exists outside time is meaningless. As humans we have no experience of a dimension devoid of time. Our universe is bound up in time and space. In fact German physicist and Nobel laureate Albert Einstein showed that time and space where two aspect of the same reality. In short, our universe and everything in it could not exist apart from time. The only god we can understand is a god in time and space. The fact that the bible claims that god has intervened numerous times in human history must depend on the notion that god acts in time. If god acts in time, god must be part of time. Remember as well that the claim of eternal existence defies our very understanding of time, which must be finite and which all of us experience as finite. Enmeshed in time, god cannot be eternal. In fact we have no evidence that anything is eternal. All reality had a beginning, and this origin marked the beginning of time. Yet god must be eternal for god to be unlimited. Therefore god does not exist. It follows that Jesus could not have been god since no god exists.

Yet Swinburne goes on, claiming that Jesus was god and preexisted his birth.[2] That is, this is the theological claim in the prologue in the gospel of John.[3] Given this conviction, it is not surprising that John had no birth

---

[1] Ibid., 21.
[2] Ibid., 41.
[3] John 1: 1-4.

narrative. With Jesus already in existence, his birth would have been an anticlimax. If Jesus predated his birth, many problems arise. First, if he predated his birth, Jesus must have existed in immaterial form. If Jesus were soul or spirit or whatever one might say, how would he have had a gender, because maleness or femaleness is a characteristic of physical beings? This is a characteristic that Jesus could not have exhibited before birth. Only at conception would his gender be set. Second, how can something that is immaterial be transformed into something material, into a physical being, that is? I can, for example, construct in my brain the image of a unicorn. Such an object, if I may call it that, exists only in my mind. If I wish to go further, I can draw a picture of this image, but nowhere in nature will I find a unicorn as a mammal evidently related to all other equines. Just as I can think of no way of converting my mental image of a unicorn into a real organism I can think of no way of transforming the immaterial being of Jesus into a real human, someone I might see at the street corner and greet. On the other hand, were Jesus merely human, no problem arises about the acquisition of a body and with it a gender. The claim that Jesus predated his birth, therefore, is untenable. The claim that Jesus was god is likewise untrue. Jesus was fully human, nothing more or less.

Swinburne also argues for the perfection of Jesus, a being who could do no wrong. Even a cursory reading of the canonical gospels challenges this claim. We have seen that according to the gospel of Mark Jesus caused a fig tree to die. Such an action is wrong because the tree was likely someone's property or perhaps a source of fruit for the neighborhood. In either case people valued the tree and Jesus had no right to deprive the community or owner of it. An even more egregious case concerns the gospel of Luke's recounting of Jesus' encounter with a possessed man. In expelling the demons, Jesus grants their request to inhabit a herd of pigs on a nearby hillside. Jesus grants the request whereby the demons cause the pigs to rush into a lake and drown. Again the destruction of property, in this case a source of sustenance, deprived an owner or the community of pork. In no way can one judge these actions good or responsible. The Infancy Gospel of Thomas contains many acts of evil, including several murders. In sum the sources about Jesus' life comfort no one.

Swinburne continues to cling to the legend of a virgin birth. Jesus obtained his divinity from god and his humanity from Mary. These suppositions do not stand scrutiny. I do not wish to rehash my arguments in chapter 2. It is enough to remind the reader that only two of the 27 books of the New Testament—the gospels of Matthew and Luke—say anything about Jesus' birth. The earliest extant documents, Paul's letters, say not a word about Jesus birth. Should not the documents closest in time to Jesus contain the best probability of harboring historical information? Yet these documents tell us nothing about Jesus' birth, probably because he was obscure as a youth, and in antiquity historians seldom wrote about the individual lives of obscure people.

Turning to probability, Swinburne claims that with the passage of sufficient time, it would be necessary for god to reveal himself in full to humanity.[1] This revelation was Jesus. I think probability arguments such as this one suffer defects. The key problem is that we have no idea what time would mark the passage of a sufficient duration to come near to guaranteeing the project of Jesus into the world. The arbitrary nature of this revelation is troubling. For example, Neanderthals existed on earth several hundreds of thousands of years. Neanderthals seem to have been the first religious people, so why did god not bless them with Jesus? That is, why is Jesus a member of *Homo sapiens* rather than Neanderthal? If there really is some hidden reason why Jesus had to be a modern human, why did he enter human history apparently so late? Anatomically modern humans have peopled the world for the last roughly 200,000 years; yet Jesus came to earth only in the last 2,000 years. Why the delay? Why did he come to the peoples of westernmost Asia rather than the peoples of the Americas? In short, lots of randomness surrounds Jesus. Is it necessary that he be inscrutable, or was his life a purely human existence in the random way that defines all our lives? After all, neither you nor I got to choose the place, time, and parentage of our existence. As a man, Jesus had no choice of these variables either.

Swinburne's basic problem is that he attempts to approach Jesus through the lens of history without reference to the fact that he is a theologian, not a historian. He believes one made find reliable information about Jesus throughout the New Testament, in the canonical gospels. Of the gospels the synoptics are particularly reliable. We have trodden this ground in chapter 1, where we found that the accounts about Jesus are legends. They are not history. We have seen that the copying process introduced errors into the original autographs, which were themselves fanciful with their miracles and talk of resurrections. We affirm that the purpose of the New Testament is to convince readers about the divinity of Jesus, not to create a historical account of the man. Swinburne must read the New Testament through the lens of faith. The methods of the sciences and history escape him. I have confessed all along that I wish to compile a more adequate treatment of Jesus through my work as a historian of science knowledgeable in historical and scientific inquiry.

Swinburne compounds this error by assuming that the canonical gospels convey a consistent account of Jesus. One may perhaps argue this

---

[1] Swinburne, *Was Jesus God?* 92.

point for the synoptics given that Matthew and Luke copied from Mark and that Matthew and Luke probably copied from another source that is no longer extant. I agree that liberal doses of copying can yield uniform results. As an instructor I experienced this phenomenon repeatedly when I read plagiarized papers. So if Mark, Matthew and Luke share passages in common then uniformity will result. But there is little uniformity between the synoptics and John. By the time one arrives at the gospel of John, grand miracles like the resurrection of Lazarus take center stage and the pithy parables of the synoptics cede ground to the long speeches perhaps modeled after the speeches of Socrates in the middle and later dialogues of Plato.

Swinburne's answer to the miracles, like the raising of Lazarus, is that god allowed Jesus to perform them.[1] If this is true, Swinburne must be courting polytheism because god emerges as the superior being who allows the inferior Jesus to do or not do particular actions. In fact if Jesus was an inferior type of god than by definition he cannot have been god because must be the perfect, unlimited being. Swinburne's Jesus is limited in his actions and so cannot have been divine. If Jesus were not god, then he must have been human alone, a position I have maintained throughout this book.

Swinburne however does not let go of the divinity myth. He asserts that Jesus claimed to be god. In contrast, this book maintains that we cannot know what Jesus claimed because the gospels are not historical records of his actions and assertions. Given this circumstance, we cannot know what Jesus said or did. We do not know that Jesus claimed to be god. We know that the Jesus in the gospel of John proclaims himself divine, but with John we are about 70 years past the death of Jesus. Any historical memory would have been lost to the aggregation of legends. In a sense the gospels produce a fossilized Jesus, not the actual Jesus. Consider the formation of a fossil. Pick your favorite dinosaur. Its fossils were formed by the gradual replacement, atom by atom, of the actual bone with the minerals that formed rock. The fossil is not bone but rock. A similar process was at work after Jesus' death. Any historical knowledge that might have existed changed word for word and story for story into the legends that now populate the accounts about him. Again one is left with a kind of fossil of Jesus, not the historical person. We can no more retrieve him than we can retrieve the bones of dinosaurs.

Concerning the claim of resurrection, Swinburne turns to the gospel of Mark. He does not believe that Mark originally ended at verse 8 of chapter 16. Instead the original and longer ending is lost. The remedy was for another anonymous writer to tack on a longer ending to preserve the original intent of the author of Mark. This is an exercise in wishful thinking. There is not the slightest evidence that Mark contained a longer ending. The earliest

---

[1] Ibid., 97.

manuscripts end at 16:8 and no amount of conjuring can wipe away this fact. This type of counterfactual theology strikes me as dangerous. Swinburne appeals in essence to hope and supposition, but these aspirations cannot replace the brute fact that Mark ended without any resurrection appearances by Jesus. Mark ends with the empty tomb, but we have seen that there is no valid reason to suppose that Jesus was ever buried.

Gerald Schroeder

Physicist Gerald Schroeder is an interesting example of a man who has tried to bridge our current understanding of the world as given by the sciences and the world as given by the bible. In a sense this argument is very old. The initial belief was that science and revelation were two ways to know reality. Each performed properly gave an understanding of the world that coincided with the other field of knowledge. For example, many naturalists held that the diversity of life revealed the sweeping magnitude of god's creative powers. An examination of nature revealed the truth of the creations stories in Genesis. It is not surprising that in the early modern eras, many ministers were amateur botanists and zoologists. They wanted to demonstrate the grandeur of god in the dazzling diversity of life. My point is that Schroeder does not propose novel ideas so much as he squares what we claim to know with the scriptures.

Part of Schroeder's aim is to bolster the design argument.[1] Again this is not new. Perhaps the best exponent of this position was British cleric and naturalist William Paley. In 1802 he formulated the design argument in a way that it still resonates with many Christians.[2] His method is admirable. He began his account by imagining that while walking, he tripped upon a stone. Someone might ask him the origin of that stone. Paley confessed he did not know, but for all the poverty of his knowledge the stone might have existed for eternity. This claim would not be easy to refute, according to Paley. Now he considered a second scenario. Imagine the same walk along some pristine path. This time Paley trod upon a watch. Having discovered this machine, Paley would not claim it to have existed for eternity. Its precision and many parts, all working to the same end of keeping time, meant that the watch had a purpose. Anything with a purpose, Paley believed, had to have a designer who constructed it to achieve that purpose. Here the analogy passed to the human body and intellect. Were not the body and intellect even more intricate and perfect in construction than was the watch? The conclusion is that some being must have made humans according to a purpose. This being

---

[1] Gerald Schroeder, *The Science of God: The Convergence of Scientific and Biblical Wisdom* (New York: The Free Press, 1997) 5.
[2] Ibid., 115.

we know as god. Paley believed therefore that the design argument proved the existence and grandeur of god and of the humans as beings created with a purpose that no other plant or animal shared.

Since Paley's day, that design argument remains popular. It is interesting to note that British naturalist Charles Darwin read Paley while a student at the University of Cambridge. In fact he occupied the room that Paley had while at Cambridge. Darwin's initial reaction was to believe Paley correct in every detail. Darwin's later insights will merit consideration later. In fact I admit to toying with the design argument elsewhere. My supposition is that the beauty of the female form may derive from some divine plan or simply from the force of natural selection. Even now, when I look at a gorgeous woman, I am not certain whether divine agency or natural selection is at work. If divine agency is the answer, then I must admit the validity of the design argument.

The design argument has taken a molecular twist in the work of American microbiologist Michael Behe. Behe has taken the simplest organisms, bacteria, to find all sorts of complexity in them. His first premise is irreducible complexity, by which he meant that basic biological structures are too complex to have arisen from natural selection alone. If natural selection cannot have formed these structures, one must affirm that god must have designed life in all its complexity.

Here Behe faced intense criticism from the standard interpretation of evolutionary biology. At this point one must return to Darwin. His belief in the design argument crumbled in the 1830s while he was on a round-the-world voyage. He came to understand that all organisms face an intense competition for scarce resources, especially food and mates. Darwin understood that all organisms vary in their characteristics. Some organisms have variations that increase their odds of survival. Imagine giraffes. Their long necks enable them to feed high in trees. Imagine that one giraffe has a slightly longer neck than its peers. It will be able to feed higher in the canopy of a tree. That is, when the food supply is exhausted at lower levels, this taller giraffe will continue feeding and so have a greater likelihood of surviving long enough to reproduce, with reproduction being the biological goal of life. This interaction between organisms and the environment is known as natural selection, and it is the process that accounts for the preservation of favorable traits in a group of organisms.

The problem for Darwin is that he did not understand how one giraffe might be taller than another. It is interesting that the answer was available Darwin's life. In 1866, German monk Gregor Mendel published a paper on his experiments in hybridizing varieties of pea plants. The key insight from this work is that pea plants, and by extension all other organism, contain hereditary particles that we know call genes. They genes code from traits. I have brown hair and brown eyes because I have genes that code for these traits. Obviously a Nordic man or woman will have genes that code for blond hair and possibly blue eyes. The point is that these genes determine who we are at the most fundamental level and so they account for the differences among us. Obviously a person like American basketball player Lebron James has the physique, strength and speed that make him a much more gifted athlete than I can ever hope to be. Simply put I did not inherit the genes he did. The synthesis of Darwinian natural selection and Mendelian genetics has given rise to modern evolutionary biology.

Behe's problem is that he has never been able to demonstrate that life is too complex for natural selection to have shaped it. He has offered conjectures that must be true without Behe ever proving them true. It is particularly interesting that the lack of proof has not killed the design argument. For a time activists attempted to introduce "intelligent design" into the public school biology curriculum. Successes at the state level had no staying power because the U.S. Supreme Court has correctly interpreted the incursion of design in biology is the invasion of a religious belief in the science classroom. The first amendment makes clear that government cannot sponsor any religion. The outcome has been the preservation of science as a unique enterprise to the dismay of fundamentalists, those who interpret scripture literally.

Into this morass of fact and faith, Gerald Schroeder, in *The Science of God*, has attempted to bring physics within the compass of a design argument. His favorite target is the Big Bang, specifically the energy of it. Remember that the Big Bang is thought to be the moment of the creation of space and time. That is, the Big Bang marked the moment of the creation of the universe. This event is to have occurred about 13.7 billion years ago. It was the moment when a dense core of matter exploded to create the first light, energy, and the incipient universe. To Schroeder the energy of the Big Bang is precisely attuned to the development of life.[1] He estimates that had the energy differed by as little as 1 part per 10^{120}, life never could have evolved because the temperature of the universe would not have permitted the existence of life. That is the universe is exquisitely tuned to the formation of life by 1 part in 10 with 120 zeros after it. It is as though, according to Schroeder, that standing on one side of the universe, a person were able to hurl a dart across the entire universe to strike at the other end a target no larger than the impression of a pencil point. Obviously the chances of this event occurring are so small as to be impossible within the realm of ordinary physics. Thus god must have created the universe and light.

[1] Ibid., 5.

One might object in two ways to this claim. First, it is impossible to know what type of universe would have formed from a slightly larger or smaller amount of energy. It is impossible to rule out the formation of life, though it seems possible that this life might not have resembled us. Would it be possible, for example, for the formation of some photosynthetic organism with cognitive abilities? Perhaps not, but we do not know enough about the Big Bang to say definitively that life would not be possible in any universe but the one we exhibit. Nonetheless, let us accommodate Schroeder as much as we can. Let us suppose that only this universe can accommodate sentient beings and that all other possible universes would be devoid of life. Although I do not believe time can be infinite for reasons I detailed earlier, time may be extremely old. The origin of time might predate anything we can fathom. In short, given a sufficient duration of time and a sufficient of universes, the formation of our universe, as a matter of probability does not seem impossible any longer. There is no reason to doubt that we are simply a chance occurrence, an improbable role of the cosmic dice. There is no need to posit a creator to necessitate the existence of life. We have done well enough without one for millions of years.

Moreover, as Schroeder admits, the principles of the physics of Quantum Uncertainty dictate that something may form from nothing.[1] This idea negates the need for a creator. We do not need the god of Thomas Aquinas to create the universe out of nothing. This notion of creation is embedded in the laws of physics. Schroeder persists, wondering whether the laws of physics could have applied amid nothingness. The laws of physics seem to require the existence of a universe in which to operate, so he is not sure that Quantum Uncertainty would hold prior to the existence of our universe. The point is that this is speculation. We cannot know whether Quantum Uncertainty would hold amid nothingness because we cannot conceive of such a state. In this context, Schroeder is willing to jettison the laws of physics but I am not.

Tenacious as ever Schroeder claims that randomness cannot have generated complex life. This attempt at reason is not new and remains flawed. By randomness he means that mutations are random events. I agree, but let us examine this randomness. By random we mean that we cannot predict when or what of mutation will occur. Mutations may be of many types, perhaps the deletion of genes, a circumstance that is usually fatal to the cell or perhaps the doubling of some length of genes, another usually fatal circumstance. That is, mutations are usually harmful. In the case of a beneficial mutation, this turn of events will produce an advantage for an organism. We noted earlier in the case of a giraffe that a beneficial mutation

---

[1] Ibid., 23-24.

would confer a survival and reproductive advantage to an organism. Imagine in this case a mutation that allows a plant to endure a greater duration of shade. In such an environment this plant will have an obvious advantage over plants that need maximum exposure to sunlight. That is, natural selection acts on mutations to preserve those mutations that confer a survival or reproductive advantage. With natural selection, there is no need to posit a creator to have made complex life. This complexity is the result of natural selection operating on mutations for the roughly 3.8 billion years that life has inhabited earth.

Schroeder pursues a related argument by claiming that carbon would not likely have formed in our universe.[1] Carbon is the building block of life so that god must have prepared the conditions necessary for the formation of carbon and life. This claim is not sound. Carbon and every element heavier than hydrogen must have formed in our stars. This claim must be true given that stars produce energy through fusion. In brief the early universe was composed of hydrogen. Through the force of gravity, these hydrogen atoms coalesced into dense, hot balls of hydrogen gas. Hydrogen is flammable, as anyone who knows about the demise of the German blimp Hindenberg may affirm, so that given sufficiently high temperatures this hydrogen ignited in the core of a new star. This heat sufficed to cause hydrogen atoms to collide with one another so ferociously that two hydrogen atoms fused to form one helium atom plus energy and light. Thus stars by their nature formed all the elements heavier than hydrogen, carbon among them. To put matters bluntly, we are the residue of dead stars. None of this process requires a creator or suggests the improbability of forming carbon and life.

Turning to life itself, Schroeder states correctly that life evolved rapidly on earth. If earth is about 4.5 billion years old and life is 3.8 billion years old, then life must have formed as soon as the molten earth cooled sufficiently to permit the formation of life. I think Schroeder is correct, but his conclusion that a creator must have formed this life because natural selection takes too long is probably wrong. Note that by the creation of life, we mean the simplest form of life, probably nothing more elaborate that a molecule of some length that could replicate itself. This is the incipient chemistry of replication, a form of reproduction. Upon the scaffolding of this molecule, natural selection built a diversity of forms. Again this natural process has no need of god.

Schroeder's point is that the idea of an abrupt origin of life corresponds with the creation accounts in Genesis, in which god simply speaks and life in all its variations appear over a span of six days. There is nothing remarkable about such claims. In fact the gods of ancient Egypt created life in the same

---

[1] Ibid., 27.

way. The Hebrews, having spent a period under Egyptian domination, likely encountered the Egyptian gods and their methods of creation. As the Hebrews did in so many cases, they borrowed these ideas, adding them to their notion of Yahweh, their god. But it seems atavistic to take one's ideas of how life arose on earth from Egyptian and Jewish myths. There is nothing scientific about such a process.

It is striking to note how brazenly Schroeder is in claiming that the Genesis creation accounts can tell us about the formation of the universe, earth, and life on it. Schroeder believe that the six days of creation represent the entire 13.6 billion years of the universe's existence.[1] Nothing warrants this type of comparison. The writers of these creation accounts thought in terms day, in terms of the roughly 12 hours of daylight, for it was the only type of day they could conceive. So for these authors six days must have meant literally the passage of six days. To credit the writers with somehow envisioning their six days as a metaphor for the passage of 13.6 billion years is beyond farfetched. It strikes me as impossible. The stories in Genesis, at their best, rise to the level of poetry. They cannot be twisted to quasi-scientific ends.

Sticking to the creation accounts, Schroeder avers that Adam was the first human to possess a soul.[2] Such a claim strikes me as wild speculation. The belief that Adam was the first to have soul must derives from Schroeder's conviction that Eve must have come after Adam, though only the second story of creation contains such information. The first story implies that the two may have been created simultaneously. I see no grounds for positing the existence of a literal Adam and Eve or the claim that Adam was the first to have a soul. Schroeder is simply modifying a type of theological literature to suit his own aspirations. When would Adam be the first to have a soul? Neanderthals seem to have been the first people to have had spiritual longings. Why not posit them as the first people to have a soul? Along these lines, Schroeder does not define the term "soul," so it is impossible to know what he means. Plato may have originated the term. In many of his dialogues "soul" seems to be the equivalent of "intellect." But I doubt this is what Schroeder means. Does he mean "disembodied person"? Probably, but I cannot be sure. Even if we confine the term soul to members of *Homo sapiens*, one must realize that our species is some 200,000 years old. Where does Adam fall in this timeline? For consistency, it would seem necessary to try to put Adam as early as possible on this timeline, for how can one have some relatively recent being possessing a soul when all his forebears did not?

---

[1] Ibid., 41.
[2] Ibid., 125.

Here Schroeder's thought is probably more unsystematic than at any other point in *The Science of God*.

Schroeder the physicist contends that evolutionary biology cannot tell us when and how humans evolved to their current state. This statement is necessary to cause us to retreat to the origin stories in Genesis. In fact it is an unfair criticism of evolutionary biology. In fact our evolution is exceptionally well documented in the fossil record. How is it possible, for example, to know much about the Neanderthals? We possess knowledge because we possess many of their fossils. Perhaps even more important we have their deoxyribose nucleic acid (DNA). Comparing their DNA to ours, we note that many of us have Neanderthal DNA. Moreover as a species we possess nearly 1/3 of the Neanderthal genome. This is powerful evidence of the kinds of intimate interactions between Neanderthals and us. This is potent and precise information about our evolution and with whom we have had sex. Given this information, Schroeder is simply wrong.

The truth is that there is no such thing as a science of god. Science seeks to understand reality as we know it. It is not capable of understanding immaterial entities. If science lacks data about them, then we must concede that we have no basis for believing in such putative things. In this sense science is antithetical to theology. Does this mean that theology is false? I cannot supply an ironclad answer, but on the basis of everything I know, theology is untrue. In the hands of gifted writers, theology can become a kind of poetry. This is justification enough for theology. The claim that it is true goes beyond the bounds of what is possible. In the case of Jesus, we encounter again a man. The temptation to make him god has yielded the worst results.

CHAPTER 7. THE DEATH OF GOD

At the end of our inquiry, we must ask what we have learned about Jesus. The answer is precious little. We know nothing about his birth besides the certainty that he had two human parents. The gospels use the names Mary and Joseph and they will suit our purposes. We know nothing about Jesus' childhood. The legendary material in the Infancy Gospel of Thomas is neither history nor factual and we must discard it. We know little about Jesus' adulthood other than the probability that he was an apocalyptic preacher. More than that, we have confidence, as second century Roman historian Tacitus wrote, that Pontius Pilate crucified Jesus during the reign of Emperor Tiberius. We are confident that Jesus did not rise from the dead, did not appear to his disciples, and did not ascend into heaven. This little paragraph tells us what we can know about Jesus apart from any statement of faith.

Jesus, the Notion of God, and the Universe

We know as well that Jesus was fully human and not at all divine. Such knowledge poses a problem for Christians, who view the denial of divinity as tantamount to atheism. But this leap is not warranted. We have taken care to show that Jesus was limited in every respect and so cannot have been god. This claim does not in itself posit that god does not exist. For god to exist one would need to propose a limitless being whose definition will become clearer as we proceed. As limitless this god cannot have been born and must have existed before the Big Bang. Could this being have caused the Big Bang? We have no idea and will not speculate. The beginning of the universe coincided with the beginning of the laws of physics, of space, and of time. These mathematical statements seem to suffice for the expansion and subsequent evolution of the universe, but these laws are not god. They merely describe how our universe came to be. Of course this universe may not have been the first. According to nineteenth century German philosopher Friedrich Nietzsche, if time is infinite and the matter in the universe is finite then all permutations and combinations must recur again and again. For all we know, this may be the 3 trillionth time you have read this sentence. But I'm not sure Nietzsche was on the right track to assume that time is infinite. Infinite time presupposes the possibility of regressing into the past without end. If one can regress without end, when will one come to a beginning from which the universe will have had its origin? The answer is never. The fact that our universe exists means that it had a beginning and that time also had a beginning. God, if it exists, must have preceded all of these events and all events in general. God must also never cease to exist. Jesus on the other hand ceased to exist at death. Again Jesus cannot have been god, and god if it exists was a completely different being than the merely human Jesus. Therefore Jesus and god cannot have been the same beings. The life and death of Jesus say nothing about the existence or absence of god.

Nonetheless, skepticism and ultimately atheism have grown in modernity. Two arguments deserve particular mention. In the nineteenth century, both German philosopher Friedrich Nietzsche and Russian novelist Fyodor Dostoevsky furthered the critique of god. Let us consider each quickly. In more than one work, notably in *Thus Spake Zarathustra*, Nietzsche claimed that we had killed god.[1] What did the death of god mean? Dostoevsky had the answer. Without god, morality vanishes. Right and wrong no longer exist and everything is permissible.[2]

Let us examine Nietzsche in greater detail. The idea that we have killed god implies that we had created god long ago. As a historical statement, Nietzsche's claim has merit. In fact humans were in prehistory probably polytheistic before they settled on monotheism. We noted earlier that the Neanderthals were likely the first humans to bury their dead. These burials were ritual events with the accompaniment of flowers and other grave goods to memorialize the dead. The fact that Neanderthals went to great trouble in burying the dead suggests, but does not prove, the belief in an afterlife. After all, why fuss over a corpse unless one believes that the person is somehow still alive in another realm? If humans survive death, do they not need a creator being to assure their continued existence? It seems then that the Neanderthals were the first theists. Our own species, remarkably similar to the Neanderthals in worldview and intellectual

---

[1] William Barrett. *Irrational Man: A Study in Existential Philosophy* (Garden City, NY: Doubleday Anchor Books, 1958) 184-185.
[2] Ibid., 135-141.

attainments, seems to have believed in god or gods for a very long time. If we ponder that modern humans are about 200,000 years old, then the belief in theism is at least this old.

The question we have skirted so far is whether we originally believed in one or many gods. The answer is not easy to determine because for most of their existence humans did not leave records of their beliefs. Matters began to change with the Neolithic Revolution: the rise of agriculture and with it civilization and writing. Although civilization requires the existence of cities, most people lived in the countryside. In fact as late as Roman antiquity, 90 percent of the population still farmed. It is a safe generalization then that most people farmed the land or raised livestock or did both. Agriculture made its own demands of people. They needed to ensure protection against drought, insects, and pathogens at a minimum. It became necessary for humans to invent protector gods. At minimum humans needed a god to ensure sunlight without which plants, being photosynthetic factories, cannot survive. There must as well have been a god to ensure sufficient rainfall or the protection of irrigation works. A variety of gods too, were necessary to protect crops and livestock from insects and diseases. For example the Romans had the god Robigus to perform an essential task in protecting wheat plants from the fungal disease known as rust. The difference today is the presence of the sciences, which promote the breeding of wheat plants resistant to rust and many other diseases. Yet because the ancients did not have these tools they needed the help of gods.

Thus arose the polytheism of the Egyptians, Greeks, Romans and others. These gods were the utility deities who served a specific purpose to benefit humanity. It seems mysterious that such an assemblage of gods would ultimately prove unattractive. The drift to monotheism seems to have been gradual. To be sure the Egyptian pharaoh Akhnaton seems to have moved in this direction, but upon his death the priests and people resumed their devotion to the Egyptian pantheon of gods. Jews and Christians tout their adherence to monotheism, but the truth is less simple. The Jews believed in their god Yahweh, but also the sons of gods mentioned in Genesis and angels, who certainly were not human. These beliefs seem more like polytheism than strict adherence to monotheism. Even the Christians were not uniform in their beliefs. Some Gnostic Christians believed in many gods. One sect even held the existence of 365 gods, one apparently for each day of the year. Those who stuck narrowly to Yahweh, Jesus, and the holy spirit had difficulty affirming that this trio was actually a single god. Only in the fourth century did the Council of Nicea finally agree on the existence of three persons or manifestations of a single god. I will consider the fourth century as the beginning of the age of monotheism, a belief that Islam also adopted. Notice that in this fourth century humans, not god or the gods, defined spirituality in terms of a single god. The three persons in one god is the very formula that moved humans beyond polytheism to monotheism.

From a philosophical position, a belief in one god rather than many allows one to define god's powers. For example god must be omniscient, a requirement that only monotheism satisfies. Imagine again our host of agrarian gods. One knows only about sunlight, the next only about water, and so forth. If god is truly omniscient it must know the totality of what these agrarian gods were thought to know. Only one god, now, will be responsible for light, water, and protection against diseases and predators. Similarly only one god can hold the totality of all powers and so be omnipotent. This is the god of eleventh-century English theologian Anselm and others who felt the need to move beyond the partitioning of powers implicit in polytheism. Only the god of Anselm can represent the totality of all knowledge, all power, and eternity. Such a god is unlimited, a definition we have stressed from the outset. As we will see Anselm tried to use his definition of god to prove its existence.

The attempt to prove the existence of god appears to have reached its apex in the thirteenth century when Italian Dominican friar Thomas Aquinas constructed five proofs for god's existence. One may note a certain vulnerability in Aquinas' approach. If one can prove the existence of god, one rigorous proof should suffice. A multiplicity of proofs suggests that one is uncertain that any single proof is beyond criticism. Hence many are needed to prop up the weakness in any single attempt to prove god's existence.

Anselm's argument is based on ontology, the study of being. That is, what do we mean when we refer to god? To Anselm the answer is obvious. We believe in an unlimited being, or as he put it, a being about whom nothing greater can be thought. Sticking to this definition, Anselm asserted that it is greater to exist in reality than merely in the imagination. Consider for example the concept of $20. We can think about this money all day long, but if we do not actually have $20, we are not any richer. The person who has this money may flash the bill in my face to prove he is richer than I am; my thought of $20 means nothing without its existence. In the case of god, one should be able to think of another being that actually exists, proving that it is greater than god if god does not exist. But this is impossible because we have already defined god as the greatest being. Being the greatest must therefore include existence in reality and not merely in the imagination. Over the centuries this argument has unleashed a fierce debate that need not concern us here. My problem is that the language can be inverted, so to speak. Instead of the greatest being, one might imagine the worst being— who is generally thought to be Satan. Of course this being is the worst only if it exists. Otherwise it cannot torment humans. The ontological argument therefore appears to prove the existence of both god and Satan. How can the same basic formula prove the existence of polar opposites? It is not clear that this is possible, leading me to doubt Anselm's argument as too slippery to be taken at face value. The argument seems to be more a game than a rigorous proof.

We have seen that Nietzsche dispensed with the notion of god. It is possible then to disbelieve in the narrow case that Jesus was god and in the larger case that no god or gods exist. The question of whether god exists has transfixed humans for millennia. Philosophers and theologians have contributed to this discourse. Their arguments are too well known to rehearse here. The question becomes whether the putative existence of god can be fashioned into a hypothesis. The crucial point, of course, is that a hypothesis must be testable. It must be possible to devise an experiment or, in this case, a line of reasoning that can falsify a hypothesis. For example Darwin recognized the kinship among humans, chimpanzees and gorillas. Because these species of ape reside only in Africa, Darwin reasoned that humans, sharing a common ancestor with them, must have originated in Africa. Since the 1920s paleoanthropologists have confirmed this hypothesis. Had the oldest human remains been discovered in Asia, however, one might have had grounds for doubting Darwinism.

In turn, can one articulate a god hypothesis? Let's start by defining this being, as has been our practice all along. Anselm provided a serviceable definition in the eleventh century. God is that being about which nothing greater can be thought. If this is true, one should be able to enumerate god's traits. It is not enough that god be powerful. He, she, or it must be omnipotent. Along the same lines god must be omniscient and all loving. The last characteristic may prove discomforting, but one might say that it is greater to love than to hate, a proposition that even Italian author Niccolò Machiavelli might have supported. One might consider other traits, but for my purposes these three suffice. Let us suppose that god is omniscient. At once a hurdle must be cleared. If god knows everything, then this being must know every action that has occurred in the past, is occurring in the present, and will occur in the future. But if god knows every future event nothing must be left to chance. Event A must in the future cause event B. This determinism means that I cannot change events as I move through a succession of presents toward my death. Freedom of choice, or free will if you prefer, must be an illusion. How can one reconcile the loss of free will with the deeply ingrained intuition that one can choose to eat hamburger or fish for dinner? If free will is an illusion, why do I believe so ardently that

I am free to choose? On an intuitive level, then, the trait of omniscience is suspect.

The case against omnipotence may be made even stronger. If god's power is limitless, then it seems reasonable to suppose that this being created the universe in its minutest detail, as the opening chapters of Genesis suggest. But why would god have created *Anopheles* mosquitoes (the italics denote a genus to which this species of mosquito belongs), which transmit malaria to humans? Notice that we are not speaking of one species, harmful as it is. Entomologists have identified more than twenty species. Why did it not suffice for god to create one killer but rather twenty variants of this killer? Why is overkill necessary? Keep in mind that *Anopheles* mosquitoes feed only on humans. They have no other host so that they only kill humans. It is as though god tailored a killer exactly to our circumstances. The same question plagues the existence of the *Aedes aegypti* mosquito, the carrier of yellow fever. Does the fact that these mosquitoes arose in Africa mean that god has special animus toward Africans? Is god a racist? But this can't be, if god is all loving. But how then does one reconcile this love with the incalculable suffering that humans have endured since their inception?

Perhaps the supreme being is really the god of *Anopheles* mosquitoes because they seem to thrive in this world. If god exists one must posit that this being is neither omniscient, nor omnipotent, nor all loving. But this is impossible because god must have these traits. To resolve this contradiction one must nullify god. The god hypothesis must be false. Atheism is still unwelcome in many places, but it is nonetheless part of the human condition. To paraphrase Nietzsche, we have survived the death of god.

Notice that our argument from the design of nature has other repugnant features. There is a type of insect for example that has offspring by normal sexual reproduction when the food supply is not large. When food is abundant, however, the female does not bother to mate but churns out offspring. These offspring, lacking the chromosomes from the male, are haploid organisms, which we saw was the case for drones and for Jesus, if his mother was truly a virgin. In this species of insect, however, the haploids, all daughters, are born within the mother's body. As they grow, they eat the mother from the inside out until she exists no more. This process repeats itself as long as food is plentiful. Daughter after daughter cannibalizes her mother. If god were all loving, why would it permit such reprehensible behavior? It is not better to posit that natural selection is responsible for this behavior and that god must not exist?

If fact, proceeding along these grounds, we can make a much stronger case for the existence of Satan rather than the conventional god of Christian morality. Either that or we must confess that god must be evil. Perhaps god, if it exists, is both good and evil. The triumph of *Anopheles* mosquitoes is a manifestation of evil. The music of Bach manifests all that is good in existence, all that is spiritual and dazzling. Yet can god be both good and evil? Can the traits of a being be polar opposites? There appears to be no good answer to these questions, leading us to simplify matters by doubting god's existence.

Yet we might tread this path carefully. Suppose that the mosquito arguments only invalidate the traits of god, not its existence. Since god cannot be all loving to have created deadly mosquitoes, one must confirm that god is evil. Such a thought is not all that revolutionary because it just means that the being we normally call Satan is really god. Only this reorientation allows us to make sense of all the evil in the world because it is a product of an evil being. From evil flows evil. Logically and experientially, an evil god accounts for the world we occupy. Rather than being a jumble of contradictory traits, perhaps god is simply evil. If this being exists it is unworthy of worship. Better to worship a plant because it provides oxygen, calories and nutrients to humans. Perhaps the potato plant is god, not some mystical and malevolent being.

There are other ways to pursue god. Another test of god is to assume eternal existence. We wrestled with this attribute while examining the prologue to the gospel of John. The key to eternity is the premise that one can move forward as well as backward through time without end. That is one may regress infinitely in time without encountering a beginning and forward in time without reaching an end. It does not appear to be possible to move infinitely in either direction. The crucial test is regression. If one can regress without end into the past, one will never reach a point of origin. For us to have reached the present it seems necessary for existence itself to have had a beginning. Otherwise, if we were infinitely far into the past, how would enough time ever elapse to reach the present? I am not writing necessarily about this universe. It is true that this universe appears to have had a beginning, but one might suppose the existence of a prior universe. The point is that one cannot entertain an infinite series of prior universes, because again, it will not be possible to reach the present. Reality, however one wishes to define it, must have had a single beginning that marked the advent of space, time, and matter.

If time had a beginning, then it is not truly eternal because, again, one cannot regress infinitely into the past while still holding out the prospect of reaching the present. But if time had a beginning, does this mean that god had a beginning too? This question is not easy to answer. Some theologians have claimed that god exists apart from time and so whatever limitations one might put on time cannot be placed on god. This assertion is clever but it does not match empirical reality. Everything we know exists in time. Indeed time is a necessary component of existence because all life goes from birth to death, a progression that cannot occur except in time. Time, to put it another way, is embedded in what we can reality. Without time there is no reality. Because we exist, we exist in time and can be confident of existing in reality. Everything that exists exists in time, so that god too must exist in time. If god exists in time, then it cannot be eternal. But to be eternal is a necessary property of god, so that god cannot exist. To put the matter differently, there is no special clause that absolves god from adhering to the laws of space and time. In fact, these laws must be a property of god so that it is vacuous to say that god exists apart from qualities and quantities that are germane to it.

Without god, what do we have? The existentialists made clear that without god there cannot be any inherent meaning to our lives or to the universe at large. We are born at random into the world without purpose or a priori aspirations. That is, we must create meaning for our lives. None is inherent to them. Once more, there is no god to give our lives meaning. This is not necessarily a recipe for despair. One might argue that the French writers André Malraux and Albert Camus imbued their lives with great meaning despite being what we might call atheistic existentialists. It is possible to hate suffering and injustice and to wish to create a better world even though we will be dead before accomplishing much. After our death we will be forgotten, but none of this robs us of the present for it is only the present that we can hope to shape. Within the finitude of our existence emerges a near infinity of possibilities.

Perhaps the only shadow of hope might come from aesthetics. In this sense I am interested in the pursuit of beauty. Consider the human female. I am not thinking of some celebrity like Selena Gomez, because I can walk through any checkout lane in any Wal-Mart and encounter a woman her equal in appearance. Notice as well that beauty cannot be restricted to a particular type. One might claim partiality toward blond-blue eyed Nordic women, but just as easily I might cite my encounters with hundreds of African American women of dazzling beauty. One might say the same of other ethnicities. How is so much beauty so widespread? Perhaps it is the result of natural selection, the Darwinian mechanism of evolution. Natural selection has accomplished much over long durations of time, but can it have created huge numbers of gorgeous women all across this planet? One need not confine treatment to humans. Whoever has walked through a deciduous forest in the temperate zone in autumn witnesses a profusion of colors and shapes. The human hand cannot match this artistry. The landscape painter cannot duplicate what nature supplies in abundance. Now go to any beach in the tropics and subtropics. See the waves lap against the shore. Feel the sun warm the flesh and the breeze temper one's sweat. Can one envision anything more beautiful? I don't think the answer is obvious. At the moment I'm agnostic and willing to entertain the possible that the god of painters and poets, if it exists, had some small but important role in creating the life, beautiful and horrid, that populates earth. This is not a proof for the existence of god, but only a confession that agnosticism may have as much merit as atheism.

In the End

Our journey complete, we must retrace our steps in an attempt to determine what we have learned about Jesus. The beginning of this chapter provided an overview, which we now expand so that the reader has no doubt where I stand. Let us begin by returning to the Roman historian Tacitus, whom we encountered in Chapter 1. Writing in the early second century CE, Tacitus summarized what he had learned about Jesus in a single formula: Roman governor Pontius Pilate had executed Jesus during the reign of Emperor Tiberius. This statement accords with the canonical gospels but does not make extreme claims. Nowhere does Tacitus claim that Jesus was divine. Nowhere does Tacitus write about miracles, not even one. He does not trump up the belief that Jesus' mother had been a virgin at his birth. Tacitus relates no childhood miracles, as does the Infancy Gospel of Thomas. There is no raising from the dead of Jarius' daughter and Lazarus. There are neither parables nor long discourses. Jesus does not rise from the dead, visit his apostles, and ascend into heaven. In short Tacitus gives us the minimalist version of Jesus. Keep in mind that the Jesus that Tacitus identifies is not much different than the Jesus in the gospel of Thomas, except that Tacitus includes Pontius Pilate, Tiberius, and Jesus' crucifixion, none of which appears in the gospel of Thomas. The key insight may be that Tacitus gave readers what he had learned about Jesus, and nothing more. Tacitus dealt with knowledge, not mere belief. This should be the creed we all preach.

It is worth asking, now that we have reached the end of our inquiry, whether it is possible to know and not merely believe more than Tacitus' dictum. In a restricted sense I think we can know a bit more about Jesus. We know for instance that he was human, so that he must have had human parents. No, god was not Jesus' father, but I think we can attempt to pinpoint Jesus' parents. Over and over the gospels and the apocrypha claim Mary to have been Jesus' mother. I am satisfied that this must be true because Jesus had to have had a mother. Even if the name Mary is inaccurate, some woman must have given birth to Jesus. Let us say provisionally that some woman, her name being Mary or a variant of that name, was Jesus' mother. Mary is often associated with her fiancé Joseph. Because Jesus had to have had a father, this companion of Mary most likely served the purpose. Again it is possible that the name Joseph is not accurate, but for lack of alternatives, let us identify him as the father of Jesus. We can know therefore the names (or a close approximation) of Jesus' parents. This is not earthshaking news, but it does go cautiously beyond what Tacitus knew.

It may be that Jesus had siblings. After all, parts of the canonical gospels and apocrypha mention the names of brothers, but the information is so sparse that I do not think it constitutes knowledge. It is not outside the realm of possibility, because there is no reason to suppose that Mary and Joseph stopped having unprotected sex after Jesus' birth. Still, this is a claim perhaps best left to the realm of belief. It may or may not be true. Either way, I do not think the claim that Jesus had siblings tells us anything about Jesus, the focus of our inquiry.

Jesus' childhood is a blank slate. We know nothing about it despite the few words of Luke and the pseudo information in the Infancy Gospel of Thomas. The information is entirely legend devoid of any historical value. Jesus' childhood might be the worst documented period of his life. No responsible historian can treat it with anything but caution. Let those who wish to believe in superstition indulge themselves, but this is no path to knowledge.

We have seen that Jesus' adulthood appears to have been better documented than his early years. But this view is a mistake. Jesus' adulthood is so cluttered with miracles that the only sane response is skepticism. We have seen that Jesus did not raise people from the dead. Jesus did not rise from the dead. Jesus did not cure the blind, expel demons, or cure any of a number of ailments. I do not claim that Jesus did not exist. I conclude that his adulthood included a public ministry, and this public ministry may be the only source of knowledge about Jesus' adulthood. Remember that Jesus must have been an apocalyptic preacher, one concerned with the coming end of days when Yahweh would rescue his chosen people and right all wrongs. Nothing of the kind happened, but that does not matter.

What matters is that apocalypticism was probably an authentic feature of Jesus' ministry. Toward the end of this ministry, Jesus appears to have disturbed the temple in Jerusalem, a holy site. If this event occurred, it might have worried Roman authorities because Passover was a delicate time when the hope for independence ran deep. To keep events in check, they quickly ended the threat by crucifying Jesus. Yet the temple disturbance remains conjecture. It may or may not be true, and so we cannot call it knowledge. The crucifixion certainly followed, but what happened to Jesus thereafter is unknown. He probably was not buried but left to rot on the cross. If predators ate him, what would have remained to rise from the dead?

Accordingly, the resurrection never happened. Instead a few of his followers, possibly Mary Magdalene and Peter (Paul being a latecomer who never knew Jesus), hallucinated the appearance of Jesus after his death. The resurrection was therefore not reality but illusion. We know nothing more about Jesus.

In the ruins of our quest for Jesus emerges an oddity, perhaps even a miracle of sorts. This shadowy figure who has left no imprint in history nevertheless left a religious legacy. The second of the three monotheistic religions, Christianity, bases its foundation on this person for whom so little evidence exists. Theologians may debate what does and does not constitute Christianity. I seek no clever definition but wish to touch upon the basics. By Christianity I mean that religion that believes that Jesus was god, that he predicted his death, that he died for the sins of all humanity and that he rose from the dead in a foreshadowing of the eternal life that awaits us all. I am not claiming that all Christians believe exactly the same dogmas. There are fissures between the Orthodox Churches and Catholicism. Both groups differ from some of the tenets of the many Protestant denominations, and not all Protestants believe alike. And Christianity has changed over time. During the era of slavery, many zealous Christians believe that it was ethical for whites to own African slaves. One hopes that today no Christian believes such rubbish.

My concern is more immediate. How did a religion formed on the shadow of a man come to be one of the most successful religions to date? There is no easy answer, and the explanations one might give have surprisingly little to do with Jesus. Perhaps this is fortunate, because Jesus was little more than a legendary figure. I will not attempt to cite all the reasons for Christianity's success, but the salient points deserve treatment.

From the outset it is clear that Christianity was expert at borrowing ideas from elsewhere. The notion of an immortal soul derives from Plato, arguably the most important philosopher in history. The notion of an evil world of the flesh and a transcendent world of the spirit is partly Plato, again, and partly Zoroastrianism. The Zoroastrian comparison is particularly sharp when one considers the need to separate the evil world of flesh and desire from the righteous world of the spirit. The opposition is clear in words attributed to Jesus. Zoroastrianism was an important link because it positioned Christianity to compete in the Mediterranean world where everything that smacked of Zoroastrianism had a head start toward success.

In the same way, the mystery cults positioned Christianity for easy access to the Mediterranean world. The cults of Egyptian deities Osiris and Isis were particularly important because Christian writers could fashion Jesus as the new Osiris, both being the gods of the Last Judgments and the gods of death and resurrection. Moreover Christianity was perfectly positioned in time at the exact midpoint of the High Roman Empire (200 BCE–200 CE). This was a period of maximum trade and diffusion of ideas, among them the stories about Jesus. In any ordinary times an itinerant preacher like Paul of Tarsus might have succumbed to piracy in his journeys across the Mediterranean Sea again and again. But this never happened because Paul and other missionaries traveled a Mediterranean world made safe from intrusions on commerce. Paul went where he wished and preached what he wanted. Christianity appeared to be new and fresh at just the right moment in history.

Christianity also benefited from the largely indifferent attitude of the Romans. Christian partisans like to exaggerate the ferocity of persecution during the Roman Empire. In fact persecution was local, sporadic and largely ineffective. Most Roman officials, Emperor Trajan made clear, did not hunt for Christians and were reluctant to charge them with offenses against the state. There was no active, organized persecution of Christians. Instead, throughout history, Christians have been persecutors. Just ask the Jews. Christianity was never as tolerant of other religions as was Islam at its apex. Today Islam in western Asia has degenerated from the successes of the Middle Ages. Probably the greatest stroke of luck came when Rome declined and then collapsed between the third and fifth centuries. In its enfeeblement, Rome could not hold together what had once been a glorious empire.

In Rome's absence, what could hold together the Mediterranean world and parts of Europe? In this context, Christianity came to the rescue. Borrowing the administrative structures of ancient Rome, Christianity almost singlehandedly held the remnants of the Roman Empire together for long stretches of the Middle Ages. The Church became wealthy and popes gained enormous power. Even though Christianity nearly collapsed in the Late Middle Ages, it was by then, to use a modern phrase, too big to fail. By the Renaissance the wealth of the Catholic Church could not truly be measured. The art treasures of the Vatican were priceless. The frescos by Italian sculptor and painter Michelangelo Bouronati are irreplaceable. We will pause here. The list could go on and on.

In sum, Christianity succeeded not because of Jesus but because someone knew how to package the religion's message in terms people readily understood and because time and events favored it. Jesus or god had nothing to do with this success. So much for the god hypothesis.

BIBLIOGRAPHY

Barrett, William. *Irrational Man: A Study in Existential Philosophy.* Garden City, NY: Doubleday Anchor Books, 1958.

Blomberg, Craig L. *Can We Still Believe the Bible? An Evangelical Engagement with Contemporary Questions.* Grand Rapids, MI: Brazos Press, 2014.

Brumbaugh, Robert S. *The Philosophers of Greece.* Albany: State University of New York Press, 1981.

Cornford, Francis M. *Before and After Socrates.* Cambridge: Cambridge University Press, 1932.

Cumo, Christopher. "The Temptation," *Swallow* magazine, 2007, 11-13.

Dewey, David. *A User's Guide to Bible Translations: Making the Most of Different Versions.* Downers Grove, IL: InterVarsity Press, 2004.

Ehrman, Bart D. *How Jesus Became God: The Exaltation of a Jewish Preacher from Galilee.* New York: Harper One, 2014.

Ehrman, Bart D. *The New Testament: A Historical Introduction to the Early Christian Writings,* 5th edition New York and Oxford: Oxford University Press, 2012.

Epictetus: "The Discourses as Reported by Arrian, the Manual, and Fragments," archives.org/pstream/epictetusdiscour01/epicuoft/epictetusdiscour01_djvu.text.

"The Gospel According to Thomas," in *The Other Gospels: Accounts of Jesus from outside the New Testament,* eds. Bart D. Ehrman and Zlatko Plese. Oxford: Oxford University Press, 2014.

"The Gospel of Pseudo Matthew," in *The Other Gospels: Accounts of Jesus from outside the New Testament*, eds. Bart D. Ehrman and Zlatko Plese. Oxford: Oxford University Press, 2014.

"The Infancy Gospel of Thomas," in *The Other Gospels: Accounts of Jesus from outside the New Testament*, eds. Bart D. Ehrman and Zlatko Plese. Oxford: Oxford University Press, 2014.

Kraut, Richard. "Aristotle's Ethics," *The Stanford Encyclopedia of Philosophy*, Spring 2016. Plato.Stanford.edu/archives/spr2016/ethics/Aristotle-ethics.

New American Bible. Washington, DC: United States Conference of Catholic Bishops (first ed. 1970).

Pannenberg, Wolfhart. *Jesus—God and Man*. Philadelphia: Westminster Press, 1977.

Placher. William C. *A History of Christian Theology: An Introduction* Philadelphia: The Westminster Press, 1983.

Plato, *The Great Dialogues of Plato*. New York: New American Library, 1955.

"The Pseudo Gospel of James," in *The Other Gospels: Accounts of Jesus from outside the New Testament*, eds. Bart D. Ehrman and Zlatko Plese. Oxford: Oxford University Press, 2014.

Rhodes, Ron. *The Complete Guide to Bible Translations*. Eugene, OR: Harvest House Publishers, 2009.

Schroeder, Gerald. *The Science of God: The Convergence of Scientific and Biblical Wisdom*. New York: The Free Press, 1997.

Swinburne, Richard. *Was Jesus God?* Oxford: Oxford University Press, 2008.

Tipler, Frank J. *The Physics of Immortality: Modern Cosmology, God and the Resurrection of the Dead*. New York: Doubleday, 1994.

Veatch, Henry B. *Aristotle: A Contemporary Appreciation*. Bloomington and London: Indiana University Press, 1974.

Worth, Roland H. Jr. *Bible Translations: A History through Source Documents*. Jefferson, NC and London: McFarland Publishers, 1992.

INDEX

A

Abraham, 105
Acts of the Apostles, 25
Adam, 70, 80, 92, 106, 120, 125, 158, 159
Afterworld, 105, 127, 134
Aknaton, 163
Alexander the Great, 34, 59, 60, 78
Allegory of the Cave, 62
American Standard Version, 41
Annals, 29
Anselm, 164, 165
Antiquity, 7, 8, 14, 16, 18-21, 24, 25, 28, 31,
   32, 37, 39, 40, 48-51, 55, 57-60, 62, 70,
   74, 77, 79, 82, 83, 86, 90, 129, 151, 163
Apocalyptic, 31, 90-93, 104, 111, 118, 127,
   133, 141, 142, 161, 170
Apocalypticism, 90, 142, 170
Apocrypha, 70, 72, 85, 102, 103, 169, 170
Apocryphon of John, 64, 65
Apollo, 61
Apollonius of Tyana, 56
Apology, 12, 26, 27, 31, 138
Aquinas, Thomas, 115, 156, 164
Aramaic, 24, 31, 32, 64, 68, 82
Aristarchus of Samos, 52
Aristotle, 13-15, 34, 65, 115, 174
Arrian, 14, 15, 173
Atheism, 13, 126, 149, 161, 162, 166, 169
Augustine of Hippo, 120
Augustus, 49, 53, 60, 61
Aurelius, Marcus, 40, 69
Autograph, 21, 22, 28

B

Bach, Anna Magdalena, 21
Bach, Johann Sebastian, 5, 6, 18, 19, 21, 50,
   71, 74, 98, 113, 167
Baptism, 92, 93
Behe, Michael, 154
Bethlehem, 8, 48-54, 56, 70, 79
Bible, 2, 15, 17, 18, 23, 31, 38-41, 55, 68, 70-
   72, 77, 94, 95, 120, 145, 149, 153, 173, 174
Bible, King James Version, 29, 40, 41
Bible, Revised Standard, 41
Big Bang, 86, 155, 156, 161
Bock, Emil, 85
Bosch, Hieronymus, 6
Brothers Karamazov, 54, 81, 97, 102
Buffon, Comte de, 108

C

Camus, Albert, 168
Catholicism, 171
Cato the Elder, 40
Cave, birth of Jesus, 52, 53
Childhood of Jesus, 8, 67, 74, 75, 79, 85
Christianity, 2, 5, 6, 9, 23, 25, 28, 30, 32,
   34, 39, 45, 54-56, 60, 63, 72, 93, 96, 110,
   113, 127, 171, 172
Christians, 3, 5, 6, 11, 28, 48, 57, 61, 63, 70,
   72, 80, 90, 92, 93, 100, 107, 109, 110, 115,
   116, 121, 125-127, 129, 131, 141, 143, 144,
   146, 153, 161, 163, 171, 172

Printed in the United States
By Bookmasters